A DAZZLING ENIGMA
The Story of Morgan Edwards

Howard R. Stewart

University Press of America, Inc.
Lanham • New York • London

Copyright © 1995 by
University Press of America,® Inc.
4720 Boston Way
Lanham, Maryland 20706

3 Henrietta Street
London, WC2E 8LU England

All rights reserved
Printed in the United States of America
British Cataloging in Publication Information Available

Library of Congress Cataloging-in-Publication Data

Stewart, Howard R.
A dazzling enigma : the story of Morgan Edwards / Howard R.
Stewart.
p. cm.
Includes bibliographical references and index.
1. Edwards, Morgan, 1722-1795. 2. Baptists--Great Britain--Clergy-
-Biography. 3. Baptists--United States--Clergy--Biography. I.
Title.
BX6495.E36S74   1995   286'.1'092--dc20   95-3457
CIP

ISBN 0-8191-9901-X (cloth: alk paper)

⊖™ The paper used in this publication meets the minimum
requirements of American National Standard for Information
Sciences—Permanence of Paper for Printed Library Materials, ANSI
Z39.48–1984.

TO

EVIE,

KEN

AND PAUL

CONTENTS

Preface	iv
Illustrations	v
Preface	vi
Acknowledgments	ix
Prologue: Meet Morgan Edwards	1
SECTION ONE: The Story in England, Ireland and Wales	
Chapter One: A People Not Subdued	7
Chapter Two: Wild Years and A New Life	23
Chapter Three: Well-Read and Well-Schooled	59
Chapter Four: Conduct Becoming A Baptist Minister	83
SECTION TWO: The Story in Philadelphia	
Chapter Five: A New Man in a New City	117
Chapter Six: Family Life and Death	135
Chapter Seven: Prime Time in Philadelphia	153
Chapter Eight: A Time to Die	189
Chapter Nine: A Leader of Leaders	207
Chapter Ten: A Motivator of Achievers	231
SECTION THREE: The Story in Delaware	
Chapter Eleven: The Matter of Loyalty	277
Chapter Twelve: Conduct Unbecoming a Baptist Minister	313
Chapter Thirteen: The Winchester Affair	337
Chapter Fourteen: A Baptist to the End	353
Epilogue: An Enigma Still	375
Sources Consulted	387
Index	405
Biographical Sketch of Author	415

ILLUSTRATIONS

Sketch of Morgan Edwards	xii
Coat of Arms of Morgan Edwards	22
Exterior of the Penygarn Baptist Church	44
Sketch of Eighteenth Century Interior of Penygarn Baptist Church	46
Twentieth Century Interior of Penygarn Baptist Church	48
Sketch of John Wesley Preaching in Trosnant	66
Sketch of Baptisterion on the Schuylkill River	156
Sketch of Philadelphia Baptist Meeting House	158
Map of the Battle of the Brandywine	304
Monument at Grave of Morgan Edwards	369
South Facing Plate on Monument	371

PREFACE

The publication of this book is the end of a forty year journey to a promised land. Morgan Edwards first captured my interest in 1955 while doing graduate study in Baptist history at the Eastern Baptist Theological Seminary. The more his name appeared in my reading the more I wanted to know about him. I made the decision to write a biographical paper, and then made a discovery.

I discovered there were no biographies on Morgan Edwards, the most prominent leader in eighteenth century American Baptist church life. My discovery brought disappointment but also a commitment to write his life story. Pastoral, teaching and family responsibilities precluded my carrying out that commitment until retirement in 1988. After four years in research in the United States and the British Isles, and two years writing the book was completed for publication in 1995, the bicentennial year of Edwards's death.

There were many institutions and persons along the way who deserve recognition for the invaluable assistance they gave during both the research and writing phases. The list of names would be intolerably long for this preface, but my debt is more than mere words can express. The libraries of the universities, colleges, seminaries and historical societies where I did research are staffed by the most caring and helpful people I have ever met.

Those who have walked the entire path with me deserve special recognition. Chief among these is Dr. Norman H. Maring, Professor Emeritus of Christian History at the Eastern Baptist Theological Seminary in Philadelphia, Pennsylvania. He, along with Dr. Robert G. Torbet, have been my mentors in the study of Baptist history. In addition, Norman was a "son of encouragement" during the forty years in the wilderness, and a member of my review team.

Joining him on the team was the Reverend D. Hugh Matthews, Principal of the South Wales Baptist College in Cardiff. He along with his lovely wife Verina, were my primary hosts during the period of research in the British Isles. Hugh gave me sure guidance along the bypaths of Baptist history in England, Ireland and Wales.

The other two members of the review team were Dr. Robert G. Gardner, late of Shorter College in Rome, Georgia, and Dr. H. Leon McBeth, Distinguished Professor of Church History at the Southwestern Baptist Theological Seminary in Fort Worth, Texas. Bob brought the very practiced eye of a seasoned college professor to the manuscript, and Leon the keen perspective of a major scholar in Baptist history.

I also wish to thank Mary Holland, retired teacher of English, for her corrective reviews of my grammar, and Thelma Kostigian for editing the typescript for publication. Closer to home I acknowledge my abiding gratitude to Evelyn, my wife of fifty years, and my two sons Kenneth and Paul and their familes for their loving affirmation and support.

In addition, I must acknowledge my indebtedness to several persons for permission to use original sketches.

Preface

The sketch of Morgan Edwards facing page one I have used through the courtesy of the artist, Mr. Erwin M. Hearne, Jr. of Dallas, Texas, and the Historical Commission of the Southern Baptist Convention in Nashville, Tennessee. The sketch of John Wesley preaching in Trosnant, Wales, I have used through the courtesy of the artist, Mr. Kenneth Haynes of Pontypool, Wales, and the authors of the book from which it was taken, Messers Arthur Crane, Bernard Derrick, and Edward Donovan, all of Pontypool. Finally, I wisk to thank Ms. Ann Nields Garstin, of Wilmington, Delaware for permission to use the map of the Battle of the Brandywine, taken from the printed version of her father's address on the occasion of the one-hundred-fiftieth anniversary of the battle. Her father was the late Federal District Judge John P. Nields.

One final word of gratitude and praise belongs to our providential God who directed my steps around many roadblocks, and who enabled me to keep my eye focused on the promised land.

Cicero is supposed to have said, "Not to know what happened before you were born is to remain always a child." The absence of a full biography on Morgan Edwards has kept the Baptists of America in a childlike perception of one of the most important persons in their magnificent heritage. Perhaps my effort to tell his story more accurately and more completely may promote a more mature understanding of Morgan Edwards and his significant place in the history of Baptists in America.

Artist's Conception of Morgan Edwards
Artist: Erwin M. Hearne, Jr.

PROLOGUE

MEET MORGAN EDWARDS

"...a man of great ability and general worth, but eccentric."
William Cathcart, 1876

Meet the man who was the most enigmatic figure of early American Baptist history, yet was its most influential leader. His name was Morgan Edwards. He has puzzled historians since the eighteenth-century--gifted for greatness, hobbled by his eccentricities. He came on the stage of Baptist church life as a player who was dazzling in his accomplishments, but puzzling in his personality. The word "enigma" comes from the Greek *aninigmos,* meaning a riddle or a dark saying, and indeed Morgan Edwards has been a puzzle.

Edwards was a Welsh Baptist minister, and after serving churches in England and Ireland from 1743 to 1761, he came to America to be pastor of the Baptist church in Philadelphia. Here he reached the zenith of his influence on Baptists as a preacher, evangelist, historian, educator, ecclesiastic, author, denominational leader, and lecturer.

The preaching of Morgan Edwards drew such large

crowds that the Philadelphia church razed its meeting house during the first year of his pastorate and began construction of a new and larger facility. His three thousand mile evangelistic tour by horseback for the Philadelphia Baptist Association resulted in many converts, stronger associations, and the collection of extensive historical data. From these materials Edwards began the first history of Baptists in America, and all other such histories would be impoverished without his work. In education Edwards has been described as the "prime mover" behind the founding of what is now Brown University.[1]

As an eccelsiastic he produced the first manual on Baptist polity and practice, and published numerous sermons and papers. He served in several offices of the Philadelphia Baptist Association when it functioned as a quasai-national Baptist body. Finally, he lectured at Rhode Island College (now Brown University) and the College of Philadelphia (now the University of Pennsylvania). But if Edwards excites historians, he also baffles them because inadequate use of available resources has given him a phanthom-like character. As one historian has described him, "He seems as elusive as the Scarlet Pimpernell."[2]

Despite the brilliance of his place in Baptist church life, Edwards's apparent idiosyncrasies cast shadows on his personal life and ministry. These included (1) a fifteen year premonition that his death would occur on March 9, 1770; (2) his desire to imbibe alcoholic beverages and to frequent the taverns for convivial company; (3) his loyalty to England as the American colonies raced toward independence; (4) his failure to provide information on his family, which was frequently visited by tragedy; and

(5) the charge that he supported the doctrine of universalism. How can we understand this man whom some have seen as so brilliant and massive, while others have perceived him as bewildering and mysterious?

David Lloyd George was Prime Minister of Great Britain from 1916 to 1922 and another puzzling Welsh Baptist. Jan Morris, the Welsh historian, says of him, "There was something hard to pin down in his character; something shifting and almost mocking, which disturbed people often and made them feel they had been hoodwinked. To foreigners he was always to remain an uncomfortable, if dazzling sort of an enigma."[3]

Morgan Edwards rose to be an outstanding leader, but who was also a person with whom others were not altogether comfortable. He, too, has remained "an uncomfortable, if dazzling sort of an enigma."

If to dazzle is to give light or to shine brightly, Morgan Edwards was dazzling in his effect on eighteenth-century Baptist church life. At the same time, he was a puzzle to his peers. He outshone all others in his influence, but he did so while marching to the beat of a different drummer. This book is an effort to tell a more enlightened version of his story as one person sees him and understands him. It is not an exhaustive study of every facet of his life, but a story which benefits from the most extensive research yet done on this very enigmatic person.

ENDNOTES

1. Reuben A. Guild, *Early History of Brown University, Including the Life, Times and Correspondence of President Manning, 1756-1791.* (Providence: Snow and Farnham, 1896), 12.
2. From a personal interview with the Rev'd D. Hugh Matthews,

Principal, South Wales Baptist College, Cardiff, May 13, 1991.
3. Jan Morris, *The Matter of Wales*. (Oxford: Oxford University Press), 167.

SECTION ONE

The Story in England, Ireland and Wales

CHAPTER ONE

A PEOPLE NOT SUBDUED

"Often conquered, but never subdued"
L.B. and J.W. Elmwood, 1951

The Durability of Welshness
On his conquering march through Wales in the twelfth century King Henry II of England entered a little village near Llandysul, Lifyed. An elderly Welsh gentleman was seated by the side of the road as the king approached. The king, thinking the old man should be impressed by the spectacle of his regal presence and the ranks of armed, uniformed troops marching in cadence for miles behind him, stopped to ask, "Old man, how long do you think Welsh opposition to English occupation will last?" The wise old man's reply was never forgotten and eventually was inscribed on his monument.[1]

This nation, O King, may now as in former times be harrassed in a great measure, and in great measure weakened and destroyed by you and other Powers...but it can never be totally subdued through the wrath of man, unless the wrath of God concur.

The old man's prophecy proved true, as an intermittent war was fought in Wales by eight English monarchs, who all failed to pacify the land. As one grim thirteenth century English soldier said, "We dwell here in watchings and fastings, in prayer, in cold and nakedness...."[2]

The legend of the "Old Man of Pencader" and the words of the unhappy trooper illustrate, in the judgment of historians L.B. and J.W. Elmwood, that "the Welsh people were often conquered, but never subdued; squeezed but never squashed."[3] The conquerors all assumed they had erased Welshness from the Welsh heart. Too late they discovered the indelible quality of the Welsh character, which could be painted over but not obliterated. The Welsh never lost their identity as a people, and their conquerors never understood them.

The Enigma of the Welsh People
It is not so strange, then, that Morgan Edwards was also an enigma, for he came from a people who were bewildering to others. Jan Morris, herself half-Welsh and half-English, describes the mystery of Welshness: "If there is such a thing as a Welsh national character it is certainly not self-evident. They are seldom simple, and tend often toward the actorial and the posed. Their personalities are in layers of self-defiance or affectation."[4]

Quoting the mother of St. David, the patron saint of Wales, Morris continues, "There is no madness like contentiousness," and she sees this contentiousness as endemic to the Welsh people. She views them "cherishing the quick riposte more than compromise and rarely reaching unanimity on anything."[5] So perhaps Thomas Armitage's description of Edwards was correct: "Morgan was so full of Welsh fire that he could not hold his tongue, which much afflicted his brethren and involved him in trouble with the American authorities."[6]

An example of the Welsh trait of the posed and actorial in Edwards is found in his *Materials Toward A History of the* Baptists. He described in the third person an encounter between a traveling Baptist minister (himself, no doubt) and several members of the gentry in April 1772 at Goochland, Virginia, about eighty miles west of Williamsburg.[7]

> ...the following conversation happened in this neighborhood at an inn, between a northern minister and a number of colonels, captains, esquires etc. who had met for public business. The minister, having ordered a feed of corn for his horse, entered the room and threw himself on the bed, being fatigued from riding.
> **Esq. U.** You seem to be much tired Sir. Have you travelled far?
> **Northern M.** From Georgia hither.
> **Col. S.** Were you at Mr. Whitefield's orphan house while there?
> **Northern M.** Yes, Sir:
> **Col. S.** Did you see Mr. Whitefield's children?
> **Northern M.** I saw fourteen orphans and about eighteen grammar-school boys.
> **Esq. U.** No, No; we ask, if you saw his own children by the squaw?
> **Northern M.** O gentlemen, you don't talk sense, nor anything like it, else I would talk with you.
> **Omnes.** [all] Ha. ha. ha.
> **Esq. U.** Pray are you not a clergyman?
> **Northern M.** Yeas, Sir.
> **Capt. L.** Of the church of England I presume?
> **Northern M.** No, Sir; I am a clergyman of a better church than that; for she is a persecutor.
> **Omnes.** Ha. ha. ha.
> **Esq. U.** You lie Sir; I mean on the bed.

Northern M. And you lie, Sir; I mean under a mistake for I but yesterday saw her prisoners in Chesterfield gaol.
Omnes. Ha. ha. ha.
Esq. U. Then you are one of the fleabitten [meaning jailed] clergy?
Northern M. Are there fleas in this bed, Sir?
Esq. U. I ask, if you are a clergyman of the itchy true blue kirk of Scotland?
Northern M. No, no, Sir; I am a clergyman of a much better church than that which has the itch.
Capt. L. (whispers). He is ashamed to own her for fear you should scratch him, 'Squire.
Esq. U. (aloud) I fancy, Sir, you are tinctured with the baptists?
Northern M. No, not tinctured; but deeply dyed with them.
Omnes. Ha. ha. ha.
    After they had found him out they began to tell very strange stories of the baptists, quite as incredible as that of Mr. Whitfield and the squaw. They made the northern minister rake up all his witts[sic], and throw it among them, preserving as much delicacy as he could in a grocer's shop. When the repartees were over, and the grog turned their attention another way, the following whispers passed between themselves.
Esq. U. He is no baptist-.
Capt. L. No by God, nor presbyterian neither.
Col. S. What do you take him to be a clergyman of our church;
Esq. U. No, I take him to be one of the Georgia lawyers.
Mr. G. For my part I believe him to be a baptist minister. There are some clever fellows among them. I heard one Jery Walker support a petition of theirs at the assembly in such a manner as surprised us all, and make our witts [sic] draw in their horns.
Major W. I confess, that they have often confounded me with their arguments and texts of Scripture; and if any other people but the baptists profess their religion I would make it my religion before tomorrow.
    After this whispering interlude, Squire U. addressed himself to the man on the bed, saying, Sir, You must go home with me, and give us a sermon; there is plenty of your sort in this neighbour-

hood.
Northern M. *Must* is for the king, Sir.
Esq. U. Well, but will you go?
Northern M. I will if I please.
However, the minister went, and met with very genteel entertainment from the Squire and his lady. The squire offered to give the minister a fresh horse instead of his own which was much harrassed with the journey; and told other people that he would never talk any more against the baptists.

The contentious, actorial character of the Welsh has been likened to art forms in their Celtic heritage.[8]

> The notorious deviousness of Welsh people, for example, finds its exact imagery in the convoluted art forms of the Celts, which depended upon illusory circles, disturbing knots and bafflingly inconclusive squiggles. There is a sort of Celtic fluidity to the outlook of the Welsh which may also be found in their music, poetry and provocative conversation, and in their ancient religious concepts.

Roman writers described the Welsh as "a volatile mixture of flamboyance, wild courage and easy discouragement."[9] Hence, a brief review of Welsh history may aid in understanding the Welsh in general and Morgan Edwards in particular. An examination of his life clearly reveals a man who fluctuated between flamboyance, wild courage, and easy discouragement.

THE HISTORY OF THE WELSH PEOPLE

The beginnings of Welsh history may seem as puzzling as the Welsh character. Some historians begin with the so-called "Red-Man of Paviland," whose eighteen thousand-year-old remains were found in a cave on the southern Coast of Gower.[10] Others, however, reach back only twenty-six hundred years to the first Celts who moved into the area.[11] To North Wales from Northern Europe came the tall, long-legged Decangli and Ordivices. Southern Wales was settled by the more passionate, darker-hued Dematae and Silures from the Iberian Peninsula.[12] The settlers in the South, whence came Morgan Edwards, have been described as "Stocky of build, and fiery temperament."[13] These same Celts doggedly resisted Roman occupation for over one hundred years before all of Wales was finally conquered by A.D. 78.[14]

The Roman Occupation
The Romans occupied Wales for four centuries but had great difficulty winning and maintaining control. The mountainous topography of the land and the intrepid character of the people bred a spirit of independence.[15] To keep control, the Romans committed one-third of their forces in the British Isles to the small area of Wales, housing them in forts throughout the land.

The degree of Roman influence on the Welsh people depended on the effectiveness of the occupation. While they managed to conquer, pacify, and exploit the land, they failed to convert the Celts into a quiet, taxable population. Their legacy to the Welsh included the Roman alphabet, but when they left in A.D. 409, the Welsh were still Welsh. Their language was still that of the dominant Brythonic or Brettonic branch of the Celts, and with few exceptions they were still observing laws which antedated Roman occupation.

Not even the Christian faith had yet gained a strong foothold.[16] As the Romans pulled back, the Welsh moved up, and in the process began establishing their own military forces for self-protection.

After the Romans

During the fifth and sixth centuries, groups of Angles, Saxons, Jutes, Suevi, Franks, and Friesians made their way into the south and east of Britain, but none of these migrations affected the people of Wales. By the seventh century, however, four main kingdoms remained in Wales. They were the remnants of the old Celtic tribal divisions and had met the invading Romans. In 655 they were cut off from their Celtic cousins in North Britain by Mercia in the battle of Winwaed Field. This event began a process of isolating Wales from other groups in the British Isles. It was climaxed by the building of a great dyke by Offa, King of Mercia, in the latter half of the eighth century, thus creating a distinct border. The English called the people living behind the dyke "Weal-as" which means foreigners, rather than the name the Welsh called themselves, "Cymry," meaning people living together in a region.[17]

While the dyke and the name change marked off and isolated the people of Wales, it also brought into being a new nation and a national identity. Three names are associated with that process: Rhodri Mawr in the ninth century, Hywel Dda in the tenth, and Gruffydd ap Llywelyn in the eleventh.

Rhodri the Great began his rule in 844 and annexed territory to the south formerly ruled by his deceased brother-in-law. Following his death, Rhodri's six sons divided the territory, but remained united for self-protection.

Hywel Dda, or Howell the Good, emerged in the tenth century as the second great leader. Though the Welsh had their own identity and language, they had no codified system of law. Howell, established a system of law by codifying the Celtic tribal laws then in practice. In addition, he brought all but three Welsh kingdoms under his rule.

Upon the death of Howell the Good, Wales began to break up as old hostilities were renewed. In the eleventh century, however, Gruffydd ap Llewelyn managed to unite all of Wales into one kingdom. His rule began in the north in 1039, but unity and the promise of better times were shortlived.

In 1063 Harold of Wessex invaded Wales, and Grufydd was killed by one of his own men. Harold, in turn, was killed by the Norman conquerors of England in 1066 at the Battle of Hastings. The Norman invaders, who quickly conquered England, needed two hundred more years to overrun Wales.

The Norman Conquest
The two centuries required for military conquest by the Normans did bring changes to the Welsh landscape and society. The Normans gradually erected splendid castles and created Earldoms along the border, which William the Conqueror handed over to friends and relatives. They made deep incursions into Wales, and took whatever they wished.

The Norman conquest of Wales rose and fell according to the degree of collaboration by Welsh chieftains and the degree of unity among the Welsh people.[18] Toward the end of the twelfth century and into the thirteenth century, the Welsh began learning how to resist the Anglo-Norman kings while accommodating to those features of Norman culture which appeared beneficial.

Resistance was not crushed and the Welsh princes went on to build their own castles. One of these princes was Lord Rhys ap Gruffudd of Deheubarth, who dominated South Wales for the second half of the twelfth century.

Welsh political aspirations rose, and Welsh culture experienced a renaissance. The laws of Hywel Dda still governed in Welsh society even among the barons in the areas bordering England.[19] By the start of the fourteenth century, however, Edward I of England ended the reigns of the Welsh princes.

England and Wales Are Merged

While he could subdue the Welsh princes, Edward soon learned he could not crush "Welshness" out of the Welsh people. As a concession to their ancient customs, he permitted the use of old Welsh laws in minor legal matters, but in more serious offenses he imposed English law with English enforcement officers. Edward began his own castle-building program, including the importation of foreign residents, and by mid-fourteenth century the social life of Wales was changing.

Professor Gwyn Williams has described this process of change.[20]

> Townspeople who had grown rich now for the first time invested money in land. The social pattern of Wales was changing; tribe and family meant less and less, money and possessions more. Money payments replaced payment by labour and...the fourteenth century saw the emergence of the typical Welsh countryman, the small farmer, who is still today the backbone of rural Wales.

It is probable that Morgan Edwards was born into the type of family brought about by such social changes. These changes also affected marriage, family, and property rights. As marriages occurred between Norman men and Welsh women titles to Welsh lands were put into Norman hands; the difference being that Normans passed on their estates to the first-born son, whereas by Welsh tradition the estate was shared among all the male offspring.[21]

Serious Welsh resistance was reborn in the fifteenth century under Owain ap Glyndwr. Welsh workers and students who had left began streaming back home; castles and towns were captured and destroyed as Welsh pride was reasserted, but King Henry IV struck quickly and with force. By 1408-9 all of Wales was once again under English rule, and Henry imposed what amounted to martial law. Finally, when Henry Tudor gained the Crown following the defeat of King Richard at Bosworth in 1485, the Welsh people had a monarch they could support because Welsh blood flowed in his veins.

With peace and security under Henry VII, many Welsh began to do better in Wales and England. But with his death in 1509, a new and less pleasant era began for the Welsh people.

When Henry VIII came to the throne, he moved toward tighter control of Wales by dispatching Bishop Rowland Lee to take over law enforcement and to deal with the remnants of opposition. Lee was a tyrant who cared not a wit for Welsh ways and traditions. Crimes committed in Wales were tried in the nearest English county, and the most sinister forms of punishment were laid on Welsh people. In back of all this violent activity was Henry's grand design to bring about a union of England and Wales.

In 1534, Henry imposed the Act of Supremacy, cutting the link with Roman Catholicism and creating the Church of England. His action, however, could not apply to Wales since both nations were legally still separate countries. So in 1536, the English parliament passed the

Act of Union making England and Wales one country. With the stroke of his pen, Henry sought to wipe out Welsh laws, customs, and the Welsh language. The union with England had a positive side, however, as many Welshmen went to England, became wealthy and sent back large sums of money for educational purposes.[22]

A temporary swing back to Roman Catholicism occurred when Mary came to the throne in 1553, and most people in Wales welcomed the change. Protestantism re-emerged with Elizabeth. She re-estabished the Church of England but knew she could not force the Welsh to accept Protestantism dressed in the English language. So, she ordered the translation of the Bible and The Book of Common Prayer into Welsh.

By the seventeenth century, the people of Wales were experiencing the downside of union with England. The Reformation in England had removed many sacred places and forced the abandonment of the Roman Catholic faith. But there was more to come.

While developments in agriculture, mining, quarrying and metal processing began to promote prosperity, the political climate was changing. In his effort to raise money, King Charles I became engaged in a fiscal tug-of-war with two Parliaments controlled by the Puritans. He did not raise more money, but raised instead the ire of his enemies. They finally clashed openly, and Charles was executed. Puritan leader Oliver Cromwell took control, and the Puritan Commonwealth was established. Even though Wales also came under Puritan control, cries for the return of the monarchy could still be heard because the Welsh felt more secure under a king favorably disposed toward them than under the Puritan Parliament.

Thus, while supporters of the Commonwealth could be

found in Wales, the royalists were numerous. Royalists were not so much supportive of a king out of love for his majesty as they were out of a desire for stability in their own land. In his time Morgan Edwards had the same outlook.

Edwards' loyalty to the crown was more practical than political. As will be shown, he believed the monarchy provided more security to the colonies than might be had in the as yet unformed nation. He also believed that a direct appeal to the King offered a more effective means of coping with the oppression of Dissenter churches by the Established churches. The experiences of the Commonwealth period seem to bear that out. Jenkins makes the point that religion thrived during the Commonwealth, but much of that religious enthusiasm was frequently backed by the power of the sword.[23]

Despite Cromwell's Welsh ancestry, the period of the Commonwealth was hard on the Welsh. It came to an end when the monarchy was restored in 1660; by the beginning of the eighteenth century, Wales seemed once again to be enjoying a relatively tranquil life, albeit as a part of England. Now the rule of England would prevail over everything Welsh, except the Welsh personality.

Giraldus Cambrensis, a twelfth-century Welsh scholar, said of his countrymen, "The best of the Welsh are unbeatable and the worst are ghastly still."[24] What others have seen as the befuddling, enigmatic features in the Welsh may be seen in their pride of having absorbed enough of Roman culture and Christianity by the fourth century to escape the barbarism of the Dark Ages which had gripped the Continent.

Yet at the same time in their religious history "the occult is crossed with the intellectual, dogma reacted against ritual and a rumor of mystery hovered over its affairs and territories."[25] The casting of spells, belief in charms, omens and contacts with spirits doggedly resisted the encroachments of both Roman Catholicism and Protestantism.[26] All the while the Welsh became a literate people by reading the Bible and other religious literature.[27] It should not be too surprising that Morgan Edwards saw no inconsistency between his Calvinistic Christian theology and the premonitions he seriously entertained of his wife's death and his own.[28]

In another matter the Puritan reformers of the Commonwealth were diligent in addressing what they saw as the sinfulness of the Welsh. They railed against such conduct as Sabbath-breaking, excessive drinking by clergy and laity alike and the prominence of the pub in Welsh society. Yet during that same period the Welsh struggled to keep their love of poetry alive by its use in public worship through Psalm chanting and sermons in verse. They also made use of pithy sayings, proverbs and epigrams to teach Christian doctrine and morality.[29] Why, then, should it be thought so strange that Morgan Edwards could at the same time rail against the traffic in rum in his *Materials Toward A History of Baptists*,[30] and still visit the taverns for his libations?

From the Romans to the English, the Welsh people were conquered by many but subdued by none. They accommodated to the rule of all but kept their own character and culture. Because of this trait, they project the impression of people who were always ahead of their conquerors and with more grace to live beyond those who would rob them of their character. Those who had the brute force to conquer them never did comprehend the true nature of Welshness, and as a result they were always a puzzle, an enigma.

The Welsh ability to accommodate to a conqueror, while outwitting and outwaiting him, is best seen in Monmouthshire, the most English of the Welsh counties, the county of Morgan Edward's birth.

ENDNOTES

1. Jan Morris, *The Matter of Wales*. (Oxford: Oxford University Press, 1964), 72.
2. Ibid., 67.
3. Tonie Butler Elmwood and J.W. Elmwood, Jr. *The Rebellious Welsh*. (Los Angeles: The Ward Ritchie Press, 1951), xxii.
4. Morris, 167.
5. Ibid., 215.
6. Thomas Armitage, *A History of the Baptists*. (New York: Bryon, Taylor and Co., 1887), 723.
7. Morgan Edwards, *Materials Towards A History of the Baptists*. (Danielsville, Ga.: Heritage Papers, 1984), I, 62,63.
8. Morris, 53.
9. Ibid.
10. Gwyn Williams, *The Land Remembers*, (London: Faber & Faber, 1977), 19-20.
11. Ibid., 29-31.
12. Morris, 45.
13. Ibid., 179.
14. Elmwood, 11.
15. Owen M. Edwards, *Wales*. (New York: G.P. Putnam's Sons, 1901), 6.
16. Williams, 31.
17. Ibid., 42.
18. Ibid., 50.
19. Ibid., 68.
20. Ibid., 68.
21. Ibid., 69.
22. Geraint H. Jenkins, *Literature, Religion and Society in Wales, 1660-1730*. (Cardiff: University of Wales Press, 1978), 42.

23. Ibid., 1-2.
24. Morris, 167.
25. Ibid., 75.
26. Jenkins, 49.
27. Ibid., 73.
28. Morgan Edwards, *A New Year's Gift, Being A Sermon Delivered at Philadelphia on January 1, 1770,* (Newport: Solomon Southwick, 1770), 6,8.
29. Jenkins, 147.
30. Morgan Edwards, *Materials Towards A History of the Baptists in the Province of South Carolina,* (Danielsville, Ga.: Heritage Papers, 1984), 126.

Coat of Arms of Morgan Edwards
The Motto in Welsh Reads: "God's Will Be Done"

CHAPTER TWO

WILD YEARS AND A NEW LIFE

"Son of Morgan Edwards of Blaenayon"
Tombstone Inscription, 1786
Waterford, Ireland

Gwent, The Place of Beginning
The place of our nativity has much to say about the events which shape our lives. Had Morgan Edwards been born in southwest Wales, he might have been less loyal to the Crown in his later years. He was born May 9, 1722, in southeast Wales, bordering England, in what was then the county of Monmouth.

Monmouthshire, the most English of the Welsh countries, occupies 570 square miles along the Southwest border of England. When the British partitioned Wales into counties in 1282 the area was left untouched.[1] Prior to then the area consisted of two cantrefs named Gwent Iscoed and Gwent Uwchoed. For centuries the people retained their identity, by fending off the hostile Welsh princes to the West and the invading Saxons to the East.[2] The name was changed to Monmouthshire when Gwent became part of England in 1536. In modern times its ancient name has been restored and by that name we shall call it--Gwent, the county of Morgan Edwards' birth.

In Morgan Edwards's youth, the county was primarily pastoral and agricultural, only lightly touched by the Industrial Revolution in the form of the Hanbury Iron Works in the town of Pontypool. The Hanburys, a well-known family of ironmasters, came to the area by 1600,[3] and had developed a manufacturing business producing ornamental ironwork by 1677.[4] A later manager of plant was to play an important role in the education of Morgan Edwards, and in his move to Philadelphia. Edwards may have known some of the Hanburys, who were active members of the Trevethin Parish where the Edwards family were also members.

Trevethin Parish
The Trevethin Parish Church was named for St. Cadoc, a sixth-century saint much loved by the Britons who had migrated to Wales. The church dates to at least 1254. There is a chapel in the church building named after the Hanbury family.[5] A concensus exists among historians that Morgan Edwards's early life in the Anglican Church influenced his more formal views of Baptist practices.

In Edwards's time the parish was served by a curate who lived in the area. (Worship services were mainly in Welsh.) The curate at that time was William Jenkins, who served the church from 1719 to 1737,[6] and thereon hangs a twist of irony in Morgan Edwards's life.

THE EDWARDS FAMILY
There are no extant records of the Edwards family, but it is known that Morgan was named after his father and had a younger brother named James who is buried in St.

John's Churchyard at Waterford, Ireland. The inscription on his tombstone reads,

> Here lieth ye Body of ye Revd. James Edwards AM. youngest son of Morgan Edwards of Blaenayon in ye parish of Trevithin in ye Co. Monmouth, 16 March 1786.

The irony is that Morgan Edwards, who was such a careful and meticulous gatherer and keeper of records throughout his life, left little information on his own family and early life. But this was not his fault.

The manuscript records of Trevethin Parish for the period when Edwards' parents may have been married are in poor condition and illegible.[7] William Jenkins, apparently was not a good record keeper. During the eighteen years of Jenkins's ministry only nine infant baptisms were recorded, and most were named Jenkins. Only one baptism was recorded for 1722 and it was that of a little girl. Dr. Geraint Jenkins of the University of Wales points out that the poverty of many Welsh parish clergy contributed to the poor quality of many parish ministries.[8] Edwards did receive the rite of infant baptism, but there exists no known record of it. The irony continues.

Years later in Cork, Ireland, where he served as assistant pastor of the Baptist church, Edwards married Mary Nun and fathered several children. One might expect to find some records here, but the practice of keeping civil records of marriages, births and deaths was not begun at Cork until 1864. Any possible notations of his marriage or the births of his children in the church records may have been destroyed by a fire which consumed some church records. These were partially reconstructed in 1755. Whatever family records Edwards himself may have maintained were no doubt destroyed when the British army torched his house in Pencader, Delaware, during the American Revolution.[9]

Edwards attached great importance to family history and lineage, as may be seen in a statement he made in his *Materials Toward a History of the Baptists*.[10]

> It is a wonder to me that there should not be some curious body in every American family to trace pedigrees, and wear the arms of their ancestors, and those of note in Europe (but are risen up to consideration in America) should not attend to the names and history of their emigrating progenitors. Heraldry will (in time) be set up in America; and the settling of America will afford a new period to command the attention of the heralds.

When Edwards wrote that statement in 1792, he may have been looking to a future, more sophisticated America than he knew in his day. He had traveled far and worked hard to collect the data for his history of the Baptists, only to encounter many gaps in church and family records. Furthermore, his statement implies that he kept such records and that his family lineage was worth preserving. Hence, had it been left to Edwards we would have good records of his family. As it is we know only the name of his father, and only a little more about his brother James.

His Brother James

James Edwards was born in 1731, nine years after Morgan's birth,[11] and died nine years before him in 1786, nine years before Morgan's death. He served twenty years as pastor of the Baptist church in Waterford, Ireland. Morgan visited his brother on his fund-raising trip to the British Isles.

James's early Christian and ministerial experiences were

at the Baptist church in Llanwenarth, Wales, where an entry in the churchbook reads,"James Edwards, Caleb Harris apprentice, was Baptized 16 July 1749 and added to the church accordingly with the laying on of hands."[12] Since James was seventeen at the time of his baptism, he would have been at the suitable age to be an apprentice. This raises at least two possible explanations for his presence in the Llanwenarth church instead of the Penygarn church where Morgan had been, namely relatives and employment.

During this period several people named Edwards are listed in the records of the Baptist church at Llanwenarth: James Edwards who was prominent in the church, and who died January 30, 1750; James Edwards the Younger, who was baptized in 1739; and Ruth Edwards, who was baptized a month later in 1739.[13] No kinship is shown with James but if they were related, that may account for his presence at the Llanwenarth church.

James's apprenticeship appears to be the reason for his presence in Llanwenarth. The churchboook notation of his baptism cited above refers to James as "Caleb Harris apprentice." Caleb Harris, the pastor, like many Baptist pastors of that time was bivocational in his ministry, i.e., practicing a trade to make a living, with James as as apprentice in that trade. James began to exercise his ministerial gifts in 1752 and entered Bristol Academy in 1754.[14] There he was listed as a Welsh student who had come from Trosnant Academy.[15] The conclusion is that James went to Llanwenarth to work as an apprentice with Caleb Harris, and his baptism occurred soon afterward. His education at Bristol Academy lasted four years, whereas his brother was there for only one. Morgan, however, had spent four years at Trosnant Academy.

Both Morgan and James were seen by their fellow Baptists as scholars.[16]

Before going to Waterford, James interned at the Baptist church in Cork under pastor Ebenezer Gibbons, which was during the closing years of his brother's ministry there as the assistant pastor.[17] While he was at Waterford a parsonage was constructed.[18]

The Father of Morgan Edwards
The inscription on James's tombstone, "son of Morgan Edwards of Blaenayon" (currently spelled "Blaenavon"). "Blaenvon" can refer to a small landholding or farm which may have long since been overtaken by a larger farm. Thus, the elder Edwards was either a yeoman who owned a small estate in land, a gentleman farmer or a freeholder, just a cut below the gentry. In any case, a yeoman worked his own land. Morgan's father, therefore, was at best a yeoman or at the least a tenant farmer. Such speculations about the senior Edwards's position were not limited to how he earned his living, but also that he was someone other than a man named Morgan.

In 1863 a Welsh Baptist named Rufus Williams wrote about Baptist academies and reported that Morgan Edwards was the brother of Miles Edwards. If true, he would be the son of the Reverend Thomas Edwards,[19] who died at thirty-four years of age in 1746. He was pastor of the Baptist church at Llanwenarth Blaneau, the same church where James Edwards was later baptized.

Two pieces of evidence counter that speculation. First, at the time of Morgan Edwards' birth, Thomas Edwards was ten years old. Second, the inscription on James's tombstone makes it clear that his father's name was Morgan. It is very possible, however, that Thomas

Edwards may have been a relative.

Welsh Baptist historian T.M. Bassett later picked up on the Thomas Edwards story, but he may simply have been reflecting the writing of Rufus Williams.[20] About the rest of Morgan Edwards' family (mother, sisters, or other brothers) nothing is known. The same is true regarding his primary education.

PRIMARY EDUCATION

The primary education of Morgan Edwards included two major components, an encouraging learning environment at home and a charity-or-church sponsored gram-mar school. Most of the Welsh minor gentry, freeholders, tenant farmers, and townspeople though not persons of great wealth did possess libraries in their homes. The Welsh always had a high regard for their own language and much of their literature would have been written in their native tongue.[21] Not only would there have been a library in Morgan Edwards' home, but in his community as well.

Jenkins points out that the growth of Welsh towns was linked to the printing, publishing, and distribution of books. Professional booksellers concentrated their efforts on the town markets and this pressured other merchants to stock books.[22] In fact, an intentional effort to create libraries throughout Wales was carried out between 1703 and 1711. The cultivation of reading was considered by dissenting ministers as essential to a truly Christian and enlightened life.[23] Morgan Edwards's voluminous reading habits began at home and in the town library. His grammar school education also took place in Pontypool.

During the Commonwealth Period, the Puritan Parliament passed the Act for the Better Propagation of the

Gospel in 1650. This legislation not only turned loose a host of itinerant Puritan preachers, but also produced the concept that education should serve the end of spiritual and moral development.[24]

The English Puritans had a low regard for the morals of the Welsh people, but recognized the need to address them in their own language if there was to be an improvement. So, they produced literature in the Welsh tongue and required a morally strict and austere lifestyle of schoolmasters on public salary.[25] With the end of the Commonwealth in 1660, the schools reverted to being charity-sponsored institutions. As Puritan clergy were turned out of their pulpits they began to establish schools to earn a living in the hostile environment. When the Declaration of Indulgence was passed in 1672, however, a climate of toleration began to evolve.

In 1674, the Welsh Trust was founded with the twofold purpose of providing devotional literature to the Welsh people and operating schools for their children. Its major flaw, so far as the Welsh were concerned, was its insistence on teaching the children to read in English rather than in Welsh.[26]

A new infusion of life into the educational process in Wales occurred in 1699, with the creation in London of the Society for Promoting Christian Knowledge (SPCK). Its goals were to spread the Gospel to foreign lands and to establish schools at home. The society's members were Anglicans and they had the backing of the Welsh bishops.[27] The SPCK schools had no language bias, since the schools in the North were conducted in Welsh and English was used in the South. All the Schools had regular teaching staffs.[28] The parish school at Trevethin was founded by Curate William Jenkins by 1726 and was probably a SPCK school. It seems safe to assume that at least the beginning of Morgan Edwards's primary education was in the parish school,[29] although he also attended another school.

By the eighteenth century, every county in Wales had primary day schools. The local gentry sent its sons to these schools and provided the financial support, with most of the funds invested and endowments established. The curriculum was primarily classical in subject matter with heavy doses of Latin and Greek.[30] There is no evidence that Pontypool had a charity school, but it did have a school which majored in teaching the classics.

About 1711 Evan Evans (or Bevan Evans) established a school in the Quaker meeting house at Pontypool. He emphasized religious principles, Latin, Greek, and geography, and the school prospered for thirty-five years until his death in 1746. There is no other way to account for Edwards' early proficiency in Latin, Greek, and classical literature than to assume he attended a school which majored in the classics. Evans' school was the only one to meet those criteria.[31] This period of Edwards life came to a close in his sixteenth year when he experienced a conversion in a contrasting religious climate of moribund churches and a continuing revival.

THE RELIGIOUS CLIMATE
Moribund Churches

The religious climate at the time of Morgan Edwards's conversion was one of slow death and fervent coming to life in the outwardly staid Anglican Church, as well as among Dissenter Churches, including Baptists. The Welsh Puritans had produced great preachers from the time of Vavasor Powell in the seventeenth century, but the harsh poverty in Wales made it the worst of all places for parish ministers.

In order to make ends meet clergymen had to be bi-vocational or serve multiple parishes. The result was the spiritual neglect of the people and the churches.[32] Bishops who did not speak Welsh were appointed to Welsh Sees, compounding the problem. Because the Welsh people had acquired a taste for great preaching during the Puritan Commonwealth, the average scholarly sermons read by many Anglican clergy were turning people away. But there were exceptions to this dismal situation.

A Continuing Revival
By 1713 people were coming in droves to hear Griffith Jones, an Anglican curate at Llanddowror. By 1720, two years before Edwards's birth, a revival burst forth in the Arbertillery area of Gwent through the preaching of two Baptists, Enoch Francis and Morgan Griffiths.[33] A revival began in earnest in 1735 in Cardiganshire, again with the preaching of Griffith Jones, and with the conversion of another Anglican clergyman named Daniel Rowland. In the neighboring county of Brecknock, an Anglican schoolmaster named Howel Harris was converted after reading a popular devotional book entitled *The Whole Duty of Man,*[34] and he began to preach with remarkable results. Two other curates who must not be overlooked were William Williams and Howell Davies, both preached with great success following their conversions. Out of these Anglican clerical and lay conversions came a number of early Methodists, as well as Baptists and Congregationalists.[35]

The upshot of all this revival activity was that thousands of average people had a spiritual awakening, mostly under the umbrella of the Anglican Church.[36] It seems logical to assume the members of St. Cadoc's in Trevethin Parish would not have escaped the fallout from the revival. The first stirrings of sixteen-year-old Morgan Edwards's conversion no doubt occurred from the revival reaching his own parish church by 1738. The Anglican revival, however was not the only contributing factor.

Both Anglican and Dissenter churches saw sermons and books as two sides of the same coin. The sermons brought the teaching to mind, and books made it possible for the teaching to be retained and meditated upon.[37] Furthermore, the combination of a growing desire for literacy, along with a good understanding of the faith, increased the importance of Christian literature.[38] The roots of this atitude toward reading are to be found in the Protestant Reformation.

The Protestant Reformation stressed the priestly role of the parents in religious matters, and the literature was geared to the father's place as head of the house. The content of the reading materials in Wales emphasized Christian living and good citizenship, meaning loyalty to the Crown. Such teaching may have influenced Edwards' loyalty to the King later in his life because at home he had been taught it was a Christian duty.

Much of the literature was designed for people in the lower economic levels, and this proably accounts for the high literacy rate among all the Welsh.[39] It does not seem too farfetched to conclude that such reading material was present in the Edwards household. The fact that both Morgan and James were later viewed as scholars is an indication of early exposure to quality literature in their home. If, however, the seed of Morgan's conversion was sown by Anglican preaching and literature, it came to full flower under the care and cultivation of the Baptists.

Two Baptist Streams
The river of Baptist life in the British Isles began with two streams flowing from the fountain of English Congregationalism. One stream stemmed from a group of Independent Congregationalists living in exile in Holland. Under the influence of Dutch Mennonites, they had accepted the concept of believer baptism, and some, led by Thomas Helwys, had returned to English soil in 1610 or 1611 to establish a Baptist church at Spitalfields near London. They were called General Baptists because they believed in the general atonement teachings of Jacobus Arminius (1560-1609), a Dutch theologian.

Arminius held that God knew beforehand who would place faith in Christ, and though Christ died for everyone (thus a general atonement), only those who believed would be saved. He held that humans could do nothing to save themselves and that salvation was solely by God's grace. This grace, however, was not irresistible, and could be accepted or rejected by anyone. Arminiaism also taught that this grace once received could be lost, an issue which seemed to trouble the young, unconverted Morgan Edwards.

A second Baptist stream flowed from an Independent Congregational church; this one at London in 1638, under John Spilsbury. Its followers were called Particular Baptists because they followed the predestinarian teachings of John Calvin.

John Calvin (1509-1564) was a French theologian who believed that no human had any good whatsoever to merit salvation, but could only be saved by the irresistible grace of God. Irresistible grace meant that once God made the decision as to who would be saved and who would be lost, those chosen for salvation could not resist God's unmerited favor extended toward them for that purpose. Indeed, even repentance and faith were gifts of God in those elected to salvation.

The sad fact was that both General and Particular Baptists were experiencing grave theological problems by the late seventeenth and early eighteenth centuries. General Baptists experienced theological contamination as the pollutants of Socinianism and Unitarianism seeped into their belief in a general atonement. Socinianism grew out of the teachings of Lelio Sozzini (Socinius 1525-1562) and Fausto Sozzini (1539-1604). This uncle-nephew team held to a rather broad teaching that salvation required only a belief in the existence of God. All humans are mortal and only the teachings of Scripture could lead them to eternal life through the life and example of Christ. Jesus, too, was a human whose goodness was rewarded by a resurrection and an imparted divinity. The weak Christology of the Socinians made them easy prey for the anti-Tinitarians and Unitarians.

Dissenters who accepted Socinian teachings moved away from the orthodox view of the Trinity. Several groups were affected, including the Presbyterians and General Baptists.[40] By the time of Morgan Edwards's conversion, the General Baptists had fallen "victim of extreme liberalism. They had no gospel to preach, and they preached no gospel."[41] Later Edwards would give scant notice to General Baptists in his writings.[42] On the other hand, Calvin's teachings of "once saved always saved" may have brought spiritual calm to a young man troubled about losing his salvation. The Calvinistic Baptists would also be giving Edwards practical help as well as theological counsel.

Morgan Edwards's conversion and early Christian experience were fostered by a newly developing, more flexible but as yet undefined, "Evangelical Calvinism." Paradoxically, both Edwards' effort for continuing education after he left Bristol Academy and his move to the Baptist church in Philadelphia were significantly aided by Dr. John Gill of London, the most visible of the rigid Calvinists. One of the puzzling aspects of Morgan Edwards's life is why Gill, rigid doctrinaire Calvinist that he was, so highly recommended him to that church in the American colonies. An effort will be made later in the story to provide a solution to that puzzle, but Gill's star role in the Baptist drama put him center stage in the unfortunate calcification of Particular Baptist theology and a fortunate place in Edwards' life.

John Gill was born to Baptist parents on November 23, 1697, at Kettering, England. He became an ardent student early in life. By eleven years of age he gained a working knowledge of Latin and Greek, and taught himself Hebrew. At that age he dropped out of grammar school rather than submit to forced daily attendance for prayers at the local parish church. He began helping his father in the woolen trade, and spent much of his spare time reading the Latin Fathers and other European authors. During his life, Gill had the reputation of either being in his study or a bookstore.[43]

Following his baptism in 1716, Gill began to preach and soon after became an intern with John Davis at Highan Ferrars. Here Gill met and married Elizabeth Negus. For a short period he returned to his home church at Kettering, when he received two grants from the managers of the Particular Baptist Fund.[44] As we shall see in chapter four, Gill's later presence on that board as chairman would bring Morgan Edwards to his attention. In the meantime Gill received a call to the Baptist church at Horsleydown, Southwark, in September 1719. He stayed there for fifty-two years until he death in 1771.[45]

Gill's ministry at Horsleydown soon led to his recognition as chief spokesman for Calvinistic Dissenters, especially the Particular Baptists. He and John Brine became widely known theological protagonists through debates and a vast array of printed material. But they also received a large share of the negative credit for the hardening of the theological arteries of the Particular Baptist Churches and the stagnation of Baptist church life.

Two reasons for the criticism of Gill's high Calvinism were that it discouraged evangelism and encouraged Antinonianism.[46] The implication of the first charge was that if God had already decided who would be saved and who would be lost there was no need to evangelize. Antinomianism held that since faith alone saved, then obedience to God's moral law was unnecessary. Neither of these criticisms of Gill may have been fair, but there seems to be little doubt that the fallout from his closely ordered Calvinism was a deterrent to evangelism and led many to justify wrong conduct.

Gill hardly preached a sermon without speaking of the absolute, irresistible grace of God. He had no place for human choice in accepting or rejecting Jesus Christ, but would inevitably return to the major themes of his high Calvinism no matter what the stated theme of his sermon. Perhaps Andrew Fuller's description of John Martin, a disciple of John Gill, best describes Gill. Fuller said of Martin, "When he lifts up his feet he always is careful to put them down in the same place."[47]

In summary, Baptist church life in the time of Morgan Edwards' youth was generally in a state of decline with General Baptists slipping numerically and assuming a shapeless mass theologically. Particular Baptists were also in a numerical downturn with their theological feet set in concrete, as was true of the Particular Baptists in Wales as well.

The Baptists of Wales

From the time of his conversion at sixteen until his death at seventy-two, Morgan Edwards lived and labored as a Baptist--a theologically orthodox but progressive Baptist. His Welsh Baptist roots provide an essential element to understanding his conversion, his early Christian experience, and his later life and ministry.

Particular Baptists began in Wales in 1648 when Baptist soldiers in Cromwell's army began spreading Baptist teachings. The first church was started at Ilston in 1649, and four more were begun within four years. After the restoration of the monarchy in 1660, Baptists were persecuted and many began migrating to America. The oldest known Baptist meeting house set apart for worship was at Llanwenarth in 1695, later to be the home church of James Edwards.

In 1690 Baptists numbered about 550, and they continued to grow at a slow, steady pace. Most of the growth occurred among the middle class along the border with England, and among the farmers and laborers in the Southwest.[48] By 1735, however, there were only seventeen Baptist churches in all of Wales, most Calvinistic in doctrine and closed communion in practice.

Many of the Welsh Baptist churches were bogged down in the swamps of a viscose Calvinism which impeded growth and spontaneous responses to the Gospel appeal. Baptists feared being labelled "enthusiasts," a rather nasty name in those days for people who relied solely on a fervent emotional response to the Gospel without the use of the mind.[49]

While it may be said that those Baptists who had developed a dependency on the theology of John Calvin had retarded Baptist growth, it did prevent them from sliding into the pit of universalism wherein many General Baptists had fallen.[50] Furthermore, it was the evangelistic activity of Particular Baptists which effected the conversion of Morgan Edwards.

THE CONVERSION OF MORGAN EDWARDS

Morgan Edwards reported in his *Materials Towards a History of the Baptists* that he "was bred a churchman [Anglican]. Embraced the principles of the baptists [sic] in 1738."[51] This was, however, more than a mental assent to a set of theological tenets. Years later he recalled his conversion experience in a sermon at Philadelphia.[52]

> I remember the time (and the place too) when I first gave myself up as a lost man; for til then I was halting between two opinions about it. Fearing it was so, made me uneasy, and hope it might not be so, kept me from yielding to it. But this sentance stuck on my mind in a light that it was not want to do, "I will by no means clear the guilty!" Then said I, I am gone, for I am guilty; if I am not damned God must be a liar. So he slew me with the word of his mouth. Then his commandment came and I died. Then I knew what sort of thing despair was. And you cannot imagine what joy I felt, when I learnt so much of the gospel as to know it was possible for me to be saved, and that God might stand to his word, and not send me to hell.

A careful reading of this testimony reveals several facts

about Edwards' conversion. He could pinpoint the specific time and place when it occurred, and it followed a period of intense inner struggle before he yielded to faith in Christ. While not stating specific sins he made clear he viewed his life as a very sinful one, and he elaborated on this matter in other sermons.

Edwards once described his preconversion lifestyle.[53]

> I was formerly as wild and as worthless as any other; and should have been so yet had not the unmerited love of God laid hold of me, and raised me to the state I am in now.

In another sermon Edwards spoke of his remorse.[54]

> My conduct from my youth up to the time of my conversion had been base and shameful. The thoughts of it make me drop the head, and the eyes together. O that what I did had not been done! that I had not been till I had been good---I possess the sins of youth---I cannot forget them.

On another occasion he reported his conduct before his conversion as "carnal, sinful, and worldly."[55]

By modern standards Edwards's wild days may have been rather tame, but we must measure by the rules of conduct of his day. One remorseful, reformed sinner spelled out his sins.[56]

> Since youth I spent many a Sunday,
> I cannot deny playing bowl or ball
> In pain and travail often;
> Playing quoits and bobbing and leaping
> And spending what I had on beer.

Many of the gentry and even clergy kept fighting cocks, and cockpits have been found in the churchyards.[57]

Edwards told the people of Philadelphia he had doubted he could change his sinful lifestyle even if he had believed in Christ.[58]

> Thinking that sinning under a profession [of faith in Christ] deterred me strongly from becoming a professor---I was taught that a relapse is worse than the disease. That kept me from vowing to be the Lord's; because I was taught it was better not to vow, than vow and not to pay.

This statement suggests that he had been exposed to teaching on the loss of salvation by itinerant Anglican preachers with an Arminian theology. A number of these, who later became Methodists, were traveling about the area at the time.

Not only did Edwards's spiritual struggle revolve around his wild life and his fear of being a hypocrite, but he also saw faith in Christ could mean a loss of freedom to do as he pleased.[59]

> To be tied to anything, and confined, bid me not to be a professor---liberty or doing as I pleased joined in the dissuassion [sic]. My friends were against it; my interest against it, my inclinations against losing my liberty.

Furthermore, Edwards resisted the idea that he was a lost person until one day the scripture text, Exodus 34:6, grabbed his attention. The enormity of his guilt was too much to endure. His statement reveals tremendous despair when this occurred, but he went from a dark night of despair to a bright day of joy when he also discovered he could be saved from eternal punishment. His experience was not too uncommon if one is to judge by Caleb Evans, who was to be one of his mentors at Trosnant Academy.[60]

> When I was only a youth I beheld with admiration my father in the pulpit, and was delighted with the heavenly sounds which flowed from his lips. Hearing the awful terrors of the law and the astonishing grace of the Gospel, I was brought into the very dust before the throne of a holy God, and enabled to magnify the riches of free grace.

On July 20, 1756, Edwards related the experience of his conversion to the congregation at Cork, Ireland.[61]

> Every good Christian can upon a retrospect of his life find some such materials to work his fears away. I can remember (says he) my convictions and conversion: I know how God in kindness broke in upon me when I like the Israelites at Mount Sinai feared and trembled; when the pains of hell got hold of me he then said to me fear not for I am thy God, be not dismayed for I am with thee: he then said to me thy sins are forgiven be of good cheer; he then seals his love to me and in the interim my heart filled with love to him, all my soul was kindness and affection, and tho' a little before I was in such bondage that [if] all the world were to tell me that God would not forgive me I would not believe; but then again if the world were to tell me that I should die eternally I could not credit them.

At this point two major influences entered Edwards's life--Miles Harry and the Penygarn Baptist Church. These helped to bring about his conversion.

The Reverend Miles Harry

All of South Wales was being crisscrossed by evangelists in the first third of the eighteenth century. Some were itinerant preachers moving from place to place, and others were new converts attached to a church and/or a pastor while trying out their spiritual wings. Still others were pastors of churches who branched out from their communities to the surrounding countryside. Such a person was Miles Harry (sometimes spelled Harri or Harris).

Miles Harry has been described as "probably the outstanding Welsh Baptist minister of his time."[62] How providential that he encountered Morgan Edwards at a troublesome time in his life!

Harry was a larger-than-life person and typical of so many Dissenter preachers. They were single-minded in their purpose to preach the gospel, possessed of boundless energy, restless in spirit, enthusiastic, enterprising, and diligent in their ministries.[63] Some of these peripatetic preachers were more famous than Miles Harry, but none outdid him in zeal.

Miles Harry was born in Blaenau Gwent in 1700. It was here he professed faith in Christ and was baptized on April 1, 1724.[64] Five years later, on October 29, 1729, Harry was ordained as a local preacher and began to preach at a number of places, including a branch of the Blaenau Church at Penygarn.[65] He preached frequently there, and soon he was invited to be their pastor. The Blaenau church was at first reluctant to part with Harry, but eventually relented. His membership was transferred May 1, 1732, and he officially became pastor at Penygarn on May 24, 1732. Thus began a whirlwind ministry which continued to his death in 1776.

It is reported that Harry baptized "hundreds of believers" in the course of his itinerant ministry.[66] He helped establish churches, set up the earliest printing press in that part of Wales, played a major role in establishing Trosnant Academy, and continued his evangelistic tours.[67]

Exterior of the Penygarn Baptist Church

Miles Harry married into the Griffiths family, who were connected with the Hanbury Ironworks at Pontypool, and fathered a son who gave him two granddaughters.[68] With advancing years he became somewhat obese,[69] but still carried his distinguished appearance into the pulpit.[70] His last years in the ministry were difficult, as the church began to lose ground, discipline was neglected, and fault was found with his conduct.[71] Perhaps Miles Harry's most enduring legacy was the covey of effective young preachers, including Morgan Edwards, who became associated with the Penygarn church and the Trosnant Academy.

At what point Miles Harry entered Edwards's life and spiritual struggle can only be guessed. He had been involved in the revivals taking place in that area, but in his earlier years his orthodoxy was questioned by his fellow Calvinistic Baptists. The criticism was mainly against his habit of inviting all sinners to repent and trust Christ.[72] He was found to be orthodox, but his more evangelistic form of Calvinism certainly must have influenced Morgan Edwards who never preached the rigid Calvinism of John Gill. In fact, Harry's new "evangelical Calvinism" would not come to full bloom until Andrew Fuller gave it shape toward the end of the eighteenth century. In between Harry and Fuller were those young men related to the Penygarn church and Trosnant Academy.

If Miles Harry was a key person in the conversion and early Christian experience of Morgan Edwards, then the Penygarn Baptist Church was where he cut his spiritual eye teeth.

The Penygarn Baptist Church
The Pontypool area assumed an early importance in Bap-

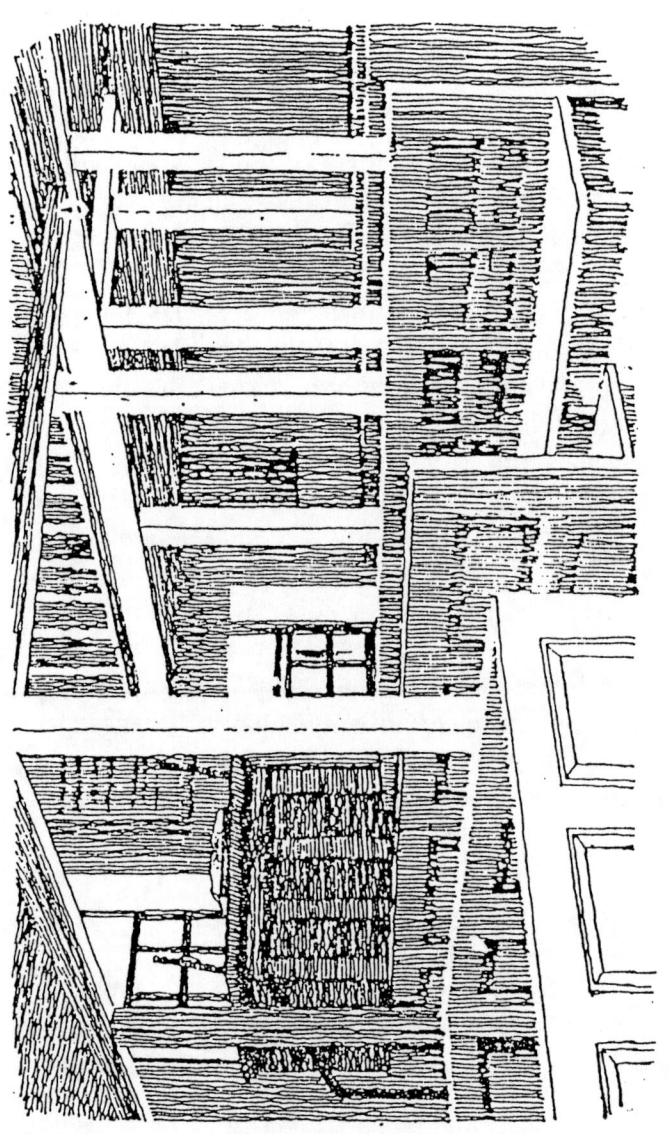

Eighteenth Century Interior of the Penygarn Baptist Church
Artist: Fred J. Rambo

tist life in South Wales, especially in grooming young men for the ministry.[73] Baptists began meeting around Pontypool as early as the late seventeenth and early eighteenth centuries. Usually they met in private houses with other Dissenter groups. From these meetings evolved a group composed of Baptists and Independents, or Congregationalists meeting at a house in Trosnant.[74]

The Trosnant group outgrew its meeting place and so separated with Miles Harry becoming the regular preacher for the Baptists and Edmund Jones for the Independents.[75] Since the Penygarn Baptists were sponsored by the church at Blaenau Gwent, members were baptized and received into that church. Harry was such a zealous evangelist that it opened a rift with Edmund Jones that broadened as Harry conducted mass baptisms.[76] It was about that time that Harry began to have difficulies with his fellow Baptists as well.

When the Penygarn church submitted its confession of faith in conjunction with applying for membership in the Welsh Association, it was carefully examined because of Harry's persistence in offering salvation to all.[77] This practice made his theology suspect to old-line Calvinists, but at the annual meeting of the association at Cilfowyr in 1726, the Pontypool Baptists proceeded to announce a desire for a meeting house of their own and requested assistance.[78] A site was obtained on Penygarn Hill for the building and construction was begun in 1727.[79] The work was completed in 1729.[80]

The exterior of the building looked like a barn while the interior resembled the style of most Dissenter chapels of the day. There were two levels of seating on three walls in the rectangular structure with the pulpit mounted on the fourth wall halfway between the two levels. There

Twentieth Century Interior of the Penygarn Baptist Church

A Dazzling Enigma 49

was a window in back of the pulpit and a preaching chair occupied the pulpit. The chair was a "high chair," having a broad arm to be lowered in front of the pastor for his notes.[81] The building, however, was not the most significant feature of the Penygarn Baptist Church.

The two most noteworthy features of life in the Penygarn Baptist Church at this period were its rapid growth among the young adults and its practice of sending out young men to test their gifts in itinerant preaching. When Harry became pastor in 1732 there were about thirty members, but the group soon grew to about two hundred.[82] Baptisms were conducted in an outdoor baptistry, which was fed by a stream near a highway about one hundred yards from the church.

Part of the folklore which surrounds the early days of the church tells of farmers, yeomen, and gentry coming with their families from miles around by horseback, carriage, wagon, and on foot. Those walking would travel single file along sheep tracks over hilltops and down slopes. They brought food for "dinner on the grounds" or in the chapel following a morning service. After eating, the singing and preaching would resume.[83] The young couples in the church even carried stones from the river Afon Llwyd to the building site for construction of their meeting house.[84]

In addition to the young couples who flocked to hear Miles Harry was a group of single young men that by 1738 included a sixteen-year-old youth named Morgan Edwards. Specific evidence is lacking to establish a chain of events linking Edwards's upbringing in the Anglican church with his eventual arrival in the Penygarn Baptist Church, but it is possible to outline a path he might have traveled.

The spiritual revival among the Anglicans has been described earlier, as well as the roles of Griffith Jones and Howel Harris in that awakening. In time, Harris became a follower of John Wesley and George Whitefield, both of whom came to the Pontypool area at Trosnant.[85] Whitefield, being a Calvinist, was more popular among the Welsh, whereas Wesley's seemingly negative attitude toward the Baptists made them wary of his revival.

With rare exception John Wesley always referred to Baptists as Anabaptists, a term offensive to them. In Morgan Edwards's time that term was still one of reproach since it recalled the radical excesses which occurred in Munster, Germany, during the Reformation. Furthermore, the name Anabaptist meant re-baptizer, and in the minds of the Baptists, they were not rebaptizing believers but administering the initial baptism. To them infant baptism was not baptism at all.

Wesley's failure to distinquish between the Anabaptists of the sixteenth century and the Baptists of the eighteenth century is understandable although regrettable. Wesley never completely divested himself of many elements in his High Church heritage, and that apparently distorted his view of the Baptists. His Arminian theology made him suspect to the more Calvinistic Welsh Baptists, and generally they resented being grouped with the Anabaptists. Morgan Edwards, however, seemed to evince a more discriminating view of the Anabaptists and the Munster episode.

In his *Materials Towards a History of the Baptists,* Edwards placed Menno Simons and the Mennonites inside the Baptist tent, and he does not use the term Anabaptist. He described the Munster rebels as the "madmen of Munster" and completely absolved Baptists of any complicity in the event.[86] Nonetheless, the Wesleyan revival among the Anglicans spilled over to touch Baptists, including Morgan Edwards.

Edwards could have met and/or heard both Wesley and Whitefield at Trosnant when he was a student at the academy. Years later he made it a point to visit Whitefield while on his evangelistic tour for the Philadelphia Baptist Association.[87] In a later sermon Edwards said, "Mr. Whitefield use to say, 'That it was easier to convert twenty abandoned sinners than one rigid moralist.'"[88] It appears, however, that neither Wesley nor Whitefield played a direct role in Edwards's conversion, but perhaps Howel Harris, the converted Anglican schoolmaster did.

At some point in his ministry, Harris met Miles Harry, and later Harry arranged for Harris to make a preaching tour in Gwent. The tour ended abruptly with Harris being thrown in jail, charged with causing a riot. Miles Harry intervened, and with the help of a deacon from the Penygarn church Harris was released on bail.[89] Harry then obtained financial aid from London Baptist leaders Joseph Stennett and Andrew Gifford and hired legal counsel, who successfully won an acquittal.[90] How does all the revival activity of that period, and especially that of Harris and Harry, relate to the conversion of Morgan Edwards?

The activities and relationships of these revivalists suggest the following scenario for their roles in the conversion of Morgan Edwards. A pre-revival to the Methodist Revival broke out among the Anglicans and was spearheaded by Griffith Jones. While Harris was not converted by Jones he was won to faith during the revival and was stromgly influenced by him. These and other converted Anglican clergy came to Gwent in their preaching tours where Morgan Edwards heard them, and he was brought under conviction.

Anglican preaching was Arminian in theology and failed to convert Edwards from his wild and carefree lifestyle. He felt tremendous guilt, but feared failure in trying to live as a Christian. In some manner he encountered Miles Harry, a Calvinist, who gave him alternatives in the doctrines of the license to believe and eternal security.

The license or warrant to believe was the label Calvinists put on the kind of spiritual distress Morgan Edwards was experiencing in his mid-teens. This conviction of sin or "divine principle within" put a positive spin on the inner turmoil fermenting in Edwards's soul because it was God's authorization for him to believe. That is, God's grace was at work in his heart, indicating he was one of the elect.

The doctrine of eternal security would have quieted his fears of losing his salvation through a spiritual relapse. If his salvation was all God's doing and none of his own, keeping it was all of God's doing as well. Hence, Harry may have resolved Edwards's dilemmas and led him to faith in Christ. Next came his baptism and membership in the Penygarn Baptist Church. Here he joined several other young men in that pool of preachers who were spreading the Gospel in the area around Pontypool.

Young men were sent out to preach as a way of testing their gifts for ministry. However, in most cases churches were very careful to examine their fitness for ministry and to send them out in orderly fashion.[91] At the meeting of the Welsh Baptist Association at Llanwenarth in 1739, the association continued to caution the churches not to send out the young men in a disorderly fashion.[92] In the case of the Penygarn church, the young men apparently were students at the new school established in connection with the church, the Trosnant Academy. With his enrollment in that school in 1738, Morgan Edwards began the second phase of his remarkable life.

ENDNOTES
1. Arthur Clarke, *The Story of Monmouthshire*, (Llandybie, Wales: Christopher Davies, 1962), II, 31.
2. Ibid.
3. E.D. Evans, *A History of Wales, 1660-1815*, (Cardiff: University of Wales Press, 1976), 148.
4. Clarke, 7.
5. Arthur Crane, Bernard Derrick, Edward Donovan, *Pontypool's Heritage in Pictures and Postcards*, (Newport, Gwent: Starling Press, 1990), 33-34.
6. J.A. Branbury, *A History of Monmouthshire*, (London: Michael Hughes and Clark, 1907), 441-442.
7. My futile search for data on the Edwards family took me to the following sources,

(1) The Gwent County Records Office at Cwmbran, Gwent, Wales to study the original Trevethin Parish Records.

(2) The Archives at the National Library of Wales at Aberystwyth, Wales.

(3) The International Geneological Society Archives at London, England. According to Mr. N.P. Harden of the Society, the Trevethin Parish Register for the years 1710 to 1725 may be missing, as no coverage is given for that period in the National Index of Parish Registers for Wales.

(4) The International Geneological Index at both Aberystwyth and the Pennsylvania Historical Society at Philadelphia.

(5) The County Recorder's Office, the Cork Archives Institute and the churchbook of the Baptist church all at Cork, Ireland.

In addition I was given invaluable aid by local historians and Anglican Church historians in England, Ireland and Wales.
8. Geraint Jenkins, *Literature, Religion and Society in Wales,*

1660-1730, (Cardiff: University of Wales Press, 1978), 7.
9. Joshua Thomas, *Materials for a History of the Baptist Churches in the Principality of Wales, 1630-1782,* (MS., Bristol Baptist College, Bristol, England: n.d.), 278.
10. Morgan Edwards, *Materials Toward a History of the Baptists, 1772,* (Danielsville, Georgia: Heritage Papers, 1984), I, 86.
11. D. Hugh Matthews, "The Students of Bernard Foskett," *The Transactions of the Welsh Baptist Historical Society,* (London: 1980), 2. This article contains a list of students at Bristol Academy and signed by Bernard Foskett. The list had been in possession of Dr. John Rippon and eventually ended up in the Congregational Memorial Library in London with his other papers. That library is now part of Dr. Williams Library in London. The catalogue number is MS. 11. C.6.a., and the document indicates the year of entry of each student, their ages and subjects studied. Both Morgan and James Edwards are listed.
12. *Llanwenarth Churchbook,* (National Library of Wales, Aberystwyth), Dep. 410B. p. 12.
13. Ibid., Dep. 409 B. 37; Dep. 410 B, 6, 10, 24.
14. D. Hugh Matthews, 3.
15. *History of Llanwenarth Baptist Church,* (MS. Written 1908. Gwent County Records Office, Cwmbran, Wales: 1908), 82. No names of authors or editors are attached, and sources cited are churchbooks and Welsh Baptist historian, Joshua Thomas.
16. Geoffrey F. Nuttall, "Welsh Students at Bristol Baptist Academy, 1720-1797," *Transaction of the Honourable Society of Cymmrodorion,* (London: 1978), 189.
17. From a loose sheet containing the registry of the pastors of the Waterford Baptist Church and kept in the Waterford Baptist Church churchbook, June 1805 to December 1914, at the Irish Baptist Historical Society, Belfast.
18. Contained in a letter from Dr. Joshua Thompson of the Irish Baptist Historical Society, dated June 12, 1991, and from the Cork Baptist Chruch churchbook, dated October 26, 1757 showing James as having gone to Waterford as pastor and Morgan to America. Morgan did not go to America until 1761 so apparently the entry was posted after 1757.
19. Rufus Williams, *The History of the Baptist Seminaries in Mon-*

mouthshire, (Aberdar: Thomas Williams, 1863), n.p.
20. T.M. Bassett, *The Welsh Baptists,* (Swansea: Ilston House, 1977), 165.
21. E.D. Evans, 36.
22. Jenkins, 249.
23. Ibid., 283.
24. Ibid., 15.
25. E.D. Evans, 42, 43.
26. Ibid., 47.
27. Ibid., 49.
28. Ibid., 53
29. Crane, et. al. 63.
30. E.D. Evans, 114-118.
31. In a personal letter to the author dated March 8, 1993, from Arthur Crane, Pontypool historian, he states that Evans school "would appear to be one of the few known sources in the area for obtaining a grounding in classical literature."
32. Jenkins, 8.
33. Dafydd Densil James Morgan, "The Development of the Baptist Movement in Wales Between 1714 and 1815 With Particular Reference to the Evangelical Revival," Unpublished D.Phil. Dissertation, (Oxford: Regents Park College, Oxford University, 1986), 224.
34. Jenkins, 123.
35. The Reverend D. Hugh Matthews, Principal of South Wales Baptist College, Cardiff, provides the following data on Griffith Jones, "the forerunner of the Methodist Revival in Wales."

> Everyone I have consulted believes him to be an Arminian. Canon Arthur Edwards [Anglican historian] says that he was too tied to the Catechism to be anything but Arminian.... Dr. J.Gwynfor Jones is of a similar opinion. The Weslyan Methodist Revival in England was Arminian - which was the theology of the Church of England, although there were some Calvinists in the Church. So why did the Methodists in Wales become as "Calvinistic Methodists?" Joshua Thomas, the eighteenth century Baptist historian, claims that it was William Herbert who persuaded Howell Harris of the truth of Calvinism. Herbert was a Congregationalist-turned-Baptist who was

assistant minister of the Baptist Church at Massyberlian. But although Herbert made a Calvinist of Harris, he failed to make a Baptist of him. Gomer M. Roberts, the Calvinistic Methodist historian, suggests that it was because Griffith Jones despised the Baptists that Howell Harris never became one himself-this may suggest that Jones was not as anti-Calvinist as he was anti-Baptist. (Letter dated November 24, 1992, and now in the possession of the the author at Alhambra, California).

It was not possible to ascertain if Howell Harris became a Calvinist before Edwards conversion.

36. Jenkins, 225
37. Ibid., 46.
38. Ibid., 123.
39. Ibid., 49.
40. Williston Walker, *A History of the Christian Church,* 1st ed., (New York: Charles Scribner's Sons, 1939), 494.
41. H. Leon McBeth, *The Baptist Heritage,* (Nashville: Broadman Press, 1987), 158
42. Morgan Edwards, I, 33. Writing about the German Baptists or "Tunkers" he states,

> They are "general Baptists" in the same sense that the phrase bears in Greatbritain; [sic] but not "Arians" or "Socinians," as most of their brethren in Holland are. General redemption they certainly hold; and withall general salvation; which tenets though wrong are consistent.

43. John Rippon, *A Brief Memoir of the Life and Writings of the Late John Gill, D.D.,* (London: 1838), 4.
44. The Manuscript Records of the Particular Baptist Fund, (Oxford: Angus Library, Regents Park College, Oxford University), I. 1st April 1718; 13th May 1718.
45. Rippon, 7.
46. Olin C. Robinson, "The Legacy of John Gill," *The Baptist Quarterly,* (London: Baptist Historical Society, 1971), XXII, No. 2, 116.
47. Ibid., 117.

48. Jenkins, 49.
49. D.D.J. Morgan, 225-226.
50. Keith Manley, "John Rippon, 1751-1836 and the Particular Baptists," Unpublished D. Phil. Dissertation, (Oxford: Regents Park College, Oxford University, 1967), 2.
51. Morgan Edwards, I, 48.
52. Morgan Edwards, 1738, (MS., Rochester: Colgate Rochester Divinity School), Sermon XVII, No. 9. n.p., Crozer Rare Books, Box 1, 252 ed. Unless otherwise indicated all sermon quotes are from the Crozer Collection.
53. Ibid., MS. "Behold What Manner of Love," (MS. loose, untied sheets)
54. Ibid., Fragment of sermon preached in Philadelphia in 1764.
55. "Behold What Manner of Love," n.p.
56. E.D. Evans, 197.
57. Ibid.
58. "Behold What Manner of Love," n.p.
59. Ibid.
60. Ernest A. Payne, "Caleb Evans, Founder of the Bristol Education Society," *The Baptist Quarterly*, (London: Baptist Historical Society, 1971), XXIV, No. 4, 176.
61. Morgan Edwards, MS. Sermon, "And Manoah Said," No. 416, n.p.
62. A.C. Underwood, *A History of the English Baptists*, (London: The Carey Kingsgate Press, Ltd., 1947), 164.
63. Jenkins, 26,27.
64. R. Jones, "Miles Harry," *Transactions of the Welsh Baptist Historical Society*, (London: 1926), 44. Translated by the Rev'd D. Hugh Matthews.
65. Selwyn Gummer, "Trosnant Academy," *The Baptist Quarterly*, (London: Baptist Union Publication Department, 1926), IX, 420.
66. Brymor P. Jones, *Sowing Beside Still Waters*, (Cwbran, Gwent, Wales: Gwent Baptist Association, 1985), 10. The Reverend Brynmor P. Jones is a pastor and local historian. He was extremely helpful to the author in transporting him to numerous locations in the Pontypool area, and in providing background information. His book on the Baptists of Gwent is good reading, but I found myself wishing it had more documentation.

67. Ibid., 10.
68. John Evans, Ed. *The Welsh Nonconformist Memorial,* (London: Sherwood, Neely and Jones, 1820), 374.
69. Ibid.
70. B.P. Jones, 12.
71. D.D.J. Morgan, 116.
72. Ibid.
73. Crane, et. al., 44.
74. Ibid.
75. Bassett, 55.
76. Peter D. Milford, *Manuscript Histories of Baptist Chapels,* (Newport: 1978), 21, 22.
77. B.P. Jones, 10.
78. Milford, 22.
79. Branbury, 452.
80. Milford, 22.
81. In an interview with Mr. Arthur Crane, Pontypool historian and a member of the Penygarn Baptist Church, he confirmed to the author, and as the sketch shows, that the interior was as I have described it. Modifications in the 1920s changed it to a different configuration.
82. D.D.J. Morgan, 108.
83. Crane, et. al., 45; Branbury, 452.
84. B.P. Jones, 12.
85. Crane, et. al., 49.
86. Edwards, I, 43.
87. _____., II, 62, 63.
88. _____., "The Prodigal Son," (MS. Sermon, n.d.), 71.
89. Crane, et. al., 49.
90. Bassett, 67; Crane, et. al., 49.
91. Joshua Thomas, 30.
92. Ibid.

CHAPTER THREE

WELL-READ AND WELL-SCHOOLED

"A Baptist Minister Possessed of Superior
Learning."
R.A. Guild, 1896

By common consent Baptist historians would concur with Reuben A. Guild, the long-time nineteenth-century librarian of Brown University, when he wrote that Morgan Edwards was a "Baptist minister possessed of superior learning."[1] On another occasion nineteenth-century Baptist writer Stephen Albert Swaine described him as a "master of scholarly attainments."[2] If Morgan Edwards is seen as one of the better educated American Baptist ministers of the eighteenth-century, it is not without reason, for he was both well read and well schooled.

A Well-Read Minister
Morgan Edwards had an abiding conviction that ministers should be both widely and deeply read which he stated in a sermon at the ordination of Samuel Jones in Philadelphia on January 2, 1763.[3]

> Reading furnishes...[ministers] with a rich variety of ideas and sentiments. I am aware that many things have been said against laying so much stress upon reading...; but I fear they amount to no more than apologies for laziness and ignorance.

The breadth and depth of his own reading is evident in Edwards's sermons, and not because he saturated them with quotations and citations. Rather, he selectively seasoned his sermons with references, quotations, and illustrations taken from a wide range of literature.

In his extant sermons Edwards drew upon a diverse field of authors to liven up his sermons and illustrate their teachings.[4] For example, in a sermon on conversion he demonstrated that he was well read on deism, the popular religious fad of his day.[5] In another sermon he took issue with the author of a book who to Edwards, appeared to advocate antinomianism, or disobedience to God's commands.[6] In a sermon entitled, "He Looketh For a City" Edwards debated rhetorically with writers who spiritualized eschatological texts and was obviously well acquainted with their arguments.[7] He made frequent references to Milton, whom he called a "half-divine poet,"[8] but he did not limit his reading to authors in religious fields.

Edwards also kept abreast with happenings in science, as he made use of the findings of Sir Isaac Newton in his preaching.[9] In addition, he apparently read books written for children, for he referred to a Mr. Janeway who wrote "Tokens For Children."[10] Sprinkled throughout his sermons are illustrations from Greek mythology as well as references to ancient writers such as Epictetus, Philo, and Josephus. Few Baptist preachers of his day had the ability to draw from such a wide-ranging field of literature, but learned eighteenth-century Dissenter ministers were expected to be well read in subjects not directly concerned with their Bibles. In the Dissenter Academies, students were trained to use such reading to enable them to make better use of the scriptures.

A Well-Schooled Minister

The superior quality of Morgan Edwards's secondary education was the result of his training at two Dissenter schools, namely Trosnant Academy in Wales and Bristol Academy in England. In her landmark book *Dissenting Academies In England,* Irene Parker described such schools as the "greatest schools of their day."[11] She is not alone in her high estimation of these institutions. Seymour J. Price reported that the "prominent place occupied by Dissenters in the history of higher education in England has very largely escaped the notice of general historians."[12] Jenkins opined, "What is clear, however, is that Dissenting Academies played vital roles in nurturing a galaxy of bright young ministers."[13] There are historical, theological, and practical reasons why Dissenting Academies of that period were superior to the universities, and thus account for Morgan Edwards being a "master of scholarly attainments."

DISSENTER ACADEMIES

Before Cromwell and the Puritans began moving toward control of the government of England in 1640, learning had been the private preserve of the upper classes. During the Commonwealth, educational activity accelerated because the Puritans were convinced of the importance of universal education. Hence, they made efforts to put it within the reach of everyone.[14] As the goal was coming into sight, however, the monarchy was restored in 1660 and the educational reform was set back two hundred years.

With the crowning of Charles II, a purging began, to root out and expel everything and everyone Puritan from the State, the Church, and the schools. The Established Church was to be supreme and freedom of thought and action in the churches and schools abolished. The year 1662 saw the reenactment of the Act of Uniformity to achieve those ends, but it also marked a new beginning for dissent and the Dissenter Academies.[15]

A series of acts, commonly called the Clarendon Code (the Corporation Act, the Conventicle Act, and the Five-Mile Act) reinforced the Act of Uniformity beginning in 1662 and required anyone who operated a school or tutored to conform to the liturgy of the Anglican Church. The immediate result was a mass exodus of many learned scholars from Anglican pulpits and university teaching posts. They, in turn, opened schools and academies of their own.[16] So, rather than weaken the Dissenters and strengthen the Anglicans, the legislation had quite the opposite effect.

The Conformity enactments drove more people into the ranks of the Dissenters and filled their academies with pupils. Sons who might otherwise have gone to the universities, were denied admission because of their refusal to become Anglicans. Instead, they enrolled in the Dissenter Academies where they were taught by very learned scholars no longer able or willing to teach at Oxford or Cambridge. But together with the historical events which led to the creating of strong Dissenter Aacdemies there was a hostile theological climate.

Dissenters and their offspring were not welcome at either Oxford or Cambridge. Both of these institutions were primarily training grounds for the clergy of the Church of England, which was their priority from the seventeenth century to well into the nineteenth century. Under these circumstances, both university communities presented a hostile environment for Nonconformists.

Beginning early in the eighteenth century, for example, townspeople of Oxford would join mobs of students in wrecking the meeting houses of the Presbyterians, Quakers, and Baptists, and they would heap vulgar abuse on Dissenters they encountered.[17] High-spirited undergraduates would attend Dissenter meetings and ridicule the worshippers.[18] If there was any restraint on these activities, it was due to fear of conversion. It is reported that students who were in the habit of attending Sunday evening lectures in the Dissenter Chapel in St. Peter-le-Bailey Parish (now the New Road Baptist Church) suddenly stopped "because it so materially impaired the gaiety of the evening."[19]

Despite such obstacles to their learning and the practice of their faith, the Dissenters continued to develop a more enlightened concept of an educated ministry, and with it schools which were mostly superior to either Oxford or Cambridge.[30] Their theological disagreements were not the only factors giving rise to schools of superior quality among the Dissenters.

Irene Parker's study reveals that freedom of conscience and a desire for a liberal education were two other compelling factors behind this development.[21] If so, then these concepts were not lost on Morgan Edwards, for these two factors are prominent in the Charter of the Rhode Island College (later Brown University) which Edwards helped to create.[22]

> And furthermore it is hereby enacted and declared, That into this liberal and catholic Institution shall never be admitted any religious tests. But on the contrary, all the members hereof shall forever enjoy full, free, absolute, and uninterrupted liberty of conscience.

Finally, there were some very practical factors which explain the superiority of the Dissenter Academies. The Nonconformist schools grew strong "because they satisfied the needs of the students with great efficiency."[23] Underlining this achievement was the Puritan principle that learning should be available to anyone who wanted it regardless of social or economic status.[24]

The aim of these academies, then, was to provide an education for life in general as well as for the ministry, and they were so successful that growing numbers of Anglicans were sending their sons to the Dissenter Academies rather than the universities.[25] Not only did the Puritan principle of education contribute to the strength of the academies, but so did the pedagogues and the progressive character of the training.

Many of the headmasters and tutors at the Dissenting Academies were men who left the universities because of the Acts of Conformity, and they were among the best scholars in the land.[26] In addition, numbers of them were specialists in their subject fields, which in turn broadened the offerings of the Academies.[27] Finally, many of these men were gifted teachers. Without question, as will be shown below, John Matthews at Trosnant and Bernard Foskett at Bristol were two such men who played large roles in the development of Morgan Edwards.

Not only were the pedagogues notable, but so was the disciplined and progressive character of the training. It was not unusual for the daily routine of an academy to include fourteen-hour days.[28] While the schools offered a progressive learning environment, they did not neglect the classics. Life on campus included conversations in Latin, and devotions in Hebrew, Greek, or French but read in English. There are academicals (formal papers) of Morgan Edwards extant from his year at Bristol which were originally presented in Latin and are in print in English.[29] Usually the orations were in Latin and English, but the learning went beyond the traditional emphasis of the classics.

Since the Dissenters were more progressive, they tended to be more student focused through offering lower tuition costs and giving special attention to the slower students. Because the student population included those training for secular careers as well as those for the ministry, the subject matter included studies in the fields of mathematics, logic, and the sciences. It is interesting to note that Morgan Edwards obtained some laboratory equipment for Rhode Island College when he made his fund raising trip for the school to the British Isles.[30]

The character of the education in the Dissenter Academies offered a break from the ancient method of teaching by lecture only. Lectures at the Dissenting Academies were followed by discussions or periods of questions and answers. The schools were not only interested in cramming facts into the minds of the students, but also "training them to think, and what is more to express their thoughts in their own tongue."[31]

Welsh historian Geraint Jenkins presented a "galaxy of bright young ministers" from the Dissenter Academies that included Morgan Edwards.[32] Hence, it is imperative that his story include a review of the two academies he attended at Trosnant and Bristol.

The Trosnant Academy
There was a time during the Puritan Commonwealth when it was hoped a university would be founded in Wales, but that hope died with the Commonwealth in 1660.[33] To meet the need for higher education, Welsh clergymen ejected by the Anglican establishment began creating

Artist's Conception of John Wesley Preaching in Trosnant
Arist: Ken Haynes

private academies. While these schools supplied ministers for Welsh churches, it was soon obvious that denominational schools were needed and wanted,[34] and by 1720 the Baptists were addressing the issue of education for the ministry.[35]

The issue of creating an institution for the education of the Baptist ministry was raised at the Welsh Baptist Association meetings in 1720.[36] A committee was formed to review the question of ministerial training and the feasibility of forming a Baptist academy.[37] One of the members of the committee was Morgan Griffiths, the pastor of the Baptist church at Hengoed. His presence on the committee was significant, as it was his son John Griffiths who began the Trosnant Academy about twelve years later,[38] although there is uncertainty about the year.

Seymour Price has described the start of Trosnant Academy,[39]

> There was an attempt of later years to set up a seminary at Pontypool for the benefit of candidates for the ministry. This year [1738] the following students: Messers Thomas Llewelyn from Hengoed, Morgan Edwards from Penygarn, Edmund Watkins of Blaenau, Jonathan Francis and Timothy Thomas of Newcastle [Emlyn] were all promising for the ministry. The prospect of a Welsh seminary, it is thought, was as flattering and animating then as ever it has been since; but it never could be brought properly to bear, though young men have received considerable assistance at Pontypool. There was some kind of instruction given to young men at Pontypool as early as 1734, though I think, no proper tutor till about 1736 or 1737.

Whatever the founding year, it was John Griffiths who provided the thrust to launch the school.

John Griffiths was not a minister but a layman who was the manager of the Iron and Japanning Ironworks at Pontypool and an active member of the Penygarn Baptist

Church.⁴⁰ He had the able assistance of his pastor, Miles Harry.⁴¹ The first Baptist academy in Wales was known as Trosnant Academy,⁴² and Griffiths rented a house in Trosnant for the school and occasional preaching services.⁴³

The Trosnant Academy was not limited to ministerial training but was "likewise a general school where farmers and tradesmens' children were educated and fitted for such different situations as their parents or friends had in view for them."⁴⁴ A second feature was to teach the ministerial students Welsh and English, acquaint them with Hebrew and Greek, and introduce them to various other branches of learning appropriate for the ministry.⁴⁵ At the outset Griffiths himself did some of the teaching, aided by Miles Harry. They were good friends and had married sisters.⁴⁶ Caleb Evans soon joined them as headmaster.

Selwyn Gummer, citing a "Dissenting Deputies" report, tells of Caleb Evans being hailed before the Bishop of Llandaff, Mathew Mawson, in 1739 for "keeping a school without a license." Gummer contended that Evans was at Trosnant, which places the incident during Edwards's second year at the school. In his appearance before the bishop, Evans was informed that the Schism Act required a license to operate a school, and it could only be granted to one who gave proof of attendance at communion in an Anglican Church.⁴⁷

Evans, however, was better informed than the bishop, for he told him the law had never been enforced and had been repealed in 1719. After this experience, Evans left Trosnant for Bristol, England, where he became associated with Bristol Academy in 1764 and where he died in 1790. In the meantime, Thomas Phillips assumed supervision of Trosnant Academy for a very brief period before the shining years of John Matthews's tenure began in 1740.[48]

Though John Matthews came to the school from Swansea in Wales, the bond between him and the school became so strong that he was buried in the churchyard of the Penygarn Baptist Church. The inscription on his headstone sheds light on his perspective of life and learning.

> "Here lyeth the Body of John/
> Matthews, School Master, late/
> of Trosnant, who departed this/
> life ye 17 of March 1744/45.
> Aged /32 years
> Long my delights perhaps like some of you
> Was various parts of learning to pursue
> But saving knowledge that alone I found
> Spring from the fountain of Immanuel's wound."

How close an association Matthews developed with Morgan Edwards is difficult to determine, since Edwards left for Bristol in 1742. Historian Rufus Jones lists him as a student of Matthews.[49]

> The services of John Matthews of Swansea, a young man of high academic standard with an attractive personality, had been secured as a tutor, and there were five students under his care. The names of three have their place on the list of famous men of Wales:- Timothy Thomas, Aberduar...; Morgan Edwards MA, the historian and chief founder of the first Baptist College in America, and Thomas Llywellen MA, LLD.

Matthews had a positive impact on the school. While he died after only five years, he saw graduates enter the ministry who later became outstanding leaders. It is possible, however, that a number of these young men were attracted to the school because of the notoriety surrounding Caleb Evans's trial before Bishop Mawson.[50] In any case, John Matthews was well qualified for his task, with about forty young men training under his tutelage during his tenure.[51] In the meantime John Griffiths, the school's founder, deemed it necessary to leave the Pontypool area.

Welsh Baptists held John Griffiths in high regard because of his amiability, generosity, usefulness to the Baptist cause, and the intensity with which he worked.[52] In 1750 he became involved in a public dispute which affected many people. Griffiths moved to Abercar where he helped found a Baptist church and began a business. He sold the business and emigrated to Philadelphia in 1759, two years before the arrival of Morgan Edwards. Griffiths was in Philadelphia when Edwards became pastor of the Baptist church there. He later moved to New York where he was able to direct his high intellectual capabilities to became a New York State judge.[53] It seems a fair assessment that four men at Trosnant must have had a significant effect on the mind and heart of Morgan Edwards, namely Miles Harry, John Griffiths, Caleb Evans, and John Matthews.

Miles Harry played a key role in Edwards's conversion and became his pastor in the Penygarn Baptist Church. Harry encouraged and sponsored Edwards and the other students at Trosnant Academy to begin itinerant preaching in that area of Wales; and this led to the creation of some new Baptist churches.[54] Harry also sent annual requests to the Particular Baptist Fund Board on behalf of Welsh Baptist ministry students, including Morgan Edwards.[55]

John Griffiths' effect on Morgan Edwards is not discernible, but some traits seem to have been common to both. Each was an ardent Baptist and tireless worker in the Baptist cause. They both experienced ostracism and "exile" for a period of their adult lives and then restoration with continued achievement. Each embraced the ideal of an educated Baptist ministry and went about the task of establishing a school of higher learning to that end. They were both learned men and taught at the schools they helped create.

The experience of Caleb Evans' trial before Bishop Mawson must have caused some disruption and dismay for the students at Trosnant Academy, including Morgan Edwards. He did learn a valuable lesson however. Years later when he put forward the idea of beginning a Baptist college in America, Edwards called for it to be situated in Rhode Island. There it would enjoy certification from the provincial government and could not legally be harrassed.[56]

Finally, we must see what scholarly and intellectual marks John Matthews left on Morgan Edwards. While Edwards was obviously blessed with a good mind and high intelligence, he was a good student before he came to Trosnant. There were three factors which indicate that the academy increased his intellectual and scholarly capabilities. First, the scholarly attainments of Trosnant graduates took a quantum leap with those who had been exposed to Matthews's influence. Second, the academicals produced by Edwards at Bristol give every evidence of a practised scholar rather than a neophyte. Third, there appears to be a body of opinion that the Trosnant Academy became a pattern for Bristol Academy when it was reconstituted in 1778, though it was the older of the two schools.[57] Whatever the quality of life and study at Trosnant, Morgan Edwards moved on to Bristol Academy after the close of the school year in 1742.

The Bristol Academy

Morgan Edwards was not the only young Welshman to cross the River Severn from Wales to attend Bristol Academy. From 1734 to the end of the eighteenth century, at least ninety students made the journey.[58] Five of these are singled out as persons of distinguished ability: Thomas Llewelyn (1741), Morgan Edwards (1742), Benjamin Francis (1753), William Richards (1775), and Morgan John Rhys (1782).[59]

Bristol Baptist Academy (now Bristol Baptist College) started in 1679, and is the oldest Baptist institution of higher learning in the world.[60] Edward Terrill, a wealthy British Baptist merchant and writing master, who was an elder of the Broadmead Baptist Church of Bristol,[61] conceived the idea of the school.

Terrill deeded a gift to his church at Broadmead to be used after his death for the support of a minister who was skillful in the use of the biblical languages of Hebrew and Greek. The chief task of this minister was to work three and one-half days a week at preparing young men for ministry in the Baptist churches of the land.[62] Terrill created the fund on June 3, 1679, a propitious time for Baptists.

At that time, Baptists, like all Dissenters, were an outlawed group and were being persecuted. It was just the year before, in 1678, that John Bunyan published *The Pilgrim's Progress,* written while imprisoned in Bedford jail for his religious convictions. It was also at this time that the Broadmead church was trying to locate a minister qualified to succeed university-trained Thomas Hardcastle. He had died at only forty-two years of age after suffering terrible hardship in prison, but he left behind the Puritan concept of an educated ministry.[63]

The Puritans believed that the "Minister of the Word of

God needed to be well educated, gifted in the knowledge of the Scriptures and able to understand them in the original languages."[64] Terrill himself had some knowledge of Hebrew and Greek, and he agreed with the Puritan understanding of an educated ministry. There were other Baptists, however, who did not accept that concept.

Throughout their history, Baptists have been ambivalent toward an educated ministry, and so there have been those who believed that education or human learning would inhibit the Holy Spirit. For example, Samuel How, a London Baptist preacher, published a pamphlet in 1639 with the lengthy title of *The Sufficiency of the Spirit's Teaching Without Humane Learning: Or a Treatise Tending to Prove Humane Learning to be No Help to the Spiritual Understanding of the Word of God.*[65]

Furthermore, these Baptists argued, it was the educated ministry of the Church of England which contributed to its state of spiritual decline and persecuted those who dissented from it. Nonetheless, other Baptists saw it differently, and in 1675 a group of ministers in London decided to act by inviting their fellow pastors in the rest of the country to a meeting to discuss an educated Baptist ministry.[66]

While the meeting could not be held until 1689 because of the persecution, they did create a fund with a threefold purpose: to provide financial support so ministers would not need to pursue secular employment, to sustain ministers involved in creating new churches, and to provide funds to enable ministers to obtain an education.[67] The churches began to supply the money for that trust, known as the Particular Baptist Fund, but it had no connection with the Broadmead Trust. The money from that bequest became available in 1697, and by 1711 was augmented by two other bequests.[68]

A call was extended by the Broadmead church in 1714 to a Mr. Caleb Jope to serve as an assistant minister, and he received aid from the Terrill Fund to further his studies at Tewkesbury Academy. In addition he would tutor ministerial students. This arrangement failed and Jope moved on to Plymouth in 1719.[69] Up to that point Edward Terrill's vision had not become a reality, but with the departure of Jope and the arrival of Bernard Foskett in 1720, the dream began to come alive.

Bernard Foskett was called to replace Jope as assistant minister of the Broadmead Church under Peter Kittrell. Since Foskett was also to benefit from the Terrill Fund, he viewed his ministerial priority to be the education of young men and his pastoral responsibility to assist Kittrell. In 1727, however, Peter Kittrell died and Foskett became the pastor of the church, which called Andrew Gifford as Foskett's assistant. Young Andrew Gifford began his work early in 1728 but stayed less than two years after which he moved to the Little Wild Street Church in London. In his history of Bristol Academy, Norman S. Moon has suggested that Gifford may have been "disappointed that more young men were not coming forward for training," but as years went by he maintained a lively interest in the school.[70]

The year after Gifford's departure for London, an eighteen-year-old Welshman named Hugh Evans came to Bristol for medical help and, through his aunt, became connected with the Broadmead church. Evans was well educated and blessed with a facility for ancient languages. While in Bristol he studied with Foskett who led him to faith in Christ and baptism. After Evans returned home fifteen months later, Foskett wrote to his father, who was a Baptist minister, and urged him to test the young man's gifts for ministry. For three years young Evans exercised his ministerial gifts, and then returned to Bristol and the Broadmead church. In 1739 the church called him to be the teaching elder.[71]

Foskett and Evans became an effective teaching team in the two houses on North Street where they lived and taught the Bristol students as well as shared meals and devotions together.[72] Three years later, a twenty-year-old Welshman would come to the Bristol Academy to study under Foskett and Evans, and his name was Morgan Edwards.

Bernard Foskett was well qualified to tutor the Bristol students. He was broadly educated and gifted with a remarkable memory. Though somewhat austere, he was a caring person. Welsh Baptist historian Joshua Thomas says of him, "Mr. F the most learned man...remarkable ...for the accomplishments and great regularity of his life and consecration."[74] Hugh Evans, on the other hand, was warm and outgoing, had a vibrant personality, and was an animated preacher.[75] Each was a powerful influence on his students, including Morgan Edwards.

Nonetheless, it appears, Foskett had the greater influence on Edwards, for he referred to him on a number of occasions, but there are no known references to Evans. If Evans majored in tutoring the biblical languages, then Edwards was already well versed in these by the time he reached Bristol. The likelihood is Edwards received most of his Bristol training under Foskett, who died in 1758. Upon Foskett's death, Evans became the principal.

Foskett's expansive learning may be gauged by the subjects covered in his lectures. These included logic, ethics, music, politics, rhetoric, history, philosophy of religion, and psychology. In addition the studies included five languages: English, Latin, Greek, Hebrew, and French. Biblical and theological studies included the Old and New

Testaments, the Baptist Catechism, Confession of Faith, and Christian doctrine.[76] Foskett indicated that Edwards studied grammar, logic and ontology.[77]

It has long been thought that Edwards spent two years at Bristol, but it is evident he was there for only one. The two chief evidences supporting the one year (1742-1743) are a series of academical exercises which he presented at Bristol in 1742 and 1743[78] and Bernard Foskett's list of students (see note 11, p. 49). The academicals consist of eight papers presented at the academy, one dated 1742 and seven dated 1743. The subjects of the papers are theological themes close to the hearts of the Calvinists of that time. They include foreknowledge, God's purpose, predestination, election, eternal security, conversion and imputed holiness.

The consensus has been that Edwards served the Boston church from 1742 to 1751, but in the light of the dating of the Academicals, he could not have served at Boston before 1743 since the papers would have been presented before his tutor and other examiners. In addition, Foskett's list shows him entering in 1742 and staying for one year. The records of the London Particular Baptist Fund may add further evidence for the one-year stay.

For several years, Miles Harry, Morgan Edwards' pastor at Penygarn, annually sent lists of deserving Welsh ministers and students to the board of the Particular Baptist Fund. However, Edwards's first entry in the records of the Fund is November 18, 1740, while he was still a student at Trosnant Academy. His name was submitted by the Reverend Joseph Stennett, Jr., of the Little Wild Street Baptist Church in London, and was for five pounds "extra." The word "extra" seems to indicate an additional amount to the fifty pounds already allocated to those on Miles Harry's list. Because Edwards's name was

A Dazzling Enigma

not initially on the list, the board had to make an "extra" allotment.[79]

The next entry specifically naming Morgan Edwards was two years later, on November 2, 1742. Stennett again presented his name for ten pounds. This request was marked "ditto" meaning the board agreed with Stennett's proposal.[80] Finally, there is an entry in July 1743, where a Mr. Wallin submitted a request from the Boston church for ten shillings, which was also marked "ditto."[81] This is the first recorded request from the Boston church, and could have been for assistance in settling Morgan on the field, or in meeting his compensation package, or in assisting with construction costs involved with the building they erected in 1742.[82] Edwards's ministry at Boston began by the summer of 1743. It was a Particular Baptist Church, i.e., Calvinistic, so the question arises, What kind of theology did Morgan carry from Bristol to Boston?

As was discussed earlier, eighteenth-century English Baptists, as well as other Christians, were drawn to theological extremes. General Baptists, who were Arminian in theology, began moving to Unitarianism, denying both the deity of Christ and the Trinity. Particular Baptists, on the other hand, were becoming more and more arid in their highly deterministic hyper-Calvinism. Among Anglicans John Wesley's revival began with Wesley traveling everywhere preaching the gospel from an Arminian point of view, meaning "whosoever will may come." In 1739 George Whitefield, though a Calvinist, invited Wesley to Bristol; in 1740 Wesley founded the first Methodist society there and built the first Methodist chapel.[83] The chapel was not far from the Broadmead Particular Baptist Church and the Bristol Academy. This theological environment may have impacted the students of the Bristol Academy.

Norman Moon, erstwhile librarian of Bristol College, believed that the effect of Wesley and Whitefield on the Bristol area was so great that it must have been felt in both the Broadmead church and the Bristol Academy.[84] He meant, of course, that the Wesleyan revival leavened Broadmead's Calvinism so that it became more evangelical. It seems clear, however, that the church was already flowing in a more evangelical Calvinistic stream before Wesley arrived on the scene.

Both the church and the academy were in the Western Association, which in its 1656 Somerset Confession called for the church "to send forth such men as are fitly gifted and qualified through the Spirit of Christ to preach the Gospel to the World."[85] The evangelical character of the Particular Baptist churches in southwest England had been established by the dynamic seventeenth-century Baptist lay preacher, Thomas Collier.[86] Another ingredient in that evangelical Calvinistic mix was Bernard Foskett, who though a Calvinist, continued the evangelical Calvinism he had known at the Little Wild Street Baptist Church in London.[87]

It seems safe, then, to conjecture that both the Broadmead church and the Bristol Academy were drinking at the fountain of an evangelical Calvinism before Wesley and well before Andrew Fuller led other Baptists to do the same. Therefore, whatever theological luggage Edwards may have carted from Bristol to Boston, it did not include the hyper-Calvinism of many other Particular Baptists. It did contain a more moderate evangelical Calvinism as is evident in the many outstanding sermons he preached during his ministry, beginning at the Particular Baptist church in Boston, Lincolnshire, England.

ENDNOTES

1. Reuben A Guild, *Early History of Brown University, Including the Life, Times and Correspondence of President Manning, 1756-1791*, (Providence: Snow and Farnham, 1896), 12.
2. Stephen A. Swaine, *Faithful Men or Memorials of Bristol Baptist College and Its Distinguished Alumni*, (London: Alexander Shephard, 1884), 68.
3. Morgan Edwards, "I Magnify My Office," (Philadelphia: Andrew Stewart, 1763), 10.
4. The author has made only selective use of instances where Morgan Edwards made referals to his reading. Those selected are from the manuscript sermons of the Crozer Collection at the Colgate Rochester, Divinity School, Rochester, N.Y.
5. Morgan Edwards, "Conversion to the Likeness of Children," (MS. Sermon, n.d.) III, 3.
6. Morgan Edwards, "Prodigal Son," (MS. Sermon, n.d.)III, 85.
7. Ibid.
8. Ibid.
9. Morgan Edwards, "Blessed Are They That Mourn," (MS. Sermon. n.p.), VI, n.d.
10. Morgan Edwards, "And Eli Perceived," (MS. Sermon, n.d.), II, n.p.
11. Irene Parker, *Dissenting Academies In England*, (New York: Octogon Books, 1969), 95.
12. Seymour J. Price, "Dissenting Academies, 1662-1820," *The Baptist Quarterly*, (London: Baptist Union Publication Department, 1932), 25.
13. Geraint Jenkins, *Literature, Religion and Society in Wales, 1660-1730*, (Cardiff: University of Wales Press, 1978), 216.
14. Parker, 42.
15. Ibid, 45-46.
16. Joshua Toulmin, *An Historical View of the State of the Protestant Dissenters in England From the Revolution to the Accession of Queen Anne*, (Bath: Richard Cuttrell, 1814), 216.
17. Walter Stevens, "Oxford's Attitude to Dissenters," 1646- 1946, *The Baptist Quarterly*, (London: Carey Kingsgate Press, 1949), XIII, 5.
18. Ibid., 6.
19. Ibid.

20. Parker, 46.
21. Ibid., 47.
22. Charter of Rhode Island College, (Providence: MS. Manning Papers. John Hay Library, Brown University, 1763), 5.
23. Parker, 46.
24. Ibid., 42
25. Seymour Price, 125.
26. Toulmin, 216.
27. Parker, 103
28. Seymour price, 126.
29. Morgan Edwards, *Res Scarae*, (Philadelphia: Pritchard and Hall, 1788) 30. Morgan Edwards, Account Letter With the Corporation, 1769, Manning Papers. John Hay Library, Brown University. n.p.
31. Parker, 103.
32. Jenkins, 216.
33. Selwyn Gummer, "Trosnant Academy," *The Baptist Quarterly*, (London: Baptist Union Publication Department, 1939), 417.
34. Ibid.
35. Ibid., 418.
36. Rufus Williams, *The History of the Baptist Seminaries*. (Aberdar: Thomas Williams, 1863), n.p. Translated from the Welsh by the Reverend D. Hugh Matthews.
37. Gummer, 418.
38. J.A. Branbury, *A History of Monmouthshire*, (London: Michael Hughes and Clark, 1907), 455.
39. Seymour Price, 31-32.
40. E.W. Price, "Dr. Thomas Thomas of Pontypool," *The Baptist Quarterly*, (London: Baptist Union Publication Department, 1926), 132.
41. Gummer, 419.
42. Branbury, 455.
43. Evans, 132.
44. E.W. Price, 135.
45. Gummer, 418.
46. Ibid., 419.
47. Ibid.
48. Ibid., 420
49. R. Jones, "Miles Harry," *Transactions of the Welsh Baptist Historical Society*, (1926), 45. Translated by the Reverend D. Hugh

Matthews.
50. Ibid.
51. E.W. Price, 135.
52. R. Williams, n.p.
53. Gummer, 419.
54. Ibid.
55. Minutes of the London Particular Baptist Fund, II, 1740- 1757., MS. Angus Library, Regents Park College, Oxford: n.p.
56. Barnas Sears, *Celebration of the One Hundreth Anniversary of the Founding of Brown University,* (Providence: Sidney S. Rider, 1865), 11.
57. R. Williams, n.p.
58. Norman S. Moon, *Education For Ministry - Bristol Baptist College, 1679-1979,* (Bristol: Bristol Baptist College, 1979), 17.
59. Ibid., 18.
60. Ibid., 1.
61. Ibid.
62. A.C. Underwood, *A History of the English Baptists,* (London: Carey Kingsgate Press, Ltd, 1947), 130.
63. Moon, 2.
64. Ibid.
65. Ibid.
66. Ibid.
67. Ibid., 3.
68. Ibid.
69. Ibid.
70. Ibid., 4.
71. Joshua Thomas, From a manuscript history of Bristol Baptist College accompanying a letter from Thomas to Dr. John Rippon. Bristol: Library, Bristol Baptist College, 1795, 3.
72. Moon, 5.
73. Thomas, 1.
74. Moon, 5.
75. Ibid, 6.
76. Morgan Edwards, "Academical Exercises, 1742-1743," (Providence): MS. McKesson Collection, John Hay Library, Brown University.
77. See endnote 11 on page 49.
78. Particular Baptist Fund, n.p.

79. Ibid.
80. Ibid.
81. Ibid.
82. Pishey Thompson, *Historical Antiquities of Boston*, (London: Longman and Company, 1865), 259.
83. Moon, 19.
84. Ibid.
85. Ibid.
86. William Lumpkin, *Baptist Confessions of Faith*, (Philadelphia: The Judson Press, 1959), 212-213.
87. Moon, 19.

CHAPTER FOUR

CONDUCT BECOMING A BAPTIST MINISTER

> "His conduct was becoming a minister of the Gospel."
> Baptist Churchbook
> Cork, Ireland, 1759

A Time For Reflection

Morgan Edwards may have wanted to race his horse at breakneck speed to put Cork behind him on that June day in 1759. As one of six delegates from the Cork Baptist Church he was on his way to the annual meetings of the Irish Baptist Association. This would be his last duty as assistant pastor to the aging and ailing Reverend Ebenezer Gibbons. Edwards was dismissed by the congregation under questionable circumstances, and those hours of riding afforded him opportunity to sort out the conflicting emotions and thoughts whirling in his heart and mind.

How could he reconcile his forced termination with the tribute paid to him and his ministry and recorded in the Cork Baptist churchbook.[1]

> We think ourselves obliged to do so much justice to this our late brother whose labours were very acceptable to a great part of the congregation to declare that it was not for any immorality or misdemeanor that he was dismissed for his conduct was becoming a minister of the Gospel.

Following the 1759 meetings in Dublin, Edwards headed toward London where his future ministry would be determined.[2] In all probability Mary traveled with him, since there were no children at that time, and it would be seven months before they settled at Rye in Sussex. He was scheduled to preach in London at the Little Wild Street Church on August 6, 1759.[3] Meanwhile he could reflect on the years in Boston, Lincolnshire, and Cork, Ireland, to assess of his ministry.

THE BOSTON YEARS

As a single, twenty-one-year-old young man, Edwards went to Boston to begin his ministry with a newly organized Particular Baptist Church, worshipping in a new meeting house.[4] The General Baptists in that area were in a state of chaos and decline.[5] Fortunately for him, Edwards's evangelical Calvinism filled a theological void in a historic locus of General Baptist Church life.[6]

Grants from the Particular Baptist Fund, enabled Edwards to continue his studies under the tutelage of three outstanding Baptist divines of that time: Dr. Joseph Stennett, Dr. Thomas Llewelyn, and Dr. John Gill.[7] The grants allowed him to further develop his library.[8] In contrast to the humiliation he suffered at Cork, it appears he went to Boston, fresh from Bristol Academy and with some youthful arrogance.

The last Academicals or formal papers Edwards presented at Bristol Academy contain statements tinctured with youthful pride. In the conclusion of one paper, Edwards had set up a straw-man Anglican minister who decried conversion. Edwards believed he had destroyed the straw-man's argument by simply quoting his text, but not so the tutor.[9]

> The master [Headmaster] signified a cold approbation [approval] of this little lecture and then added 'You admire the last text you refered [sic] to as a picture of a true convert: we presume you do not admire without reason & we expect to join in your admiration when you exhibit the picture in that desk: Let that be next week.

His life and ministry at Boston would not only moderate his pride but would mature his mind and his ministry.

Boston in Lincolnshire

Boston gave its name to the capital of the Massachusetts Bay Colony through the role her merchants played in sponsoring that colony.[10] It is located in the Eastern Midlands of England in Lincoln County. Lincoln was a name adopted into common usage from the Roman compound Lindum Colonia.[11] The town had been a military center during the Roman occupation.[12] Danish people, who came later, developed the area into prosperous farming country by the tenth century.[13] The General Baptists, who came later still, played out much of their history in Lincolnshire, especially in the General Baptist Church at Boston.

Filling a Void

Morgan Edwards was a Calvinist. His ministry as pastor of the Particular Baptist Church in Boston enjoyed success in part because of the state of upheaval among the General Baptist Churches in that part of England. As described earlier, numbers of General Baptist churches and pastors had been drifting from their Baptist moorings for many years as they set their sails more and more toward the winds of Unitarianism. By the time Edwards had come to Boston, the slippage was approaching a critical stage, for two reasons.

The General Baptists were more connectional than the Particular Baptists; in their organizational structure, i.e. they were a more centralized denomination. They formed more associations and amalgamated these into a General Assembly.[14] In addition there was a three fold order to the ministry: Messengers, who functioned as "Associational Ministers"; Elders who were pastors of local churches; and Deacons.[15] This resulted in frequent conflicts over the role of the Messenger and the autonomy of the local church.

The major problem facing the General Baptists was theological and dated from the seventeenth century. In 1651 thirty General Baptist congregations met in the Midlands to produce a Confession of Faith which they presented to the King in 1660.[16] It was inadequate, however, to offset the influence of a General Baptist pastor named Matthew Caffyn in Horsham, Sussex, who was preaching Socinianism. To counter his effect, representatives of the General Baptist churches met in 1678 and produced "An Orthodox Creed," moderately Calvinistic in its tone.[17]

With all this turmoil, the General Baptists were unable to define clearly their theological position. At the 1686 General Assembly they settled for unity over orthodoxy by accepting the six principles in Hebrews 6:1-2. They became known as the "Six-Principle Baptists."[18] Thereafter, splits and reunions occurred and reoccurred until 1731 when they reunited on the basis of the Six Principles.[19] Meanwhile, the orthodox churches continued to view the General Assembly with suspicion.[20] One of these churches was in the town of Boston.

Baptists in Boston

Baptist work in Boston began with the witness of Colonel John Hutchison, an officer in Cromwell's army. Later Sir Henry Vane gathered his neighbors to start a Baptist Church at South Marsh that eventually centered in Boston.[21] Out of the Boston General Baptist church came Thomas Grantham, described as the "General Baptists' most gifted leader" in the seventeenth century.[22] Because of its history and Grantham's importance, the Boston General Baptist Church gained prominence among General Baptists.

In 1738, the year Morgan Edwards was converted and began his studies at Trosnant Academy, John Goode became pastor of the Boston General Baptist church. Five years later, in 1743, Edwards became pastor of the fledgling Independent (Particular) Baptist Church,[23] meeting in its new chapel off Heslam's Alley. Goode continued as pastor until his death in 1751,[24] but his Boston ministry years straddled those of Morgan Edwards. One might safely assume they knew each other and shared some common theological ground. Still Edwards never paid much attention to the General Baptists in his writings--and no doubt because of their theological compromise and dying condition.

Given the continued dispute, it would be easy to imagine a dwindling of members from the General Baptist church to the Particular Baptist church. In view of the soft theology of most General Baptists, the clear biblical theology in Morgan Edwards's preaching may have drawn other General Baptists to his church as well. Apart from this speculation, little is known about the Particular Baptist church or Edwards's ministry as its pastor.

What Church Did Edwards Serve?

Because the General Baptist Church dominates the pages of Baptist history in Boston, Lincolnshire, there has always been a question as to which church Morgan Edwards actually served. Historian Arthur S. Langley states, that "the Particular Baptist Church [in Boston] did not organize til 1770"; [25] historian Josiah Thompson reports there were two Baptist churches in Boston in 1773.[26] Neither historian made an effort to identify them. While little is found in Baptist historical materials, some information is provided by a local historian and in the records of the Particular Baptist Ministers Fund.

In the town history of Boston, published in 1865, Mr. Pishey Thompson states,

> A little below White Horse Lane at the same side of High Street is a narrow entrance called Heslam's Alley, which leads to a small chapel, founded before 1727, by the Independent Baptists. The present day building was erected in 1742, on land which was the property of William Heslam from whom the place has its name.[27]

Later, Thompson writes of a second Particular Baptist Church called Salem Chapel which erected a large building in 1801 on Liquor Pond Street. A little distance down the street was another chapel called Ebenezer Chapel, built in 1838 and occupied by the Particular Baptists who formerly occupied the chapel in Heslam's Alley.[28] The original chapel in Heslam's Alley had been purchased by the General Baptist Church for use as a schoolroom.[29]

It appears there were three Baptist churches in Boston by the early nineteenth century, one General and two Particular. The Salem church may have been a breakaway from the Ebenezer church, which was started by 1727, and therefore the one served by Morgan Edwards. The above suggests that the Particular Baptist church cited by Langley as organized in 1770 was the Salem church.

There is additional information in the records of the Particular Baptist Fund. An entry for July 17, 1744, reads, "Agreed to receive the case of the People at Boston as to building a meetinghouse and that it be considered after the case at Crockerton."[30] At some time, the board loaned the Boston church five pounds since there is an entry in the 1747 year-end report, indicating the church had paid five shillings on the five pound loan. Other entries include:

```
1743                ten shillings
August 7, 1744      ten shillings
August 6, 1745      eight shillings
September 2, 1746   seven shillings and six pence
September 7, 1748   seven shillings.[31]
```

In summary, it appears that Particular Baptists began to meet at Boston by 1727. Later they organized themselves into a church and, by 1742, had erected a meeting house at Heslam's Alley. During this time they received a five pound loan for the project from the Particular Baptist Fund and repaid the loan in regular installments. Either at the time of their organization or later, they became known as the Ebenezer Baptist Church. As with the church, so with the year Edwards began his ministry at Boston. We must rely on the records of the Particular Baptist Fund.

It is apparent that Morgan Edwards intended to maintain a continuing education program. This is evidenced from the aid from the Particular Baptist Fund. One year after Edwards arrived at Boston, there is an entry in the fund records for July 17, 1744, which reads, "The Minister at Boston...1:0:0."[32]

There is little question that Edwards received that one pound. While there is no indication it was for educational expenses, the next entry hints that it could have been either to repay money owed to Bristol Academy or for continued study. Two years later a Mr. Wilson, a member of the board, submitted a request on June 3, 1746, for three pounds to enable "Mr. Edwards (of Boston)" to buy books.[33] The last entries were made in the final quarter of 1749.

The final fund record entries for Morgan Edwards begin with October 4, 1749, which reads, "The Case of Mr. Edwards of Boston was proposed by Mr. Wallin, but some Objections being made it was agreed to be postponed."[34] The action was again postponed, at the November 7th meeting, but at a meeting on November 21st the entry reads, "Agreed that the case of Mr. Edwards of Boston be postponed to the next meeting, and be considered."[35] Finally, on December 3rd he was voted a grant of seven shillings,[36] but why the delay?

The delay in awarding the grant was probably because the Boston church had not made a payment on its loan for that year. It was common practice for the board not to act on a request for aid if a church was behind in its repayment. There is no hint of any doctrinal consideration in the delay which the records usually reflected when such occasions arose. If the church was unable to meet its financial obligations to its pastor, it would be the onset of a problem that would follow Edwards through his pastoral years.

The Particular Baptist church at Boston was like most eighteenth-century Dissenter churches--it was small and could not offer full salary support. Therefore, it was quite common for pastors to be bivocational. Welsh Baptist historian T.M. Bassett illustrated the problem.[37]

> But the most significant change of all was the number of craftsmen in the ministry. Thomas Edwards, father of Miles Edwards, was a craftsman and Joshua Thomas had said rather patronizingly of him, 'that with more time to study and more money to buy books he would have made a good minister.' It was this very class which provided the denomination with many of its preachers and missionaries in the last quarter of the century.[37]

Bassett then presented an extensive list of such pastors and their secular vocations.

If Morgan Edwards worked outside his pastoral duties, it may have been as a teacher or tutor. He never spoke of any vocation, but in later years he lectured at both Rhode Island College and the College of Philadelphia. Given the times, there is little doubt that Edwards had some form of work in addition to his pastoral ministry at both Boston and at Cork.

There is the possibility that Morgan Edwards carried on an itinerant evangelism ministry while at Boston and Cork. Selwyn Gummer claims he traveled through towns and villages of England and Ireland as an evangelist.[38] There are no known records of churches that may have started from such evangelistic activity, but we do have some records of his life and ministry at Cork, Ireland.

THE YEARS AT CORK

When Edwards went to Cork in 1750, he was a single twenty-nine-year-old man; but when he left in 1759, he was married. He knew the joy of marriage to Mary Nun, but also the sorrow, of losing children in childbirth and infancy. His work with Mr. Gibbons was surely a learning experience, but it is believed the senior pastor betrayed his trust and failed to support Morgan against the cabal which ousted him. It was at Cork where he was ordained and where he served for a time with his brother James on the church pastoral staff. Cork was also the site of that dreaded premonition of his own death and where his wife had a similar experience. They had many friends in the congregation and years later he would return to Cork in a successful effort to raise funds for the infant Rhode Island College. While the Baptist witness in Cork was weak, it was present in Ireland for over one hundred years.

The Baptist Church at Cork

Oliver Cromwell's army arrived in Ireland in 1649. With it came Particular Baptist soldiers and chaplains who established churches in ten or eleven garrison towns including Waterford and Cork during the 1650s.[39] The congregations were made up mostly of army and government people as well as new settlers.[40]

The general population was not reached because of Irish hostility to Cromwell's army and the Calvinistic doctrine of the churches.[41] A review of the churchbooks reveals mostly English and Welsh names.[42] With the return of the English monarchy in 1660, the Cromwell army disappeared from Ireland and only a few small churches survived, including Waterford and Cork.[43]

The Cork churchbook for the years 1653-1875 details some of the beginnings of the church, although parts of the record are not original. Some church records were destroyed by a fire in 1729, but Mr. Joseph Fowke, who joined the church in 1755, reconstructed the records from remnants and interviews with older members of the church.[44] Mr. Fowke recorded that he used the papers of the pastor, Rev. Ebenezer Gibbons, and the memory of "an ancient member of the Baptist church now living aged about 89 and yet in a good state of health and the faculties of her mind was perfect as ever viz. 24 March 1757."[45]

Fowke reported that the church was founded by Edward Riggs, Esquire, of Riggsdale, about seven miles from Cork. Mr. Riggs was a member of Parliament in the mid-seventeenth century during the Commonwealth era, and he had developed the practice of frequently gathering his neighbors on Sundays to preach to them.[46] It was Riggs's widow Ann who left a legacy which sustained the Cork church through difficult times.[47]

The oldest report on the Cork Baptists was in a letter sent to London from a team of English Baptists in 1653.[48] They reported that the brethren of Cork were walking "orderly together, though in a place of much opposition by such as slight the ways of the Lord." Joseph Petit became pastor of the church in 1704 and stayed until 1729. His successor was Ebenezer Gibbons, who served from 1729 to 1764.[49]

The Reverend Ebenezer Gibbons
Ebenezer Gibbons had been the assistant pastor at the

Swift's Alley church in Dublin before coming to Cork in 1729.[50] The Cork church had forty-seven members, but by 1755, Gibbons had baptized seventy-six others.[51] The Swift's Alley church was only moderately Calvinistic[52] but did have an interest in an educated ministry, which led to the establishment of an educational fund from which James Edwards received almost seventy pounds between 1756 and 1762.[53]

How much influence the support of an educated ministry had on Gibbons can only be guessed, but he seems to have taken younger, unordained men as his assistants at Cork, including both Morgan and James Edwards. Gibbons was pastor in 1746, when the Wesleyan revival rolled into Cork which caused considerable stress for the Baptist church. Baptists who heard Charles and John Wesley preach were in awe and became disenchanted with Gibbons and life in the Baptist church. In one such case we may gain an insight into Gibbons's personality, his teaching of Baptist principles, and his leadership style. His passive personality and leadership style were to be important factors later in two matters related to Morgan Edwards.

The Bentley Affair

A Mrs. Bentley, who had been a regular attendee at the Baptist church on the verge of baptism, became so enthralled with Charles Wesley that she asked him to baptize her. She spoke with Gibbons about it, and he saw no problem with her request. He even offered to cooperate with Charles Wesley in the preparations. Charles Wesley at first agreed, but he delayed the baptism until he left Cork, leaving Mrs. Bentley unbaptized. Mr. Bentley was an apothecary and a man with a violent temper who disapproved of his wife's plan for believer baptism.

Shortly thereafter John Wesley arrived in Cork. Gibbons advised Mrs. Bentley to make her request of him, which she did. Wesley not only refused to baptize her, but said her desire for believer baptism by immersion was a "delusion of the devil."[54] Meanwhile, Mr. Bentley was so enraged by the whole episode that he threatened both Gibbons and his wife were the baptism to take place.[55] Mrs. Bentley was well informed on believer baptism, and she impressed Charles Wesley with this knowledge. Since she was the only one in her family who identified with the Baptist church, she must have come by her knowledge by listening to Ebenezer Gibbons at the Baptist church. Gibbons seemed to be able to teach Christian doctrine effectively.

Six years later, on October 2, 1752, Gibbons secretly baptized Mrs. Bentley, with only three witnesses. To keep peace in her family she continued in communion with the Anglican church.[56] Gibbons came under fire for baptizing her in secret, yet knowing she would still take communion at the Anglican church. He defended himself by citing similar cases which had occurred in other Baptist churches.[57] The experience indicated an passive response by Gibbons in the face of strong personalities such as the Wesleys, assertive people in the church, and physical threats issued by Mr. Bentley.

Gibbons's passivity would resurface seven years later, when he faced another crisis which involved Morgan Edwards. Then, his aging, ailing body would cripple his ability to manage the conflict. Apart from this, however, his congregation had good reason to love him.

The churchbook includes records of several occasions when Ebenezer Gibbons provided very caring help to people in times of crisis. There is little question but that he was sensitive to his peoples' needs, and quick to respond in the fullest measure. One of the needs he no doubt met in Edwards's life of was to perform the marriage ceremony for him and his bride, Mary Nun.

The Wife of Morgan Edwards

Mary Edwards (nee Nun or Nunn) has been as much of a puzzle to Baptist historians as her husband Morgan. There is little information about her, and it is not certain she was ever a member of a Baptist church. The records of the Cork Baptist church list several persons by the name of Nun or Nunn being baptized, but none has the name of Mary. Joshua and Ruth Nun were baptized in August 1730.[58] They were Mary's parents. The youngest child of Morgan and Mary was named Joshua after her father.

Further, in correspondence with Reuben A. Guild of Brown University, the grandson and namesake of Morgan Edwards and son of Joshua Edwards, stated that his grandmother was the daughter of Joshua Nunn of Cork.[59] A Sarah Nunn is also listed as baptized, possibly in 1742, which raises some questions. Is Sarah really Mary by another name? Or is Sarah a relative, such as a sister, cousin or aunt? Since Joshua and Ruth Nun were Mary's parents, it is assumed Mary was baptized, though no clear record exists. There is yet another missing piece to this puzzle.

In the records of the First Baptist Church of Philadelphia is the following entry for June 1, 1761.[60]

> Morgan Edwards received as a member and minister of the church by a letter dismissive and recommendatory from Penygarn

A Dazzling Enigma 97

in Monmouthshire, South Wales, Jos Moor being first delegated of the church to do so.

There are two puzzling aspects to this entry in that Morgan apparently never transferred his membership to any of the three churches he served prior to coming to Philadelphia; and no mention is made of Mary's membership. Following her death in 1769, Mary was buried with some of her deceased children under the aisle of the Philadelphia church meeting house, where Morgan would join her following his death in 1795.[61] One must conclude that Mary was a Baptist church member, but there is no written record of her baptism and joining the church.

The Edwards's marriage resulted in a number of pregnancies while they were at Cork, but none survived childbirth. Mary and Morgan apparently had a loving marriage, for her death in 1769 affected him greatly. According to his son Joshua, Morgan was extremely distressed by Mary's death.[62] This information is found in a letter dated July 20, 1853, from a Presbyterian minister, Rev. Richard Webster of Mauch Chunk, Pennsylvania, to historian Horatio Gates Jones. Webster was an acquaintance of Joshua Edwards, then living in New Jersey. He reports, from the youngest son of Morgan and Mary Edwards, that "...the death of his first wife is supposed to have impaired his mind for a time."[63]

Joshua would not have been able to confirm the details firsthand since he would have been about four years old when his mother died, but the general impression of the event would have been clear. The effect of Mary's death will be discussed later in greater detail. It is clear that Edwards was devastated. He once stated that she was "very near and dear to me."[64]

Morgan Edwards Is Ordained

While there was much sadness in his family life at Cork, in Cork Morgan Edwards was finally ordained to the Gospel ministry, June 1, 1757. Present-day Baptists may be puzzled that Morgan Edwards served in the ministry for fourteen years before he was ordained, but Dissenters in the eighteenth century did not rush their candidates for the ministry into ordination. Some insight is provided by an extensive statement from a Congregational ordination service.[65]

> It very rarely happens, that a minister among us is admitted to the pastoral office, till he hath spent some years as a kind of candidate for it; and, so far as I can recollect more undertake it after, than before their twenty-sixth year is completed. An unordained minister is seldom chosen to the pastoral office in any of our churches, for in the members of each of these societies the whole right of election lies, till he has resided among them some months or perhaps some years; preaching statedly to them, and performing most other ministerial offices, excepting the administration of the sacraments.

There was a clear line of difference between Dissenters and Anglicans in their views of ordination. Whereas Anglicans saw ordination as bestowing the ability to preach, Dissenters believed it "signified that a man had already been endowed with ministerial gifts which were now being acknowledged."[66] As important as his ordination was to Edwards there is no known record of it. Though endued by the Holy Spirit, gifted for ministry, and ordained, Morgan Edwards would find himself the target of a conspiracy by some members of the Cork church who were aiming at his ouster.

The Forced Termination of Morgan Edwards
Edwards's dismissal from the church is described in the churchbook.[67]

> Mr. Morgan Edwards who for several years has assisted our Pastor in this place being dismissed by the Subscribing members took Dublin in his way to England. We think ourselves obliged to do So much justice to this our late brother whose labours were very Acceptable to a great part of the congregation to declare that it was not for any immorality or misdemeanor that he has been dismissed for his conduct was becoming a minister of the Gospel-- but the necessity of our affairs Seemed to require it, for many years past we have been in a declining condition Several useful members droping [sic] off by death & no addition of any new member, Some were for ascribing this to the heavy manner in which Mr. Edwards delivers himself but whatever was the cause there seemed to be a majority to look out for a popular man who might be agreeable to other denominations.

The congregation had a legitimate concern because Ebenezer Gibbons had been too old and too ill to attend the association meeting the year before and was not listed as a representative in 1758.[68] Even though he would live to 1764, it was obvious to the members that his days as their pastor were numbered, and they were thinking about a successor. It was quite common for assistants to be considered as a successor in such circumstances. In fact they could see the church was already declining. Many believed Morgan Edwards was not the man to draw more people into the church because of the "heavy manner in which Mr. Edwards delivers himself." What they seemed to be saying is that Edwards's sermons were too sophisticated for people in Cork.

To make a comparison between Edwards's preaching and Ebenezer Gibbons's would be rather difficult. While there are at least three dozen of Edwards's Cork sermons extant, none by Gibbons can be found. There are two funeral orations in the churchbook--one by Gibbons, one by Edwards. In the first Gibbons delivered a eulogy at the funeral of Mr. John Rogers, who died March 14, 1758.[69] He talked of the grave being our house and corruption our parent, and of raging diseases and groans of dead friends. He talked of the frailty and short duration of life; not even a hale and hearty constitution could stop death. He augmented these words with equally depressing quotes from Scripture. Gibbons then praised Mr. Rogers for the loving and friendly manner in which he lived, and for his faith in Christ. There is little in the message to comfort, inspire and uplift.

 Three months later, on June 4, 1758, Edwards delivered a funeral oration for ninety-year-old Lucy Rose.[70] He began by assuring his hearers that Mrs. Rose had arrived at her heavenly rest after fighting a good fight, keeping the faith, and finishing her course. Based on Scripture, Edwards portrays her as having received her heavenly crown after a lifetime of poverty and obscurity, and that she now sat with Christ in His heavenly kingdom. He continued, paying tribute to her integrity and diligence in this life, averring that she had faithfully walked with God all of her days. He related examples of her Christlike character and knowledge of Christian doctrine.

 While it is easy to see the superior quality of Edwards's message, it is not easy to determine why some felt his sermons would fail to bring people into the church. There is evidence that his preaching at Rye and later at Philadelphia drew large crowds, and there is every reason to believe the same occurred in Boston. At Cork he was the assistant and did not preach on a regular basis. There were at least two occasions when he preached a series of sermons, implying Gibbons's absence from the pulpit for an extended period. Those sermon manuscripts from Cork bear the same quality and character as those he preached at Rye and Philadelphia. If we are going to look for more substantial reasons why Edwards was dismissed from Cork, we need look no further than the churchbook for a record of the sinister manipulations which brought about his termination.[71]

The churchbook clearly states that the majority of the members liked Morgan Edwards, but they were persuaded to seek a person who might have more popular appeal. It appears that the people who wanted him ousted already had a replacement in mind and his name was John Knight.

Though a Baptist, Knight came to Cork to candidate for the Presbyterian church. They did not know he was a Baptist. After he preached the Presbyterians were ready to call him, but his Baptist identity was known by then. He offered to be their pastor if he would not be required to conduct infant baptism. That was out of the question. Some of the Presbyterians remarked that he was the most acceptable of the candidates for the pulpit, but even if he were an angel from heaven, they would reject him if he would not baptize their children.

Knight had been strongly recommended to Gibbons and the deacons by Mr. Eleasor Edwards of London. The leading members of the Baptist church attended the service at the Presbyterian church when Knight preached. When the Presbyterians rejected him, the Baptists offered him the job as Gibbons's assistant. He said he would accept if the salary were adequate; he was given a unanimous call at a congregational meeting. He finally began his ministry at Cork as Gibbons's co-pastor in December 1759. He did not last long, however, for by 1763 he was pastor of the Particular Baptist church at Moreton Hampstead in England.[72] The whole episode was not handled with much grace, but there may have been another less obvious factor at work, which is not mentioned in the churchbook.

On March 9, 1755, as Edwards was "calmly sitting in meditation, the Notion or Tho't instantly rushed into his Mind with distinct clearness, in a singular manner, he knew not how, but giving him a fixt indubitable Persuassion of the future fact, the year when he should die, viz., 1770 and the very day of the year."[73] Thus we are introduced to one of the major mysteries of Edwards's enigmatic life. There is an interesting timing which may relate it to his dismissal from the Cork church.

In his famous, so-called "Death Sermon" on January 1, 1770, he reported that four years after he had this experience he told a friend about it.[74] He continued, "that friend endeavouring to rally him [Edwards] out of the notion, made the thing known abroad." Edwards had kept the experience to himself for four years, and no doubt then told the one person he most trusted, his mentor Ebenezer Gibbons. Edwards put the kindest face on his confidence being betrayed, but one must speculate on a possible connection between Edwards confiding his experience in 1759, in all probability to Gibbons, and his being dismissed in 1759.

When Edwards was asked to leave in 1759, his replacement was waiting in the wings, in full favor with Gibbons, the deacons, and some principal members of the church. Small wonder that in 1781 when a large group of members in the Baptist church of Philadelphia were circulating a petition in the congregation to dismiss Elhanan Winchester for preaching Universalism, Edwards signed the petition thus, "Morgan Edwards signs this protest against the doctrine of Universal Salvation under the character only of a doctrine that he does not believe."[75] He was opposing Universalism but stopping short of endorsing the dismissal of Winchester. He had been down that road, and he knew the pain.

THE YEAR AT RYE

Joseph Ivimey, a British Baptist pastor who published a four-volume history of English Baptists in the nineteenth-century, referred to the Particular Baptist church at Rye.[76]

> The names of its pastors, their settlements and removals, form the principal events in the history of the church.

Name	When ordained	When Removed
Charles Rodgers	November 1750	November 1758
_____ Edwards	1758	Removed to America, 1759
Christopher Hall	1760	_____ 1762

In 1904 the Reverend A. Hedley Brown gave a lecture on the history of Rye Baptists and included in his reference to Morgan Edwards are these words, "Whence Mr. Edwards came and thither [sic] he went, we know not,..."[77]

A Successful Ministry

Mystery and puzzlement seemed to hang over Morgan Edwards like a rain cloud, even in a pastorate which lasted only from March 1760 to February 1761.[78] A major Baptist historian does not know his first name and has the wrong dates for his ordination and departure from the

Rye church. A pastor of the church, writing about him more than one hundred forty years later, cannot report his previous pastorate or the place to which he moved. Yet, judging by Edwards's farewell sermon at Rye, his ministry there was significant and rewarding, even if it did last only one year.

In his farewell sermon, Edwards listed many encouraging elements of his twelve-month stay. He cited the "unusual gathering of people to this place" and the "frequent free-will-offerings." In addition he spoke of people who "have been added to the church,...A number so considerable, as to equal the number that met in communion, when I first administered the Lord's Supper in this place." He spoke of unity by saying, "breeches have been made up, and varying parties reconciled." Finally, he said, "strong prejudices against us as a community have been happily removed: so that they who hated us have shewn us favours."[79]

Also in this sermon we have Edwards's tribute to the congregation for the wonderful way in which they treated him. He said, "your satisfaction in me, and kindness to me were manifest;...Your efforts to raise me a competent salary were such indeed as I had read of, but never saw before." He went on to speak of the tears that flowed when he first received proposals to go to America, and their efforts to offset that possibility, including raising his salary "were augments of the sincerity of your friendship."[80]

The townspeople were also kind to Edwards. When a few people harassed him after his arrival in Rye, the leaders of the community rallied round. They invited him as their guest to public events and in their homes, gave him sound advice when his family was in danger, aided him when he was ill and allowed him the use of their carriages. They asked him not to leave and offered money to increase his support.[81] Considering the state of the town and the checkered history of the church all these tributes are the more significant.

The Town of Rye

The town of Rye, judging from the writings of Daniel Dafoe, had little to recommend it. Dafoe's description was written in 1724, only thirty-six years before Edwards's arrival.[82]

> ...the towns of Rye, Winchelsea and Hastings have little in them to deserve more than a bare mention; Rye would flourish again if her harbour, which was once able to receive the royal navy, cou'd be restored; but as it is, the bar is so loaded with sand cast up by the sea, that ships of 200 tun chuse [sic] to ride it out....

Rye, then, was a town by-passed by history, but the church was young and fiesty.

The Rye Baptist Church

The Baptist church in Rye was a young church, but it was the oldest Dissenter church in the town. Though the church was founded in 1750, Baptists had been in the area for over one hundred years.[83] Baptists arrived in the Kent-Sussex area in 1633, when Archbishop William Laud began imprisoning people for nonconformity. Among the arrivals were some who advocated believer baptism, and by their witness to their fellow-prisoners, converts were made. Soon there were Baptists preaching throughout the region, and among the converts were two Anglican vicars, Francis Cornwell and Christopher Blackwood. About twenty churches were formed during this initial outburst of evangelism, and most were General Baptists. Those which were Calvinistic began associating together in 1700.[84] The Rolvenden Church (also called Sandhurst) was one of those churches.[85] A meeting house was erected in 1731, and the congregation included people from Rye.

In 1733 Thomas Petter became pastor at Sandhurst. He continued the tradition started by Francis Cornwell of laying hands on those who had been baptized--practiced in many Particular Baptist churches. Petter, however, expanded the laying on of hands to include the ordination of ministers and deacons. Some members disliked the practice because it hinted too much at sacramentalism, and they raised issues related to discipline and communion.[86] In November, 1750, eleven people in that group formed themselves into the Particular Baptist church at Rye.[87] The break with Sandhurst was not amicable, as the Rye group charged the others with being in error.[88]

Before then the Rye Baptists would meet periodically with the Presbyterians. In 1749, the Presbyterians suggested the Baptists call their own pastor. Charles Rogers was called and settled at Rye on November 8, 1750.[89]

The Baptists at Rye met at the Friends Meetinghouse until it was purchased by a Baptist deacon, George Quested. The building was demolished and subscriptions taken for a new building on Mermaid Street.[90] In 1754 they built a new chapel, with men in one gallery and women in the other. The members sat "on forms unless they were willing to build their own pews."[91] However, financial stress brought on by the construction of a new church, began to take a toll on the membership.

The church encountered difficulty providing an adequate salary for the pastor and paying off the indebtedness, and apparently was unable to do either. Rodgers resigned in November, 1758.[92] Brown reports there were no communion services during the next two years. The church lacked an ordained minister and there was much division in the congregation.[93] On an early spring Sunday in 1760, the church's fortunes took a turn for the better.

On March 23, 1760, Morgan Edwards presided over the Lord's Supper with thirteen members of the Rye Baptist Church. While the rest of the members were aloof, Edwards made his beginning with this feisty, squabbling young church. His twelve month stay at the church was a welcome hiatus from the stress of preceding years. Edwards left in 1761 and was succeeded by Christopher Hall. His brother, Robert Hall, became one of England's great Baptist preachers. Hall stayed only a few months and left Rye for Luton in Bedfordshire.[94] On the surface it appeared the church reverted to its old habits, but Hall's successor, Thomas Purdy, stayed until 1817.[95]

Morgan Edwards's farewell sermon is the only measure we have to gauge the results of his ministry in Rye. The Rye churchbook, now at the Angus Library of Regents Park College, Oxford, dates only to 1768, when Thomas Purdy was pastor. There are two statements, however, in the printed edition of Edwards's farewell sermon which tell of the strong bonds which he developed with the Rye congregation in that brief period.

On the title page is the statement, "And printed by them that heard it, in testimony of their Affection to their late Minister."[96] Given their willingness to extend themselves to provide a greater inducement for him to stay and the preceding warm witness of affection, there can be little doubt of their love for Morgan Edwards. His sermon makes clear his affection for his congregation.[97]

> And the general regret at my departure which wets so many cheeks in this assembly, gives my heart very sensible touches of sympathy-- This being the case, you may be sure I leave the town, and this congregation with great reluctance.

Edwards's sermon reveals he had no illusions of what he faced in leaving Rye for Philadelphia.[98]

> The dangers before me are not few. The quitting of my native country, friends and relations (probably) for ever, is grievous. And yet after a mature consideration; and consulting my honoured friends; and brethren in the ministry, it appears to me I ought to go. And as I cannot suspect your friendship for me, give me leave to tell you, That I shall esteem this the highest instance of it, viz. To pray God to give me success in my office in the place whither I am going.

In summary it is seen that the Baptist church in Rye had experienced a revival under the-one year pastorate of Morgan Edwards. Before his arrival, it was a church obsessed with doctrinal disputes with other churches, held in disrepute in the community, rent by internal squabbles, unable to support a pastor, and in a dying condition.

When Edwards left they were at peace with their sister churches, respected in the community, reconciled to each other, able to pay a full salary, and growing. One questions why he left such a wonderful situation and all that had been important in his life to travel to a distant colony of the British Empire.

Like many others before him, he felt genuinely called of God to go, but he would return to his native land a few years hence. In retrospect, his first thirty-nine years in the British Isles appear as a prelude to the dramatic years to follow. In May 1761 he arrived in Philadelphia and there lived among mostly the Welsh, English, and Irish, as he had at home. He would be able to speak in both the English and Welsh languages and conduct business in British currency as he had all his life. Edwards's final words also show he had made a momentous decision.[99]

> ...the time of my departure is come: and I go a great distance; and to a habitation far asunder from yours: a distance that forms a great part of the circumference of this huge globe: a habitation as wide from yours, that the Earth itself will interpose between us."

With that distance being so far, the question arises as to what prompted John Gill to recommend Morgan Edwards to the Philadelphia church. It is one of the puzzling questions about his life.

ENDNOTES

1. Cork Baptist Churchbook, (MS., 1759), n.p.
2. Ibid.
3. Morgan Edwards, *Christ Our Life*, (MS. Sermon, August 6, 1759)
4. Pishey Thompson, *History and Antiquities of Boston*, (London: Longman and Co., 1865), 259.
5. Adam Taylor, *The History of The English General Baptists*, (London: T. Bore, 1818), 98-114.
6. A.C. Underwood, *A History of The English Baptists*, (London: Carey Kingsgate Press), 73.
7. Reuben A. Guild, *Early History of Brown University Including the Life, Times, and Correspondence of President Manning*, (Providence: Snow and Farnham), 14.
8. M.S., "Minutes of the Particular Baptist Fund, II. 1740- 1757", (Angus Library, Regents Park College, Oxford University), n.p.
9. Morgan Edwards, *Conversion*, (MS., Academical), 1743, 74, McKesson Collection. John Hay Library, Brown University, Providence, Rhode Island.

10. John R. Green, *England*, (New York: Peter Fenlon Collin, 1958), III, 174.
11. Frank M. Stenton, *Anglo Saxon England*, (Oxford: Oxford University Press, 1847), 49.
12. Ibid., 518.
13. Ibid., 506.
14. Robert G. Torbet, *A History of the Baptists*, (Valley Forge: Judson Press, 1963), 64
15. Underwood, 139.
16. Ibid.
17. William L. Lumpkin, *Baptist Confessions of Faith*, (Philadelphia: The Judson Press, 1959), 295-296.
18. Torbet, 65.
19. H. Leon McBeth, *The Baptist Heritage*, (Nashville: The Broadman Press, 1987), 157.
20. Torbet. p. 66.
21. J.H. Wood, *A Condensed History of the General Baptists of the New Connection*, (London: Wood, Simkin, Marshall and Company, 1847), 182. 22.Taylor, 99.
23. The church in Heslam's Alley was called the "Independent" Baptist Church to distinquish it from the more connectional General Baptist Church. It was, however, a Particular Baptist Church.
24. Taylor. 111.
25. Arthur S. Langley, "Baptist Ministers In England About 1750 A.D.", *Transactions of the Baptist Historical Society*, (London: Baptist Union Publication Society, 1918-1919), 153.
26. Josiah Thompson, "A View of English Nonconformity in 1773," *Transactions of the Congregational Historical Society*, (London: T.G. Crippen, Thacker, 1911-1912), II, 264.
27. Pishey Thompson, 259.
28. Ibid., 269-270.
29. Ibid, 259.
30. Ministers Fund, II. 1740-1757, n.p.
31. Ibid.
32. Ibid.
33. Ibid.
34. Ibid.
35. Ibid.

36. Ibid.
37. T.M. Bassett, *The Welsh Baptists,* (Swansea: Ilston House, 1977), 94.
38. Selwyn Gummer, "Trosnant Academy," *The Baptist Quarterly,* (London: Baptist Union Publication Department, 1939), IX, 422.
39. Joshua Thompson, "Baptists In Ireland, 1792-1922" (Unpublished D.Ph. dissertation, Angus Library, Regents Park College, 1988), 10.
40. Ibid.
41. McBeth, 312.
42. Ibid, 313.
43. Irish Baptist Historical Society Journal, 1968-69, I, 4- 19.
44. Cork Baptist Churchbook, n.p.
45. Ibid.
46. Ibid.
47. Ibid.
48. Joseph Ivimey, *A History of the English Baptists,* (London: Issac Taylor Hinton, 1811), I, 240.
49. Joshua Thompson, 10.
50. Ibid., 9.
51. Cork Baptist Churchbook, 27-30.
52. Joshua Thompson, 9.
53. Joshua Thompson in a letter to the author dated June 12, 1991.
54. Cork Baptist Churchbook, 63.
55. Ibid.
56. Ibid., 35
57. Ibid., 42.
58. Ibid., 27.
59. Guild, 15.
60. Churchbook, First Baptist Church, Philadelphia, 13.
61. William Rogers, "Memorial Sermon," *Rippon's Register,* (London: January 1796), 310.
62. MS. Letter, Richard Webster to Horatio Gates Jones, July 20, 1853, Horatio Gates Jones, Jr., Collection, File #1, American Baptist Historical Society, Rochester.
63. Guild, 15.
64. Morgan Edwards, *A New Year's Gift,* (Newport: Solomon Southwick, 1770), 8.
65. Frederick W. Harris, "The Life and Work of Phiilip Doddridge,

As Illustrating the Internal and External Relationships of the English Independent Churches During the First Half of the Eighteenth Century", (Unpublished doctoral dissertation, Appendix C).
66. D. Densil Morgan, "Smoke, Fire and Light", *The Baptist Quarterly*, (London: Baptist Historical Society, 1988), XXXII, No. 5, 228.
67. Cork Baptist Churchbook, 57.
68. Ibid., 56,57.
69. Ibid., 53,54.
70. Ibid., 54,55
71. Ibid., 57,58.
72. Ivimey, IV, 19.
73. F.B. Dexter, ed. *The Literary Diary of Ezra Stiles*, (New York: 3 Vols., 1901), 24,25.
74. Morgan Edwards, *A New Year's Gift*. p. 8.
75. Philadelphia Baptist Churchbook, March 5, 1781, n.p.
76. Ivimey, IV, 239.
77. A. Hedley Brown, *The Rye Baptists 1750 to 1904*, (Rye: Deacon's Printing and Publishing Works, 1904), 12.
78. Ibid.
79. Morgan Edwards, *A Farewell Discourse*, (Dublin: S. Powell, 1761), 12,13.
80. Ibid., 13,14.
81. Ibid., 14.
82. Richard Muir, *The Lost Villages of Britain*, (London: Michael Joseph, 1982), 98, 99.
83. G.J. Ballard. *Connecting Links of About 200 Years History of the Sandhurst Baptists*, (Rye: Adams and Sons, n.d.), 12.
84. W.T. Whitely, "Sandhurst Bicentenary," *The Baptist Quarterly*, (London: Baptist Union Publication Department, 1930-1931), V, 322.
85. Ibid., 324.
86. Frank Buffard, *Kent and Sussex Baptist Association*, (Faversham, Eng.: E. Vinson, n.d.), 50.
87. Ballard, 12.
88. Ivimey, IV, 538.
89. Brown, 5.
90. Geoffrey F. Nuttall, "The Letter Book of John Davis (1731-1795) of Waltham Abbey," *The Baptist Quarterly*, (London: Baptist

Historical Society, 1971), 58-59.
91. Brown, 8.
92. Buffard, 50.
93. Ivimey, IV, 538-539.
94. Brown, 12.
95. Ivimey, IV, 239.
96. Ibid.
97. Edwards, *A Farewell Discourse*, Title Page
98. Ibid, 15.
99. Ibid.

SECTION TWO

The Story in Philadelphia

CHAPTER FIVE

A NEW MAN IN A NEW CITY

> "They required so many accomplishments...The Dr. could not find a man in England who would answer their requirements; Mr Morgan Edwards came the nearest..."
> David Benedict, 1855
> (Quoting John Gill, 1761)

The Baptist Church of Philadelphia must have been viewed with suspicion in 1760, for it had drawn up demanding criteria to measure any candidate for its vacant pulpit. It was certainly not the most attractive Baptist pulpit in the American colonies. For that matter, the city of Philadelphia was not the most loving place for Baptists, which its founder, William Penn, envisioned for all people.

So why would Morgan Edwards leave a promising situation in Rye after only one year and travel three thousand miles to a city still struggling to cast off its frontier image to serve a church unable to find a pastor on its own shores? The answer is found with those who were responsible for bringing him to the church.

The Call to Philadelphia

Upon receiving a letter from the Philadelphia Baptist Church, John Gill and members of the Particular Baptist Fund Board recommended Morgan Edwards's call to the pulpit vacated by the death of Jenkin Jones. Historian David Benedict described Gill's response to the church's list of demanding standards for their new pastor.[1]

> It is said that the church in Philadelphia sent to Dr. Gill to assist them in obtaining a pastor; but that they required so many accomplishments to be united in him, that the Dr. wrote them back that he did not know as he could find a man in England who would answer their description; informing them, at the same time, that Mr. Morgan Edwards, who was then preaching in Rye, in the County of Sussex, came the nearest of anyone who could be obtained.

In Gill's eyes, there were others who might meet the standards but who were not available. Among these were some of Gill's very prominent fellow board members. Gill had good reason to believe that Edwards was worthy of the standards and was also "obtainable." The question of Gill's recommendation of Edwards has puzzled Baptist historians, but when all the components of that call are considered, it does not appear so mysterious.

Gill's recommendation included four major elements: first, Gill himself and the Particular Baptist Fund Board of London; second, the board's full knowledge of Morgan Edwards the man, and his pastoral record; third, Edwards's close acquaintance with many members of the board; and fourth, John Griffiths, who had moved to Philadelphia from Wales.

In 1717, the Particular Baptists of London established a fund to assist needy ministers and to help with the education of ministerial candidates.[2] The fund's board served not only as a financial resource but also as a clearing house in recommending men to churches with vacant pulpits. John Gill, the well-known chairman of the board for many years, was the natural contact between the churches and the board. A recommendation signed by Gill carried great weight.

It was the practice to submit names of the most promising young ministers to the Particular Baptist Fund Board; John Gill, himself, had been through the selection process. Gill came to the attention of the board in 1718 as a young assistant to John Davis at Higham Ferrar, recommended for a grant from John Noble. Though a year later he received a second grant, he was already well known to the board as a promising young minister.[3] Edwards's name came before the board through the same process, it having been included on the annual "Welsh List" submitted by Miles Harry.

The first record of Edwards's name coming before the board was in 1740,[4] but it would have been on the Welsh List in 1738 when he entered Trosnant Academy. The individual names on the Welsh List were not usually included in the records. Edwards's name appeared separately in 1740 because it was an addition to the list. It was submitted by Joseph Stennett, member of the board and pastor of the Little Wild Street Church in London. He was one of the most eloquent preachers of the day, as well as one of the better educated.[5]

Indeed, Stennett was one of the trio of outstanding Baptist ministers who mentored Morgan Edwards in his continuing education program after he left the Bristol

Baptist Academy in 1743. The other two were John Gill, and Thomas Llewellyn.[6] As was stated earlier, John Gill was the outstanding Baptist minister and theologian of the period, and Thomas Llewellyn, a major Baptist figure.

Llewellyn was a leading promoter of evangelism in Northern Wales, and director and tutor at a Baptist school in London. He was active in the "Society for Promoting Christian Knowledge," and, in 1771, mediated with King George on behalf of the Baptists of Ashfield, Massachusetts. Llewellyn influenced the Fund board in London on behalf of several worthy students and causes.[7]

By 1761 the board had known of Edwards and his pastoral performance record for twenty-three years because the annual Welsh List carried Miles Harry's evaluations with it. Welsh Baptist historian Joshua Thomas reports,[8]

> He [Harry] used to send to the FUNDEES in London, a very particular and friendly account of the Baptist ministers in Wales, their function; who most useful & C., and this he did annually soon after each association.

Every year, then, Edwards was on a ratings list, at least until he left Bristol Academy in 1743. It is clear that Morgan Edwards was well known to the board since 1738 because of the continual flow of data they received from Miles Harry.

It is evident that Edwards was personally acquainted with members of the board. In May 1762, one year after he arrived in Philadelphia, he cosigned a letter with Peter Van Horn from the Philadelphia Baptist Association to the London board, reestablishing a relationship which had been moribund since 1734. The help sought in the form of money, books, and "apparatus" for the Hopewell Academy, and requested that future correspondence be addressed to Morgan Edwards.[9] His boldness in renewing contact with the London board is a clear indication of his close relationship its members. Almost all the board members were outstanding persons in Baptist church life of the day.

As chairman of the board, John Gill received frequent requests for help from churches in finding a new pastor. Not even Gill's backing, however, was a guarantee of good pastoral leadership. Walter Richards came to the Devonshire Square Church in London with high marks from his training pastor in Birmingham, James Turner. Gill preached Richard's ordination sermon on December 16, 1762, the year after Edwards went to Philadelphia. Richards's preaching, however, was so unsatisfactory that he was forced to resign eighteen months later. He settled finally at the Baptist Church in Cork, succeeding John Knight who replaced Edwards there. He was known as a man of "unsettled principles and eccentric habits and but of little use."[10] Besides the board and John Gill, there was an additional element that brought Edwards's name to the Philadelphia church.

John Griffiths, who started the Trosnant Academy, left Wales for Philadelphia in 1759, two years before Morgan Edwards. Griffiths, was an ardent Baptist layman and active in the Philadelphia Baptist church. At a church meeting on March 13, 1760, he was appointed to write a letter to the Particular Baptist Fund Board in London requesting them to send a minister to Philadelphia. The letter was signed by those members present.[11] A number of factors contributed to his selection as the letter writer.

Like Edwards, Griffiths was well known to the London board, for he was widely respected among Baptists in the British Isles. In addition, his years at the Trosnant

Academy brought him into frequent communication with the board as they attempted to meet the educational needs of ministerial students. It was Griffiths who composed the letter and developed the criteria to be used in the selection of a minister. His keen interest in ministerial education would lead him to include high educational qualifications.

Given the relatively low education level of most Baptist ministers in the American colonies at the time, it is no wonder that some candidates took offense when they learned of the high standards the church was requiring.[12] In addition, most pastors in England who met these standards were not "obtainable," as they would already hold prominent pastorates in the larger churches. It is not so strange then that Gill's finger would point in Morgan Edwards's direction.

Gill's recommendation of Edwards to the Philadelphia church does not appear to be as perplexing as it once seemed. The board was a resource for such recommendations and Edwards' pastoral and educational record were well known to Gill and the board for many years. Edwards personally knew each board member and had even preached in their churches on a number of occasions. John Griffiths, who developed the standards, was a man dedicated to the education of Baptist ministers and an acquaintance of Morgan Edwards. By September 1760 John Gill's letter recommending Morgan Edwards had been received by the church.

On September 15, 1760 Isaac Jones, Esq., Stephen Anthony, Ebenezer Kinnersly, and H. Woodrow were appointed to "invite Mr. Edwards to come over, or any other gentlemen of like character, to take ministerial charge of the church."[13] As time passed all these gentlemen were highly visible in Edwards's pastorate, but at this time they were to set the stage for his arrival.

Morgan and Mary Edwards got their first glimpse of Philadelphia as they sailed up the Delaware River on May 23, 1761.[14] The view has been described by Philadelphia historian E.P. Oberhaltzer as a city dominated by five steeples, which indicated its importance. These prominences were the State House (later Independence Hall), Christ's Church, the Presbyterian Church, the Courthouse, and the College of Philadelphia.[15] The Baptist church would meet a different type of minister than they had ever known, and the Edwardses would live in a different kind of city than they had ever known.

The City of Philadelphia
When Morgan and Mary Edwards stepped off that ship onto the soil of Philadelphia on May 23, 1761, they began a new life in an "exciting and exuberant town."[16] Between 1681 and 1776, the city had been transformed from the few scattered farms of the first Swedish settlers to the second largest city of the British Empire, second only to London.[17]

Philadelphia was first settled by less than one hundred Swedish immigrants in 1643; within fifty years there were one hundred eighty-eight families numbering nine hundred fifty-two Swedes. In 1682, one year after William Penn established his "greene country towne," brisk land sales would launch an accelerated development; by 1700, the population would reach five thousand.[18] By 1761, the Philadelphia area population had reached forty thousand.

Penn laid out the streets in straight lines, to intersect at right angles. He included a square or park in each quadrant of the city, with the marketing area near the waterfront on the Delaware River. His holy experiment of providing a haven for the religiously persecuted brought thousands from Europe with their diverse manufacturing skills.[19] Thus, the city thrived in its commercial, religious, and cultural life, but not without some stress.

By 1739 the demand for wheat, flour, and bread was so great that over two hundred ships annually tied up to the Philadelphia docks. One October day in 1754, there were one hundred seventeen large ships docked at the city's sixty-six wharves.[20] The swelling tide of commerce was offset by the seamy traffic in vice which developed in the caves along the Delaware River.[21] The degree and quality of sin in Philadelphia was shocking to newly arrived religious leaders.

Henry Melchior Muhlenberg was a Lutheran missionary sent from Halle, Saxony in 1742 to minister to German Lutherans. In 1750 he reported.[22]

> It is almost impossible to describe how few good and how many exceptionally godless, wicked people have come into this country every year. The whole country is flooded with ordinary, extraordinary and unprecedented wickedness and crimes. Surely the rod of God cannot be spared much longer.
>
> Our old residents are mere stupid children in sin compared with the new arrivals! Oh, what a fearful thing it is to have so many thousands of unruly and brazen sinners come into this free and unfenced country.

If the religious people in the Quaker city of brotherly love were shocked by the sins of the nonreligious, they were also very pointed in the barbs they directed at each other. An amusing example of this is found on a headstone in the graveyard of Trinity Church, Oxford, then outside the city limits. It bears the inscription of Elizabeth, the wife of John Roberts, who died May 6, 1708, at age forty-one.[23]

> Here by these lines is testified
> No Quaker was she when she dy'd
> So far was she from Quakerism
> That she desired to have baptism.

Though people of many different denominations settled in Philadelphia, the religious scene was not always as it was designed to be. When George Whitefield came to the city in 1739, he created a sensation--his great voice and eloquent, bold preaching created a clamor of enthusiasm in the quiet town.

He began his preaching at Christ Church (Church of England), but was soon denied that pulpit, and before long the pulpits of all other churches. Whitefield resorted to preaching from the balcony of the court house and in the public squares and open fields. Meanwhile a building was erected for him, which later became the home of the College of Philadelphia.[24]

Morgan and Mary Edwards found their new city making significant urban progress. By 1750 most of the streets were paved with flagstone sidewalks,[25] but the residents were still placing their trash in front of their homes. The resulting filth created a terrible stench and posed severe health problems. Eventually Benjamin Franklin initiated a successful effort to raise funds to hire street cleaners, and before long all the center city streets were paved and trash free. In addition, street lamps had been installed by 1749.[26]

In the early eighteenth century the city experienced some terrible fires, but by 1730 a good stock of firefighting equipment was on hand and the first fire company was formed by 1736. In the meantime, progress was being made in the medical field.

Though the city still suffered intermittent scourges of yellow fever and influenza, an inoculation program began in 1756 to combat small pox. In December 1756 the Pennsylvania Hospital opened its doors as the struggle continued against other diseases such as whooping cough, measles and malaria.

The Edwardses discovered Philadelphia's cultural side as well. A theater was erected in 1760, and by 1763 the city could count some forty music teachers. The eighteenth century saw Philadelphia blossom into a city of painters with such great painters as West, Peale, and Stuart. Morgan Edwards commissioned a portrait painting, which apparently survived the destruction of his home in Delaware during the Revolution.[27]

When Morgan and Mary arrived in Philadelphia, they were probably met by a number of old friends, since many Welsh Baptists had migrated to Philadelphia. It is likely that John Griffiths met them, as he was the logical person to introduce them to the Philadelphia Baptist Church.

The Baptist Church at Philadelphia

What is today the First Baptist Church of Philadelphia was in 1761 the second Baptist church constituted in the Philadelphia area. Founded in 1698 it is only ten years younger than the oldest Baptist church at Pennepek (Lower Dublin)[28] and the eleventh oldest Baptist church in the United States.[29] The Philadelphia church was sixty-three years old when Morgan Edwards arrived. The early Baptists of Philadelphia, however, traced their roots to other regions.

The first Baptists arrived in the Philadelphia area in

1684 under the leadership of Rev. Thomas Dungan.[30] They settled at Cold Spring, Bucks County, but dissolved the congregation in 1702. The remaining members joined the Pennepek church.[31]

Rev. Elias Keach and eleven others organized the Pennepek church in 1684.[32] Keach was the son of the renowned Benjamin Keach of London. When the young man arrived in Philadelphia in 1686, he dressed as a man of the cloth, though he was neither a believer nor a minister. He attempted to carry on the charade by preaching in public, but he fell under such deep conviction after starting the sermon that he confessed his deception to the crowd. They gathered round him in support, and he professed faith in Christ. He then went to Cold Spring where Dungan baptized him. He later returned to Pennepek and helped to constitute the church, and from there he carried on an itinerant evangelistic ministry. Keach returned to England in 1692.[33]

Some of the first members of the Pennepek church moved to Philadelphia for better employment, and they occasionally met on the Lord's Day.[34] Nine members formed the Baptist church of Philadelphia "on the second Sunday in Dec. [December 11] 1698." Rev. John Watts, then pastor at the Pennepek church presided at the Lord's Table,[35] and he continued to serve them on a regular basis.

The new church held its meetings in an abandoned warehouse of the Barbadoes Trading Company at Second and Chestnut Streets, which they shared with the Presbyterians.[36] Watts and a Presbyterian minister preached every other Sunday to the combined group.[37] Before long the Presbyterians called a resident minister and requested that the Baptists vacate the premises. Characteristically,

Morgan Edwards was straightforward in his description of the event.[38]

> But when Jedidiah Andrews came to the latter [the Presbyterian congregation] they in a manner drove the baptists [sic] away. Several letters passed between the two societies on the occasion, which are yet extant. There was also a deputation of three baptists appointed to remonstrate with the presbyterians for so unkind and rightless a conduct; but to no purpose.

Keen later described the correspondence as "spicy,"[39] but after their eviction from the Barbadoes property the Baptists met in the Brewhouse of Anthony Morris, "near the draw-bridge."[40] That location at Water and Dock Streets is now covered by an interstate highway, but the brewhouse served the Baptists for eight years until 1707. The Keithian Quakers moved to another location and offered the Baptists the use of their old building at Second Street and LaGrange Place. The Keithians (Quakers who felt a kinship with Baptists) erected the building in 1692, and the Baptists used it until 1731 when they razed it and constructed a new brick building, 42 feet by 30 feet.[41]

It was during this period that the Pennepek-Philadelphia church joined with four other churches to create the Philadelphia Baptist Association in 1707. Five Baptist churches had met together annually since 1688, and in 1707 they formed the first continuing Baptist association in America.[40] It would be on the stage of the Philadelphia Association that Morgan Edwards would later play his star role as a leader of American Baptists.

In 1734, three years after entering their new building the Baptists found themselves involved in a legal dispute to hold the property on which the building stood. The Keithians were not an incorporated body and the property they offered the Baptists was held by four trustees. By 1723 the Keithians had practically ceased to exist, and only one trustee was still living. He deeded the property to Christ Church (Anglican), whose property was adjacent to that of the Baptists.

When Mr. Thomas Peart, the trustee, died in 1734, the Vestry of Christ Church demanded possession. As expected, the Baptists refused and brought suit before the Assembly. The Anglicans relented and offered to sell their claim for 50 pounds. The Baptists quickly accepted the offer.[42] Meanwhile the congregation continued to function under a succession of pastors who served both the Pennepek and Philadelphia churches.

The practice of shared ministry ended in 1746 during the tenure of Rev. Jenkin Jones. Jones came to America from Wales in 1710 and was called to the ministry at the Welsh Tract church in 1724. He became pastor of the Pennepek and Philadelphia congregations in 1725 and served the dual pastorate until 1746.[43] In that year, a dispute arose between the two congregations over the legacies left the Philadelphia church.

The Pennepek church believed it had a right to benefit from the legacies to the Philadelphia church because it was a branch of the Pennepek church. To forestall any possibility that the benefactors' intentions might be diverted, "the Church at Philadelphia did, May 15, 1746, formally incorporate, which had only been done implicitly in December 16, 1698."[44] The month before on April 5, they petitioned the Pennepek church for a separation, which was approved at a church meeting the following month.[45] Since he lived in the city Jenkin Jones was among those separated.[45] He became the sole pastor of the Philadelphia church until his death on July 6, 1760.

Morgan Edwards, in his history, took special note of Jones's ministry by citing the services he accomplished:[46]

> (1) He secured to them the possession of their valuable lot and place of worship.
> (2) He was the moving cause for altering the direction of licenses so as to enable dissenting ministers to perform marriages by them.
> (3) He built a parsonage house partly at his own charge.
> (4) He gave a handsome legacy towards puchasing a silver cup for the Lord's table...

Another incident occurred during Jenkin Jones's pastorate which reflects both the church's commitment to religious freedom and an ecumenical spirit. David Spencer's description of the episode, offers a view of a religious climate which would suit Morgan Edwards.[47]

> A few families of the Roman Catholic faith, had arrived and erected a small chapel in Philadelphia. The colonial officers were alarmed at this movement, and Governor Gordon brought the matter before the Council, and informed them that a house had been lately built on Walnut Street in Philadelphia, wherein mass was openly celebrated by a Catholic priest, contrary to the laws of England. The citizens of the Baptist persuasion and others claimed that Catholics and all other sects were protected by the laws which had been established by William Penn, and all were entitled to religious liberty. The Council, therefore wisely refrained from any interference.

During the closing years of Jones's thirty-five-year-long pastorate--the longest in the church's history--his health and strength were failing as was that of the church.[48] As early as 1757 entries in the church records reveal an increasing tempo of censure for improper behavior and more wrangling at congregational meetings. By September 1758 (twenty months before Jones died), the church petitioned the Philadelphia Association to persuade several ministers "to come and settle among us."[49]

Jones was in such poor health that the church needed a interim pastor. The best they could arrange, however, was a series of men filling the pulpit several weeks at a time. Worship attendance was down to about a dozen people, and several months passed without a church meeting.[50]

Finally, four months before Jones died, the congregation voted to request help from the board of the Particular Baptist Fund in London in finding a pastor.[51] The person motivating the church to take that step was John Griffiths. He was familiar with the practice of making such requests, he knew the members of the board, and he was the obvious choice to make the contact. His letter to Dr. John Gill and the board solicited a response which included the name of Morgan Edwards. At the September 1760 church meeting, Isaac Jones was empowered to invite Edwards "to come over...and take ministerial charge of the church."[52]

On the surface it appears Morgan Edwards had been invited to become pastor of a church which was ready for its own demise. The fact that he was immediately successful in restoring life, health, and growth to the church created a tremendous reservoir of goodwill toward him in the congregation. Eventually he exhausted that reserve, but it kept him in good stead for many years. In the later years of his life he was able to restore it. The record of his pastorate in Philadelphia is one of the most remarkable chapters of his most remarkable story. .

ENDNOTES

1. David Benedict, *General History of the Baptist Denomination in*

America, (New York: Sheldon, Lamport and Blakeman, 1855), 602.
2. A.C. Underwood, *A History of the English Baptists*, (London: The Carey Kingsgate Press, 1947), 131.
3. Barrington R. White, "John Gill in London," *The Baptist Quarterly*, (London: The Baptist Historical Society, 1967), XXII, 73.
4. MS. "Minutes of the London Particular Baptist Fund, II. 1740-1757," (Angus Library, Regents Park College, Oxford University), n.p.
5. Underwood, 148.
6. Reuben A. Guild, *Early History Of Brown University, Including the Life, Times, and Correspondence of President Manning. 1756-1791*. (Providence: Snow and Farnham, 1897), 15.
7. T.M. Bassett, *The Welsh Baptists*, (Swansea: Ilston House, 1977), 68, 83, 100-101.
8. Joshua Thomas, *History of the Welsh Baptist Association*, (London: 1795), 55.
9. A.D. Gillettte, ed. *Minutes of the Philadelphia Baptist Association from A.D. 1707 to A.D. 1807*, (Philadelphia: The American Baptist Publication Society, 1851), 84 - 85.
10. Joseph Ivimey, *A History of the English Baptists*, (London: Issac Taylor Hinton, 1811), IV, 317 - 318.
11. Philadelphia Baptist Churchbook, Entry March 13, 1760, 9.
12. Stephen Gano, ed., *Biographical Memoirs of the Late Rev. John Gano*, (New York: Southwick and Hardcastle, 1806), 86.
13. Churchbook, 10.
14. Morgan Edwards, *Materials Towards a History of the Baptists*, (Philadelphia: James Crukshank and Isaac Collins, 1770), I, 41.
15. E.P. Oberholtzer, *Philadelphia: A History of the City and Its People*, (Philadelphia: S.J. Clark Publishing Corporation, n.d.), 187.
16. Joseph T. Kelly, Jr., *Life and Times In Colonial Philadelphia*. (Harrisburg: The Stackpole Company, 1973), 12.
17. Ibid.
18. Ibid. 49.
19. Ibid., 33.
20. Ibid., 46 - 48.
21. Ibid., 138 - 139.
22. Ibid.
23. William W. Keen, *The Bi-Centennial Celebration of the Founding*

of the First Baptist Church of Philadelphia, (Philadelphia: The American Baptist Publication Society, 1899), 36
24. Horace M. Lippincott, *Early Philadelphia, Its People, Life and Progress,* (Philadelphia: J.B. Lippincott, 1917), 73- 75.
25. Kelly, 49,
26, Ibid., 51.
27. MS. Letter. Richard Webster to Horatio Gates Jones, Jr., (Mauch Chunk, Pennsylvania: July 20, 1853). There is a reference to a portrait in this letter. Mr. Webster was a friend of Joshua Edwards, and at the end of the letter he states, "The M.S.S. & the Portrait are to go to Brown University." In the context it is obvious he is refering to manuscripts of Morgan Edwards' sermons and his portrait. No trace of that portrait could be found even though the author made a diligent search has been made for it.
28. Edwards, 42.
29. Keen, 13.
30. William D. Thompson, *Philadelphia's First Baptists,* (Philadelphia: First Baptist Church, 1989), 5.
31. Edwards, 41.
32. Ibid.
33. Ibid.
34. Thompson, 5.
35. Ibid.
36. Edwards, 42.
37. Ibid.
38. Ibid.
39. Keen, 40.
40. Edwards, 44.
41. Robert G. Torbet, *A History of the Baptists, 3rd ed.,* (Valley Forge: Judson Press, 1963), 211-212.
42. Edwards, 45.
43. Ibid., 46.
44. Ibid., 43. There is an apparent discrepancy between the December 11 date of Morgan Edwards and the December 16 date of William Keen. Edwards gave the second Sunday of December as the day as well as December 11. According to Keen, however, the second Sunday of December in 1698 would have been the 11th rather than the 16th. He thinks Edwards erred which he sometimes did.

45. Pennepek Churchbook, Entries for April 5 amd May 3, 1746.
46. Edwards, 47.
47. David Spencer, *The Early Baptists of Philadelphia,* (Philadelphia: William Sychelmore, 1877), 63.
48. Thompson, 12.
49. Philadelphia Churchbook, Entry for September 7, 1758, 5.
50. Ibid., Entries for May 10, 1759 and March 13, 1760, 7,9.
51. Ibid., 9.
52. Ibid., Entry for September 15, 1760, 10.

CHAPTER SIX

FAMILY LIFE AND DEATH

"A fond and pious parent!"
William Rogers, 1795

William Rogers, the successor to Morgan Edwards at the Philadelphia Baptist church and a professor for many years at the College of Philadelphia, delivered Edwards' memorial sermon on February 22, 1795. The sermon included comments about the Edwards family.[1]

> Our worthy friend departed this life, at Pencador, Newcastle county, Delaware State, on Wednesday the 28th of January last in the 73rd year of his age, and was buried, agreeable to his own desire, in the aisle of this meetinghouse, with his first wife and their children; her maiden name was Mary Nunn, originally of Cork, Ireland, by whom he had several children, all of whom are dead, except two sons, William and Joshua: the first, if alive, is a military officer in the British service; the other is now present with us, paying his last public tribute of filial affection to the memory of a fond and pious parent!

Rogers continued, mentioning Mrs. Elizabeth Singleton as Edwards's second wife, who was also dead and by whom he had no children.² He made no reference to Edwards's third wife, the widow of Washington Nathaniel Evans, who also preceded him in death. We are able to form a picture of the Edwards family from what we know of him as a father and by what we know of his two sons, William and Joshua.

The Story of Billy Edwards

William "Billy" Edwards was the first of only two Edwards children to survive childbirth or infancy. Mary Edwards died on August 16, 1769, pregnant with her eighth child.³ At least one child was interred with Mary under the aisle of the Baptist church; however, two or more of the six ill-fated children may have been buried there.⁴ William Rogers used "children" in his reference to the Edwards's crypt.⁵ In his history of the church, Keen reported,

> In spite of frequent mention of rates for a burial in the aisle, which would pre-suppose its frequency, Morgan Edwards and *some* [emphasis mine] of his family are the only persons whose burial in the aisle I have discovered.⁶

It has been difficult to determine the birth years of Billy and his younger brother Joshua.

By eight years of age Billy was enrolled in James Manning's academy at Rhode Island College. This is confirmed in a report in the *Providence Gazette* for September 8, 1770 on the second commencement of the college.⁷

> On Wednesday, was celebrated the second Commencement in Rhode Island College. The parties concerned met at the Court House about 10 o'clock from whence they proceeded to the Rev.

Joseph Snow's meeting-house. The members of the Grammar School joined in the procession. Before the assembly broke-up, a piece from Homer was pronounced by Master Billy Edwards, one of the Grammar School boys, not nine years old.

In commenting on this report, a later president of Brown University named Barnas Sears said, "This promising boy was the son of Rev. Morgan Edwards."[8] Apparently eight-year old William was following in his father's footsteps in his mastery of classical literature.

James Manning had established his academy in 1764 when he became pastor of the Baptist church in Warren, Rhode Island. In 1770, the school was moved with the college to Providence in 1770, and Manning continued to teach and oversee the academy for many years, in addition to fulfilling his presidential and pastoral responsibilities.[9] Billy's education, however, probably did not begin with Manning's Latin School.

At the time, Ebenezer Kinnersley operated an academy in Philadelphia. He was an associate of Benjamin Franklin in his experiments with electricity, taught at the College of Philadelphia, and was a member of the Baptist Church. Billy attended the school for the first two years of his grammar school education; Joshua attended later.

Joshua stated that his father had strong educational convictions, including the "settled opinion" that education could not begin too soon nor be too actively pursued. Morgan Edwards was a close friend of Kinnersley, and enrolled Joshua in his school in 1770, when Joshua was six years old.[10] Thus, if Billy began his education at the same age as Joshua it would have been in 1768.

Joshua reported in a brief autobiography years later that both he and Billy had a difficult time in their early school years.[11] In Billy's case, that difficulty included coping with the tragic loss of his mother on August 16, 1769, and leaving home soon after. For Joshua the negative effect of his mother's death was not too apparent.

When Mary died, Edwards must have struggled over how he would care for his two young sons. He had many commitments, including those at Rhode Island College. The commencement schedule required him to be in Warren, Rhode Island, on September 6, 1769, to attend the board meeting and to receive an honorary degree the next day at the commencement. He was also to preach the first annual sermon.[12] Cancelling these commitments was out of the question.

The *Providence Gazette* report implies that Billy was a student at Manning's academy the preceding year, and thus the following sequence of events seems to have occurred after Mrs. Edwards died. After her funeral Edwards took Billy to Warren and registered him at the Latin School operated by Manning. He attended the board meeting and the commencement, and then returned to Philadelphia. Billy, only seven or eight years old, was left in Warren, still trying to cope with his grief and a new environment. The trauma of his wife's death was yet another instance of Edwards being conquered, but not subdued. The same can be said for Billy.

It is not too difficult to imagine what young Billy was feeling as he saw his father ride off down the road toward Philadelphia. He had lost his mother three weeks before and he was separated from his brother several days later when he and his father left for Rhode Island. Now he was in a totally alien environment, many miles from his home. But before the end of his first year, Billy would have to cope with another problem.

On January 1, 1770, Morgan Edwards preached what

has been called his own "funeral sermon." This event will receive more detailed treatment later. The sermon was put into print, and a much wider audience waited to see if the prediction of his death to occur on March 9, 1770, was correct. After all, Mary Edwards had a premonition she would die while pregnant with her eighth child, and she did. But what effect did all this have on Billy?

James Manning and others in Rhode Island knew of Edwards's premonition, and now it was in public print for all to read. To be sure, Billy must have known of his mother's premonition because she had talked about it freely. Now it seemed to have come true, at least in the mind of an eight-year-old boy. As March 9, drew near, Billy must have had a reprise of all the fears he had known the year before. He was no doubt subjected to ridicule by his classmates. He would be hundreds of miles from home when his father died, and all the while plagued by the thought of never seeing him again. Who would care for young Joshua, at home alone, when his father died? Edwards did not die as predicted, but it must have been a very difficult time for Billy.

William Edwards graduated from Rhode Island College in 1776[13] when he was fourteen years old.[14] While it may appear to be a young age to be graduated from college, one must remember there were no accrediting agencies at the time to set and maintain uniform standards. What is more important in this case is that Manning opened his Latin School "with an ultimate view to college instruction."[15] Manning intentionally connected the Latin School with the College with a view to move students through to the College courses. Billy Edwards, along with Daniel Gano and John Hart, all sons of well-known Baptist ministers, were admitted to their Bachelor of Arts studies on that basis. However, their conduct created many problems.

The students' behavior was the subject of a vote at the college board meeting in September 1775.[16]

> ...the president write to the parents of Daniel Gano, John Hart and William Edwards informing them, that upon their sons applying at some future Commencement, and passing the usual examination, together with their bringing recommendations of good conduct, they may be admitted to the honors of this College.

The requirement for "recommendations of good conduct" was not without warrant.

On March 2, 1774, President James Manning summoned the college family to the college hall and read a public admonition against William Edwards and four of his classmates for violating the "Laws of the College."[17] The five offenders were called forward and told their names were being entered into the "Black Book." All but William Edwards were charged with multiple violations; he was guilty only of not keeping study hours.

The enforcement of prescribed study hours was something of a problem to the infant colleges in America. In England the tutors dined with the students. The quadranglar shape of the college buildings enabled the sole exit to be under constant surveillance. The American schools attempted to solve the problem of students skipping out during evening study hours by requiring the tutors to visit the students' rooms frequently and irregularly. As a result of the students' misbehavior, Rhode Island College established a new rule in 1774.[18]

> That no Student refuse to open his Door when he shall hear the stamp of the Foot or Staff at his Door of Entry, which shall be a

Token that Some Officer of Instruction desires admission, which Token every Student is forbid to Counterfit, or imitate under any Pretense whatever.

Apparently the public admonition in the hall and the record of his misbehavior in the Black Book did not immediately deter William from further violating the rules governing study hours. On August 19, 1775, Nicholas Brown wrote to Morgan Edwards concerning William's behavior. Brown, a wealthy businessman, and a generous benefactor of the college, was a friend of Edwards. The letter was sensitive to the father's feelings and concern for his son. Brown believed William would not complete his education if he did not do so at that time because of the worsening relations between the American colonies and England. Brown reported to Edwards that William had stopped studying altogether, and that the next step was expulsion.[19] Edwards had renounced his loyalty to the Crown only two weeks before receiving Brown's letter. William must have become unsettled by the gathering political storm because he shared his father's loyalty to the Crown, and lived on a campus alive with patriotic fervor.

Judging by correspondence from James Manning to Samuel Jones, Billy was in Jones's care. Edwards had left Billy in his care while he was on an evangelistic tour of the South. Manning's letter was very solicitous of Billy's welfare[20]

> Yours of ye 8th Ansd: came by Mr: [Master] Edwards, I will take particular care to comply with your Requests, repecting his conduct. I find him an amiable young Man, & I hope he will prove an honor to the College___ I wish he had been forward enough to enter College: for he promises usefulness___ I am very

sensible that change in outward circumstances have an amazing Influence on young Minds: But we are favoured with a Number of really pious young Christians, Members of College, with whom he has already formed a connection; which I hope will be for his Advantage; especially as some of them are possessed of good natural Abilities.

Then, on March 7, 1774, Manning wrote to Jones, "We expect Edwards will enter college next Fall."[21] This assurance followed by five days the public reprimand in the dormitory hall, and preceded by three months Nicholas Brown's letter to Billy's father. What is learned from this correspondence is that Billy entered the college program in September 1774, at a younger age than the other college students, and he graduated two years later. In September of 1775 he was cleared for graduation. Despite all his problems William Edwards was entrusted by Manning and others with letters and packages as he made periodic trips between Rhode Island and Philadelphia.[22]

All the efforts to encourage William and dissuade him from misbehavior had an effect. At the Corporation meeting one month after Nicholas Brown wrote his letter, the board voted, that the president should write to the parents of "Daniel Gano, John Hart and William Edwards they [be] admitted to the honors of the College."[23] One year later on September 7, 1776, William Edwards graduated from Rhode Island College, with the valedictorian theme of liberty resounding in his ears.[24] This was to be the college's last public commencement until after the Revolution.

Four months earlier, in May 1776, Rhode Island renounced all allegiance to King George III; on July 4, all the colonies, acting through their chosen representatives, declared their independence from England. The political climate was becoming more and more uncomfortable for the loyalists to the King. At some point subsequent to his graduation, Billy persuaded his father to send him to Wales or Ireland where he would stay with his paternal or maternal grandparents. Later he enlisted in the British Army and eventually was promoted to the rank of colonel.

William Edwards may have outlived his father, who died January 28, 1795. Rev. William Rogers's sermon at Morgan Edwards's memorial service on February 22, 1795, suggested William might have been alive at the time of his father's death.[24]

> ...he [Morgan Edwards] had several children, all of whom are dead, except two sons, William and Joshua: the first, if alive, is a military officer in the British service; the other is now present with us, paying this last public tribute of filial affection to the memory of a fond and pious parent.

Morgan Edwards may have made a second trip to England in 1791 to look for Billy (see chapter fourteen). It remained for his brother Joshua to discover any existing evidence as to what had happened to Billy.

The most specific information available about William Edwards's disappearance is contained in a letter from Richard Webster, a friend of Joshua Edwards, to Horatio Gates Jones in 1853. Joshua was eighty-eight years old at the time. Webster reports,

> His [Joshua] brother Wm. was an officer in the British army & having taken passage in the coach from Plymouth, Eng. with a view to visit Ireland to recover his mother's estate, disappeared & was never heard of.

Webster goes on to say that Joshua himself spent many

years in England.[26] The estate was evidently one left to Mrs. Edwards upon the death of her father, Joshua, in Cork. Since she had already passed away, her children would have been her heirs. While there is no information to outline a course of events, it is possible to suggest what probably took place.

After Morgan Edwards's death in January 1795, Joshua disposed of his father's holdings in Delaware by July 28, 1795.[27] He then went to England to trace his brother's path and to determine the final disposition of his mother's estate. Joshua had some success concerning his brother; he learned that Billy had taken "the coach from Plymouth," which would have taken him to Bristol where he would board a ship to Cork or Dublin.

Likewise, Joshua made a final settlement of his mother's estate and then stayed in England for many years. He inherited ample estates from his mother, his father, and possibly his brother.[28] One wonder's how much Joshua may have yearned for more years with his brother. They were separated early in life when William went to Rhode Island and then again when William went to England and disappeared some years later.

William perpetuates the Edwards mystique. So little is known about him-he seems to have disappeared without a trace. Born and reared in America he shared his father's loyalty to the Crown and left the land of his birth never to return. He was a lad of great promise who inherited his father's classical mind and brilliant intellect. Bereft of his mother at age seven and separated from his father and brother at age eight, he crossed the Atlantic as a young man to serve the mother country.

On the day he waved goodbye to his father and brother at the docks in Philadelphia, he created a permanent physical separation from them. In the British Isles, he established relations with his paternal and maternal grandparents. It is known that he served in the British army, but there is no evidence to indicate he returned to fight on the side of the British in the American Revolution. William Keen's sad description of William was appropriate when he wrote, "Poor Billy Edwards."[29]

Fine-Looking Joshua Edwards

There is some controversy about the year of Joshua's birth. Joshua's son Morgan, Mr. E. R. Siewers (great grandson of Morgan Edwards), and Joshua's friend Richard Webster all provide different dates. In his history of Brown University, Reuben A. Guild writes of correspondence he had with Rev. Morgan Edwards, a son of Joshua and a grandson of Morgan Edwards.

In the mid-nineteenth century Joshua's son was living in Burlington, Iowa. Guild received from him a generous amount of biographical material, which was lifted from the sermon preached at Joshua's funeral in 1854. Relying on this material, Guild gives Joshua's birthdate as December 29, 1769.[30] Since Joshua's mother died on August 13, 1769 this would be impossible.[31] Joshua was reported to be aged five years and nine months on August 7, 1775 when his father recanted his Toryism.[32] If correct, Joshua would have been born in November 1769. Again, this date is ruled out by the date of his mother's death.

Mr. E. R. Siewers, Joshua's grandson, reports that his grandfather was sixty-eight-years old when he began to receive a pension from the U.S. Navy in 1832. He also declared that Joshua died on February 9, 1854, at ninety years of age.[33] Both of these dates put Joshua's year of birth in 1764. In addition, on November 9, 1764, Edwards wrote to Gardner Thurston, his friend and fellow Baptist pastor in Newport, Rhode Island, "I soon expect an increase in my private family."[34]

Richard Webster, Joshua's Presbyterian minister friend, states that Joshua was eighty-eight years old on July 20, 1853. Thus, Joshua would have been born in 1765 and died at the age of eighty-nine.[35]

Obviously, the birth year given by Guild is not accurate and the dates offered by Siewers and Webster are but a year apart. The best evidence favors 1764 as the year of Joshua's birth; thus, he would have been two years younger than Billy.

At six years old Joshua was enrolled in Rev. Kinnersley's academy where he began receiving the same classical education under the same rigid discipline as Billy. School continued through the summer months, when two additional morning hours were added.[36]

Joshua was eleven years old in 1775 working in an apothecary store in Philadelphia when officers of the Committee of Safety entered, demanding to know where his father was hiding. Edwards was being sought for arrest because of his Tory views. At the time Joshua was unaware that one of Philadelphia's most prominent patriots, Colonel Samuel Miles, had hidden his father in his home until he could have an open hearing before a Committee of Safety. Miles may also have wanted time to persuade Edwards to renounce his loyalty to the Crown. The officers questioned Joshua thoroughly, and failing to obtain the desired information, confined him to the city until he revealed his father's whereabouts.[37]

Morgan Edwards renounced his loyalty to the Crown on August 7, 1775. Seven years later, in 1782, Joshua enlisted in the American navy as a surgeon's mate. His work in the apothecary shop no doubt qualified him for this assignment, but what an ironic twist of fortunes: William serving in the British army, Joshua serving in the American navy, and Morgan in limbo as a come-lately patriot.

Joshua served first on the sixteen gun "Hyder Ally" and then on the twenty-gun "Duc de Lauzon." While we do not know how long he was in the navy, it was long enough to earn a pension which he began receiving in 1832 at age sixty-eight.[38]

After Joshua returned from England, he married and went into business in Philadelphia, probably as an apothecary. He fathered five daughters and one son, whom he named after his father.[39] Like grandfather, like grandson, according to Reuben A. Guild, who says of Joshua's son, "A son of his, Rev. Morgan Edwards, an eccentric Baptist preacher and evangelist, was living some years ago in Burlington, Iowa."[40] He has also been described as a "desolute [sic] youth and has not seen his father in 21 years."[41] If so, then he must have run away to sea at age fourteen. There was, however, another view of Joshua's son.

Grandson Morgan Edwards died on August 29, 1893, at the age of eighty-five. He was known as the "sailor preacher" probably because he too served in the American navy. He was ordained in Illinois in 1843, at the age of thirty-five and was an evangelist all through his ministry from the Atlantic Coast to the Missouri River. As many as ten thousand conversions are attributed to him. He has been described as "a man of strong faith, an earnest worker and a preacher of rare gifts." The younger Morgan Edwards used a number of his grandfather's sermons, and he preached his last sermon at the age of seventy-nine. He was confined to his home in ill-health for the last six years of his life.[42]

His father Joshua, on the other hand, was in a good state of health physically and mentally until his death. He retained all his faculties, was remarkably strong, and presented a fine looking, gentlemanly appearance. At some point in his life he professed faith in Christ and was baptized by Rev. J. P. Wilcox of Philadelphia. In his last years he lived alone on his pension in a boardinghouse. He retained to his last days his beautiful script and his resolute Welsh character.[43]

After the death of his first wife, Morgan Edwards waited twenty-one months before he remarried on May 3, 1771. He was only six days short of his fiftieth birthday. His bride was Elizabeth Singleton, widow of John Singleton, Newark, Delaware, landholder. Eventually they moved to Delaware, but more will be said later about his life in Delaware. Elizabeth died in 1772 and he married the widow of Washington Nathaniel Evans of the Welsh Tract in Delaware in 1774.[43] There is no record of her first name.

It is curious that all three of Morgan Edwards' marriages were to women of some wealth. Mary was wealthy enough in her own right to bequeath fifty pounds to the Philadelphia Baptist Church.[44] While all his marriages appear to have been successful, there is a haze over his role as a father.

The paucity of information about Morgan Edwards as a father leaves one the option of seeing him through a mist. William Rogers' assessment of him as "a fond and pious parent" does imply certain positive qualities. If a fond parent, then a loving and lovable parent. There is every reason to believe that Edwards was loving and concerned for the eight children his wife conceived. He surely experienced emotional pain when she suffered either miscarriages or the loss of full-term children.

Though Edwards placed Billy in Manning's Latin School only days after Mary's death, he must have thought it best for the lad. He seems also to have helped Billy through his time of misbehavior, even though he may have seen him only on vacations or on the occasions of the annual meetings of the Corporation in September. His firm convictions about the importance of education motivated Edwards to begin the boys' schooling early in life. Edwards gave Billy freedom to pursue his own convictions when it came to independence for the American colonies.

Joshua seems to have been more like his father than was Billy. In 1849 Horatio Gates asked Richard Webster to obtain one of Edwards' sermon manuscripts from Joshua. Webster's letter brought a negative response.[45]

> I handed your request to Mr. Edwards [Joshua] & on receiving it he took the matter into consideration & gave me his answer yesterday. "I have decided to give them nothing." This is irrevocable-I pleaded for a single sermon for you-He returned the same answer.

For historical purposes, Gates wanted the extant volumes of Morgan Edwards's sermons but Joshua refused to release them. Like his father, he was thoughtful and could be adamant. Like his father, also, he realized the extreme historical value of these manuscripts.

Furthermore Morgan must have allowed Joshua some latitude in his activities, as he was working in an apothecary shop at eleven years of age. It does not suggest, however, loose parental oversight. There is no evidence that either son led other than a morally upright life in spite of serving many years in the military.

Rogers also described Morgan as a pious parent, which seems to say he did not neglect to teach his sons the truths of the faith, by precept and example. Though we have only a record of Joshua's confession of faith in Christ through his baptism, we can safely assume Billy also took that step. There are instances in Edwards' sermons where he stressed the importance of Christian teaching and Christian living in the home. He surely practiced what he preached, as both Billy and Joshua seem to have grown to be good Christian men.

If Edwards failed in any area as a father, it may have been in his long absences from home. His almost two-year absence on a fund-raising tour in the British Isles for the College must have left a gap in the Edwards' family life. Then, too, Edwards wanted to be an itinerant evangelist following his resignation from the pastorate of the Baptist church in Philadelphia in 1771. He was appointed as a traveling evangelist for the Philadelphia Baptist Association, and began a three-thousand-mile evangelistic tour which lasted many months. Again, Joshua at age seven, was left at home, only now with neither father nor mother. Edwards left Joshua in the care of Samuel Jones, but the lad surely felt the need for his father.

Perhaps the clearest indicators of the esteem and love Billy and Joshua held for their father may be seen in single acts each took in his own life. Billy adopted his father's loyalty to the crown at great cost to himself, for it separated him from his family and home for the rest of his life. Joshua named his only son after his father and so imbued him with his father's greatness as a minister of the Gospel that the younger Morgan followed in his grandfather's footsteps.

Though the picture we have of Morgan Edwards as a father is far from complete, the one we have of him as a pastor is fleshed-out in many details.

ENDNOTES
1. John Rippon, ed. *Baptist Annual Register*, London: 1796, 310. Memorial Sermon, William Rogers, February 22, 1795.
2. Ibid., 310-311.
3. Morgan Edwards. *A New Year's Gift*. (Newport: Solomon Southwick, 1770), 6.
4. Philadelphia Baptist Churchbook, Entry August 4, 1764, 55.
5. Rippon, 310.
6. William W. Keen. *The Bi-Centennial Celebration of the Founding of the First Baptist Church of Philadelphia, 1898*. (Philadelphia: American Baptist Publication Society, 1899), 171
7. Reuben A. Build, *Early History of Brown University Including the Life, Times and Correspondence of President Manning, 1764-1791*. (Providence: Snow and Farnham, 1897), 165.
8. Barnas Sears, *Celebration of the One Hundredth Anniversary of The Founding of Brown University, September 6, 1864*, (Providence: Sidney Rider & Co., 1865), 22.
9. Guild, 51,52.
10. Keen, 48.
11. Ibid.
12. Guild, 81-85.
13. Ibid., 291.
14. Ibid., 14.
15. Ibid., 51.
16. Ibid., 288.
17. MS. Manning Papers, (John Hay Library, Brown University, Providence, R.I.) Vol. 1, No. 191.
18. Walter C. Bronson. *The History of Brown University, 1764-1914*, (Providence: Brown University, 1914), 112.
19. MS. Letter of Nicholas Brown to Morgan Edwards, August 19, 1775, Manning Papers, (John Hay Library, Brown University, Provi-

dence, R.I.), OL 74-77 M.
20. MS. Letter from James Manning to Samuel Jones, May 31, 1773, Manning Papers, (John Hay Library, Brown University, Providence).
21. MS. Letter from James Manning to Samuel Jones, March 7, 1774, Manning Papers.
22. MS. Letters from James Manning to Samuel Jones, May 17, 1774; Manning Papers; and from John Gano to James Manning, September 14, 1775, (John Carter Brown Library, Brown University, Providence) L74 76M.
23. Guild, 288.
24. Ibid., 291.
25. Rippon, 310.
26. MS. Letter of Richard Webster to Horatio Gates Jones, July 20, 1853. Horatio Gates Jones, Jr. Collection, (American Baptist Historical Society, Rochester, N.Y.), File 1.
27. Newcastle County Deeds, V. 2, 180-183, Delaware State Archives, Dover, Delaware.
28. Guild, 14.
29. Keen, 48.
30. Guild, 14.
31. Edwards, 6.
32. Guild, 15,16.
33. Keen, 51.
34. MS. Letter of Morgan Edwards to Gardner Thurston, November 9, 1764, Manning Papers, (John Hay Library, Brown University, Providence, R.I.), 2.
35. Webster, 3.
36. Keen, 48,
37. Webster, 2.
38. Keen, 51.
39. Webster, 3.
40. Guild, 14.
41. Webster, 3.
42. Annual report, Iowa Baptist State Convention, 1893. 48.
43. Webster, 3, 1.
44. Guild, 16.
45. Philadelphia Baptist Churchbook, 1769-1775, Entry, October 1, 1771.
46. Webster, 1.

CHAPTER SEVEN

PRIME TIME IN PHILADELPHIA

> "His is one of the most illustrious
> names in the line of distinguished
> men who have served this church."
> William W. Keen, 1899

A New Era of Action

Morgan Edwards's ten-year pastorate of the Philadelphia Baptist church has been aptly described by Baptist historian David Spencer.[1]

> This decade ushered in a marked advance in all that pertains to real progress. It is crowded with incidents all indicative of this fact. New men appeared on the scene and new measures were inaugurated. It was not merely a decade of hope and expectation but one of real action. And the one man, of all others, who really planned the work, then worked the plans was Rev. Morgan Edwards.

A more laudatory view of Edwards can be found in a carefully researched bicentennial history of the First Baptist Church in Philadelphia written by William Keen in 1898.[2]

In 1761, in response to their letter, from Great Britain came Morgan Edwards, a man who was to fill a large place in the history, not only of this church, but of the entire Baptist Church in America, leaving a mark both in letters, education, executive ability, and personal influence such as few have ever made. His is one of the most illustrious names in the line of distinguished men who have ministered to this church.

Morgan Edwards's ten-year pastorate of was indeed an era of action, but not all of it positive. True, Edwards was one of the most distinguished ministers to serve that historic and important church, but it is also true that he was very difficult to understand at times. Renowned Baptist historian Henry C. Vedder has attempted a more balanced view of the man.[3]

There was, however, one noted exception: Scholarly, laborious, warm-hearted, eccentric, choleric Morgan Edwards, one of the most interesting of the early Baptist ministers of our country and one of the most deserving of honor. His very faults had a leaning toward virtue's side, and in good works he was exceeded by none in his day, if indeed by any of any day.

Life in the Philadelphia Baptist Church took a one-hundred-eighty degree turn in 1761 with the arrival of Morgan Edwards as pastor. Excitement began to build even before he and his wife Mary arrived on May 23. In April and May, Samuel Burkloe was authorized to install a new roof on the parsonage kitchen and to paint and reapir the house.[4]

Eight days after his arrival Morgan was received as a member and the pastor of the church. He was elected moderator on June 1, 1761.[5] The following week he was reimbursed for his travel expenses, his salary was increased from 100 pounds to 160 pounds to reflect the higher cost of living in America, and he was allowed to live in the parsonage rent free.[6] In short order, under his leadership changes would occur in the worship services, church discipline, recruiting of new ministers, administration, community involvement, and the preaching.

The Worship Services
When Morgan Edwards came to America, he brought his Welsh love of singing with him. The singing of psalms, hymns, and spiritual songs was a part of the heritage of the Philadelphia church and was affirmed in the Philadelphia Baptist Confession of 1742.[7] Singing in many Baptist churches consisted of a cantor reciting Psalms, line-by-line, followed by the congregation.

The Quaker emphasis on education had created a more literate climate in Philadelphia, so Edwards requested that the practice of a cantor reciting the lines be discontinued and that all members purchase their own Psalters. His sermons averaged forty minutes; and if reciting were discontinued there would be more time for the sermon.[8] Over a period of, time the change was fully implemented.[9]

Meanwhile a chorister named Benjamin Hellings would lead the congregation in hymn singing. At first he heard the usual complaints about unfamiliar hymns, but the problem was solved when Edwards and others assisted Hellings with the hymn selections.[10] Edwards expanded the music ministry by obtaining approval for "hymn-sings." Hellings was paid seven pounds to serve as chorister for the events.[11] To further support the music ministry, Edwards encouraged the members to purchase hymnbooks.[12] His love of singing, however, was not the only facet of worship Edwards brought to America.

Edwards held a high view of baptism and the Lord's Supper. In his *Customs of the Primitive Churches*, he de-

156 A Dazzling Enigma

Baptisterion on the Schuykill River

A Dazzling Enigma

voted several pages to the meaning and administration of believer baptism.[13] He took upon himself the task of examining candidates for baptism, raising some eyebrows in the Philadelphia Association.[14] The church, however, voted on candidates for baptism after they had been examined by Edwards.

To personalize and highlight the baptismal experience, Edwards designed a baptism certificate in 1762. It incorporated a statement on the importance of the vows made at baptism, including the surrender of one's life to Christ. Then followed commitments to practice holy living, accept church discipline, keep the faith, faithfully attend worship, and support the ministry of the church. It also included a pledge to live in peace and follow the biblical pattern for effecting reconciliation. After the vows were affirmed in writing, the individual was baptized. Edwards's name was printed at the bottom along with a notation that the baptism took place at a site along the Schuylkill River.[15]

The baptismal site is pictured in an old print in Edwards's *Material Towards a History of the Baptists* which depicts the "Baptisterion" of the Philadelphia Baptists one and one-half miles outside the western limits of the city.[16] The site was surrounded by a stand of large oak trees which the British army cut down during the occupation of the city. Edwards compared the site with the Jordan in its beauty and importance.

The church first used the site in Jenkin Jones's tenure, and it was a popular place picnics and recreation. A structure was erected at the site. It had three permanent walls with one side open facing the river which was curtained off during baptism. Another curtain divided the space for dressing rooms. Nearby a large rock which had been levelled on the top as a small platform for the preacher, pro-

New Baptist Meeting House at Second Street and LaGrange Place

truded from the ground. A baptismal hymn of five stanzas was sung during the service.[17]

Edwards also made changes affecting the monthly communion services. The church printed and distributed twelve "tickets" each year to every member. These tickets were to be placed in 'the offering box on Communion Sundays.[18] Morgan believed communion should be observed every Sunday,[19] but made no issue over the practice of monthly communion. A large two-handled silver communion chalice was purchased and inscribed with Jones's name provided for in the will of Jenkin Jones.[20]

Masses of people came to hear Edwards preach. The congregations were intergenerational and included people from all walks of life. Edwards's sermons were directed to all ages from children to seniors, to sailors and merchants, to rich and poor. Much evidence exists attesting to the dramatic explosion in attendance at the services.

Perhaps the most startling evidence of a newly crowded church was the action taken by the church on August 3, 1761, to raze the old meeting house and construct a new and larger building.[21] One can only imagine the intoxicating feelings of the members as they voted for such a bold move, recalling that their church had been on the verge of extinction only a few months before.

Evidence for packed pews is also found in the action taken to collect past-due pew rentals from members who had allowed their rentals fall into arrears. Now new faces were appearing in these accustomed places so that returning members had no place to sit. In November 1763, the church appointed two deacons to collect past due pew rentals and thus restore some order to the seating chaos.[22]

The statistical report in the associational minutes for 1761 shows the Philadelphia church with 700 "hearers" in addition to the members. Though the church was only the sixth largest in the association at that time, it had the second largest number of auditors.[23]

One external factor contributed to the upsurge in attendance. New people coming to Philadelphia from Europe found themselves in a strange new climate of religious freedom. There was no state church, and they were free to worship where they pleased, or not to worship at all. Many, like Benjamin Franklin, would attend services where they liked the preaching. As one member of Lutheran minister Melchior Muhlenberg's parish said, "I pay [the parson] by the year, but if his preaching does not please my taste, I'll go to another church where I can get it for nothing."[24]

One other problem created by the crowded conditions affected the long-time members who were habitually tardy. In October 1761 the church authorized the deacons to admonish members who persistently arrived late for services.[25] The tardy worshippers were, no doubt, creating disturbances as they slithered into tightly packed pews. With Edwards's arrival, the deacons found themselves with an increasing load of disciplinary cases.

Church Discipline

Morgan Edwards was an advocate of church discipline along biblical guidelines. Three years after his arrival at the church a committee was appointed to review the New Testament and glean every passage related to church discipline.[26] The texts were to be organized under proper headings and submitted to the church for approval. Three years later Edwards published his *The Customs of the Primitive Churches*, and this book, no doubt, included the work of the review committee.

Despite his advocacy of church discipline, Edwards enjoyed a good relationship with his people, and they rewarded him with bonuses on each anniversary of his pastorate.[27] For his part, Edwards practiced courtesy and appreciation toward the members of his flock.[28] As will be seen later, the congregation seemed endowed with an abundance of patience, and under his leadership the discipline was handled with compassion and in an orderly manner.

Typical of the orderliness and compassion with which the church dealt with members facing discipline is the case which arose at the November 3, 1766, church meeting.[29] It concerned two men and two women, about whom gossip was running rampant. Philip Thomas, Benjamin Davis, Martha Mason and Hester Moore were suspended from the church, and the deacons were assigned to look into the matter. The committee reported to the December meeting, and the matter was turned over to the newly elected ruling elders. Before the church could settle the disciplinary business, Morgan would be crossing the Atlantic Ocean on a fund-raising trip to Europe for the Rhode Island College.

On February 2, 1767, the elders reported that Philip Thomas had extorted twelve hundred and twenty pounds from fellow church member, Septimus Levering, for which he was publicly suspended. The matter concerning Benjamin Davis was continued, and Hester Moore had to face several counts of misconduct. She was charged with keeping apprentices in her home at unreasonable hours, receiving stolen property, and theft. She was excommunicated.

Martha Mason had given birth to a child out of wedlock, but the church could not agree on the discipline to be imposed, and the decision was postponed until the next meeting. The vote to continue her suspension was not taken until September; in the meantime, all the members were asked to watch over her and talk with her. Rather than excommunicate her, the church chose to nurture and care for her until it felt it was time to lift the suspension.[30] Discipline problems, however, were not limited to the people in the pews.

New Ministers
Besides Morgan Edwards, four men who were members of the church served in the church's ministry. Two, Ebenezer Kinnersley and Samuel Jones were outstanding individuals; the other two, Dr. George Weed and Stephen Watts, Jr. were themselves the subject of church discipline.

Ebenezer Kinnersley was born in Gloucester, England, and came to America in 1714 and was ordained to the Baptist ministry in 1743. He assisted Jenkin Jones at the Pennepak and Philadelphia churches and gained some unfortunate notoriety for opposing the preaching style of George Whitefield when he came to Philadelphia. Because of the negative the reaction to an anti-Whitfield sermon he preached on July 6, 1740, he was forbidden to take communion at the Baptist church. For a short time, he attended the Episcopal church next door but a reconciliation was soon effected. He later played a leading role in the 1746 formal organization of the Baptist church in Philadelphia.[31]

Kinnersley began experiments in electricity in 1746, which put him in touch with Benjamin Franklin. They began working together, with Kinnersley gaining fame in his own right as an outstanding scientist and lecturer. He discovered that electricity emitted heat[32] and was a member of the American Philosophical Society and professor of "English Tongue and Oratory" at the College of Philadelphia.[33] Both William and Joshua Edwards attended his academy.

The second person involved in the ministry was Samuel Jones. He was a member of the church and had set his sights on the ministry before enrolling at the College of Philadelphia, from which he graduated.[34] He was called to exercise his gifts on June 12, 1762, and licensed on August 31. The license certified him as regularly called by the church to preach.[35]

Jones was ordained on Sunday, January 2, 1763, at the College of Philadelphia where the church gathered during construction. Morgan Edwards preached the sermon and directed the service, assisted by Isaac Eaton and Samuel Stillman. The sermon and service were both put into print and provide an excellent insight into the Baptist understanding of the ministry at the time.[36] Jones then became pastor of the Pennepak Baptist Church, developed into a prominent Baptist leader, and remained a lifelong friend of Morgan Edwards.

Dr. George Weed, a member of the church, was a medical doctor on the staff of the Pennsylvania Hospital. He had been the church clerk prior to Edwards's pastorate. Weed conducted small group meetings at the hospital which included prayer, Scripture readings, and some teaching by him. In September 1762 he offered to preach occasionally at the church and his offer was duly considered and graciously declined.[37] Weed did not, however, accept the rejection with much grace.

A few months later, in 1763, news traveled back to the church that Weed was inviting people to attend his meetings at the hospital. In the eyes of the church, Weed was passing himself off as a minister of the Baptist church. They reaffirmed and encouraged his meetings with the hospital staff and patients, but inviting outsiders to attend, especially Baptist church members, was forbidden. In addition, they believed he was compromising his own witness and that of the church by enlarging the scope of his meetings. In fact, the church feared censure by the hospital trustees. These sentiments were expressed in a letter to Dr. Weed.[38]

The Weed affair continued until the spring of 1765, when Morgan Edwards and Samuel Davis called on him to request his presence at the next congregational meeting or to submit a written explanation of his actions. He sent a note in which he stated he saw no point in attending the meeting. Inexplicibly the issue was dropped after the church made two monetary gifts to Weed to enable him to pursue his theological studies.[39]

The case of Stephen Watts was to prove more difficult than that of George Weed. Stephen Watts, Jr., was called by the church to preach in 1762, following Samuel Jones. The call was issued on October 2, and Watts promised to respond at the November church meeting.[40] He consented to preach a trial sermon, but declined to be licensed because of his youth, his need for more theological training, and his "present manner of living."[41] Watts was a gifted person, but as time unfolded he was viewed as a very troubled young man.

The church licensed Watts on March 5, 1763, and notified other churches of his availability. At the June church meeting, they voted him a bonus of fifteen pounds and called him to be Edwards's assistant. The vote was not unanimous.

By July the church received a curious letter of acceptance from Watts. He limited the call as assistant to one year (not unusual at the time) and stated he would drop his studies at the College of Philadelphia. The letter, as was all of his correspondence, was verbose and flowery, defensive and apologetic.

At the same meeting sexton John Biddle accused Watts of being unsound in doctrine. He was joined by John Perkins, the graveyard caretaker, who charged that Watts was not fit to preach and it would be better to burn his one hundred pound salary. Both men were suspended from membership.

The church voted to have Edwards and Watts share the pulpit equally (Morgan had requested help) and share equal pew space for their families. Stephen Watts must have been impressive in the pulpit, as many churches invited him to preach after he was licensed. These opportunities interferred with his assisting Edwards, who still complained two months later about the burden of preparing three fresh discourses every week.[42]

In the meantime the committee appointed to negotiate salary with Watts was unable to do so and resigned in August. John Biddle attended the October meeting and requested his membership be restored, after asking Watts and the church to forgive him. This was done.

Perkins appeared at the November meeting and retracted his statement about burning the money, but stood by his statement that Watts was not fit to preach. He maintained that Watts broke his covenant with the church by his frequent absences. Watts also wanted to renegotiate his salary, which was only one-half of what Edwards was receiving. Perkins's membership was not restored, because his assertion was unproven, but it soon would be.

The Watts affair reappeared in March 1764. Three deacons, who had been asked to call on him, reported on their visit.[43] Watts said he had stopped preaching (apparently without notice) because he presumed the church was not satisfied with his preaching, and that the church might be adversely affected if he continued. The congregation viewed his absence as a violation of his covenant with them. One is forced to conclude that the lowly sexton and the humble gravedigger had uncovered a flaw behind Watts's flowery oratory which the more sophisticated members did not detect.

The church's problems with Watts continued for several years, with the church demonstrating an amazing amount of patience with a young man whom it thought might be salvaged for the Lord. In August 1768 he was finally suspended from membership, and in September excommunicated.[44] The Philadelphia Baptists took seriously the keeping of a commitment. While they were quick to suspend, they were less speedy to excommunicate and ever ready to forgive and restore upon valid evidence of change.

The compassion of the congregation extended beyond matters of discipline. Beginning in April 1767 there was a decided upswing in the number of requests to aid people in need. These requests included cloth for clothing, wood for heat and cooking, and money. The church always responded without reluctance.

Administrative Improvements

William Keen's appraisal of Morgan Edwards's "executive ability" points to a phase of his ministry which is generally overlooked. However, long before coming to Philadelphia he had thought through the organizational life of a church. This he related in a 1765 letter to Gardner Thurston, in Newport, Rhode Island.[45]

> If you remember, I mentioned to you that I had many years ago, formed offices for my own direction in performing the several branches of a ministers work....

A Dazzling Enigma 167

Upon his arrival at the church in May, 1761, Edwards began doing everything "decently and in order," by organizing the church's chaotic records, and keeping them in order. In the new churchbook, which he kept with his own precise hand, he wrote, "But no regular accounts, could be found of their proceedings [the church's] till the year 1760. What fragments fell into my hands, related to the proceedings of those 14 years [1746-1760] begin this book."[46] To keep the church records and papers organized, he had the church construct pigeon-holes for the filing of papers and records.[47]

In addition to bringing order to the church records, Edwards introduced the Marriage Book, used to this day by the First Baptist Church of Philadelphia. The first marriage recorded in the book is of Thomas James and Thamar Edwards on June 25, 1761, only one month after Edwards's arrival. One-hundred-fifty-eight marriages are recorded in the book.

His most challenging administrative problem was not record keeping. Edwards's most sensitive administrative problem during his first three years was the right of women to vote at church meetings. By 1762 the names of those attending church meetings appeared in the minutes, but they were only men's names. Women were denied the vote, and did not attend church meetings. This had not always been the case.

In 1761, just before the death of Edwards's predecessor, Jenkin Jones, the church lacked regular pastoral leadership. At a church meeting presided over by Deacon Davis, the men took away the women's right to vote.[48] Davis simply asked the men who were present to elect three deacons, ignoring the women who were present. Before then, women had voted for many years.

Most of the congregation were Welsh and in Wales at

the time Baptist churches convened the "Cwrdd Brodyr" or "Brothers' Meeting," which excluded the sisters. Some Welsh churches continue the practice.[49] After Edwards's arrival the women informed him of the ill-treatment they received. He was unaware that women once had voting rights and promised to do all he could to put things right. Uncharacteristically, Edwards did not act on this issue, and in 1764 the problem resurfaced.

At the March 3, 1764, church meeting, Deacon Davis raised the issue again, claiming he did so on behalf of "some of the sisters." Following the debate, the men voted to postpone the question until the next meeting.[50] Before the next meeting convened, a group of men prepared a statement addressing women's rights and passed it unanimously. Davis was deputized to inform the women of its contents.

In essence, the statement denied any desire by the men to rob women of rights granted in scripture. They acknowledged that women previously had the vote but inferred this was contrary to I Timothy 2 and I Corinthians 14. The men agreed that when women attended the meetings their views would be heard, and "when anything is to be transacted which touches the interest of their souls" they would be invited to attend.

After Deacon Davis informed the women of the statement, they held their own meeting on May 4, one day before the next church meeting. The women composed a letter over the signature of Johannah Anthony, in which they women disavowed any desire to disobey the scriptures by teaching or usurping authority. They saw no biblical warrant to prohibit them from voting, and indeed, they contended that the men's statement did not clarify whether or not women could vote.

The sisters believed they were unjustly criticized for

waiting two and one-half years to raise the issue. They had been waiting for Morgan Edwards to get settled. One woman did speak with Deacon Davis, and he raised the matter at the March meeting. Following the reading of the women's letter at the May church meeting, it was voted twelve to four in favor to allow the women to vote.[51] Beginning with the August meeting women's names were included in the minutes.

One has to read between the lines to see what occurred. Before Edwards became pastor, a few men used some of Paul's writings to establish a no-vote-for-women policy. This may have been common practice in Welsh Baptist churches and church meetings. Although the women spoke to Edwards about it, he did not act on it for two years. He may have been too busy, or it may have slipped his mind. Perhaps he hoped the matter would simply just go away.

Finally, one woman spoke to Deacon Davis since he led the action against them in 1761. Edwards must have redeemed his pledge to help the women recover their right to vote; if he had opposed, it would not have been restored. He had no qualms about women serving in church offices as elders and deacons because he did not question the practice in the Baptist church at Haw River, North Carolina, when he wrote about that church.[52]

In addition, Edwards believed that women could serve as female elders in ministry to women, but could not teach or preach among men without being veiled. He also held the view that deaconesses were equal to deacons, but served in different areas of need.[53]

Morgan Edwards triggered action in a number of other administrative areas as well. In October 1761, he upgraded the organizational structure of the church by the election of six new deacons. The congregation decided also to change the church meeting time from Sunday to the Saturday before the first Sunday of the month.[54]

Edwards provided leadership to the financial life of the church as well when two deacons were assigned to collect overdue rents on pews and the houses owned by the church. The church also called to a meeting all of its creditors and debtors to square accounts.[55] This occurred in November 1761. By the December meeting the deacons reported almost seventy pounds were collected in back rentals. The offerings for the month had brought in over sixty pounds.[56]

The houses on Third Street were deeded to the church years before and the rents provided part of Edwards's salary. They were managed by trustees elected by the church. By November 1763, however, there was only one trustee. Since deacons were elected to life terms, Edwards suggested they serve as trustees for the properties. Since he was authorized to do so he had the necessary papers drawn up for the transfer of funds.[57] In the meantime in 1763 he led the church to another organizational change.

On July 2, 1763, he had the church create a "Committee of Seven" for the church year 1763-1764.[58] The purpose of this committee is not known, but the persons appointed were church leaders, suggesting it was to be a "pastoral relations committee" or "cabinet."

The committee members were probably the church leaders Edwards referred to in his resignation letter in July 1771.[59] One committee member was Samuel Miles, who years later would help Edwards escape the clutches of a mob of overzealous patriots. He eventually became a major military leader in Philadelphia during the Revolution, and later was elected mayor of the city. By 1763 he had risen to a leadership position in the Baptist church.[60]

A Dazzling Enigma 171

By 1766 the church was facing financial problems. The churchbook hints at an economic recession caused by the political upheaval with England. Many members were unable to pay their pew rentals.[61] As will be seen, this situation continued to Edwards's resignation in 1771.

In 1766 the church elected three ruling elders, an action not widely practiced among Baptists.[62] The Broadmead Church in Bristol, England, had successfully used ruling elders, and Edwards may have been influenced by that church from his days at the Bristol Academy. Perhaps more influential was the practice of the Welsh Baptists that included in the ministry the Pastor, Teaching Elders, *Ruling Elders* [italics mine], Deacons, Widows, and Ordinary Prophets.[63] In any case, it did not work well in Philadelphia, and apart from handling some discipline matters, they are rarely reported in the minutes.

Edwards encountered another administrative problem that seemed to take forever to solve. In mid-February 1767 Edwards left for Europe to raise funds for the newly-established Rhode Island College, and he did not return until December 1768. One month before he left, the church approved a new privy for the parsonage. The plans were to be readied and presented at the February church meeting before Edwards left.

Approval was granted and two men authorized to oversee the work. For some unrecorded reason, final action was postponed until the April meeting, and again to May. It was postponed again and again, and the privy was not completed until March of 1768.[64] One wonders how serious the problem was, and how Mary Edwards and the boys coped if the outhouse was unusable.

The church faced problems in the construction of the new meeting house as well. During the demolition of the old meeting house and the erection of the new, beginning in 1762, the church moved its services to the College of Philadelphia.

The college building was located at Fourth Street south of Arch Street, less than three blocks from the Baptist meeting house site at Second and LaGrange. The building was originally erected for George Whitefield and was known as Whitefield's church. An Academy and Charitable School was launched in the city in 1749 and used the building. A year later it was used as a Latin School; in 1755 it was chartered as "The College, Academy and Charitable School of Philadelphia," and in 1779, the University of Pennsylvania.

The change in meeting place did not hinder the church's growth as the membership increased from eighty-two to one-hundred-sixteen, with seventeen new members added through baptism.[65] During construction, boundary disputes developed with Dr. John Redman, who owned property on the north line, and with Mr. Benjamin Davis, who had property on the south line. In each case Morgan Edwards headed a team, which successfully negotiated amicable settlements.[66]

A second problem occurred when the contractors stopped construction while waiting for roofing lumber to arrive at the site. The membership discussed the delay at a church meeting and decided work could proceed in other phases. They authorized the church clerk to write to the contractors requesting them to proceed with the fabricating of the windows and the construction of the gallery. If additional workmen were needed, the contractor was authorized to hire them.[67]

Community Involvement

As he had in Rye, Sussex, so in Philadelphia--Morgan Edwards became well known to the leaders of the community. He knew Benjamin Franklin well enough to ask for and receive a donation while on his fund-raising tour in the British Isles. Edwards's relations with important people will unfold in detail later, but his contact with Franklin was probably because of his relationship with Ebenezer Kinnersley.

Kinnersley influenced the decision of the faculty of the College of Philadelphia to recommend Edwards for an honorary Master of Arts degree on May 11, 1762, less than one year after his arrival from England. Edwards also made a friend of Francis Alison, minister of the First Presbyterian Church, a professor at the college and one who had high regard for Edwards.[68] Five other persons were named with Edwards to receive honorary degrees, but the list created a problem with the trustees.

The faculty list included three ministers, a former student who was now a successful Boston merchant, and two current students. When the ten trustees saw the names of the students, they were very unhappy. They were "unanimously of opinion [sic] they ought not be conferred but upon people of great learning & merit."[69]

The board inquired of Alison, the faculty representative, as to the merit of each candidate. Then they, "with utmost Regret agree [sic] to the whole list."[70] The trustees, nonetheless, made it clear to Alison that the college might be compromising its reputation by conferring too many honorary degrees. Hereafter, no person would be approved whose name had not been submitted first to the trustees. Alison was a highly respected person, and his contacts with Edwards would continue for some years.

Francis Alison had been minister of a Presbyterian church near New London, Pennsylvania where he began an academy in 1743, and was known throughout the colonies as a classical scholar. In fact Ezra Stiles described

Alison as "the greatest classical scholar" in America, especially in Greek.[71] Stiles later became president of Yale, and we shall meet him again in chapters nine and ten.

In 1752 Benjamin Franklin invited Alison to Philadelphia to head the Latin department at the College of Philadelphia. He accepted and later occupied the Chair of Philosophy.[72] Alison's New London academy moved to Newark, Delaware, in 1765, and became the forerunner of the University of Delaware. In 1774, Edwards sold a tract of land to the Newark Academy for the sum of one hundred fifty pounds.[73]

Alison's importance in the story is in the awarding of Edwards's honorary degree and later in inviting him to lecture at the college. Edwards did not overlook the kindness of the college in allowing the church to use its building during construction of the new meeting house.

A sermon manuscript dated July 17, 1763, and entitled "Through the Tender Mercies of Our Lord,"[74] has a note on page seventeen overwritten by the sermon. It is an incomplete statement in Morgan Edwards's beautiful script. It says, "To the Trustees of the College of Philadelphia. Gentlemen, We the ministers of the Baptist character in this city on our own behalf and on behalf of said church..."

Edwards had begun a note of appreciation to the college for the use of the building and then decided to reword it. He set aside that piece of paper and used it later for a sermon. With the note on that particular sermon we may infer the church moved into its new meeting house in July 1763.

Under Edwards the church not only practiced such courtesies with the college but with important political figures as well. On November 6, 1763, he and Ebenezer

Kinnersley were asked to draw up an address to John Penn, the new colonial governor of Pennsylvania, on behalf of the church. Attorney Isaac Jones was to accompany them when the address was presented.[75] Though Edwards had many contacts with leading citizens, it was his sermons and preaching which drew the crowds to the church.

Outstanding Sermons

Morgan Edwards was a perfectionist when it came to sermons. When William Rogers preached the sermon for Edwards's memorial service February 22, 1795, he revealed some of Morgan's views on preaching. Morgan believed he should master his subject completely, write the sermon in full, but not read it in the pulpit. He was adamant about what he called "barbarisms" in the pulpit, and he saw no excuse for anyone to use poor English. He said, "for an American with an English grammar in his hand, a learned friend at his elbow, and a close application for six months, might make himself master of the mother tongue."[76]

In the pulpit, Morgan Edwards was very deliberate, if we are to judge by his friend Oliver Hart of Charleston, South Carolina. In a letter to Hezekiah Smith of Haverhill, Massachusetts, he said of Edwards, "some say he preaches too slow."[77] If he was slow and deliberate, he was also more formal than most of his contemporaries, for he wore the gown of his honorary degree in the pulpit.[78] The fact is Edwards worked hard in preparing his sermons and he held the attention of his hearers by what he said and the way he said it.

In his Philadelphia sermons, Edwards did not cling to pet themes. There was an evangelistic note sounded in almost every sermon, and he covered such subjects as worship, Christian living, eternal security, adversity, regeneration, forgiveness, love, and the Lord's Supper. While his sermons were laden with doctrine and excellent biblical interpretation, Edwards often brought a measure of human warmth and vulnerability to his preaching.

His sermon of August 1, 1762, affords us a rare glimpse of how he experienced his relationship with God.[79]

> . I have such a knowledge of God, of his Christ, and of his Spirit as I never had before: I am acquainted with him in such manner as I never was till now. Such a knowledge as makes me adore him, [sic] and love him: and makes me sorry that I have ever offended; and as makes me resolve never to displease him again: such a knowledge as raises in me unusual, but strong desires to be better acquainted with him; and I seek it by all means: and blessed be God I have it.

Edwards demonstrated an insightful awareness of human nature as in his sermon on July 17, 1763.[80]

> Appetites, lusts, habits and propensities...Some of these are natural: some are acquired ___ the natural are to be mortified no further that they grow exhorbitant ___ for instance ___ the drunkard must not cease to drink at all ___ nor the glutton to forebear eating ___ nor the whoremonger subdue that which is honourable in all ___ These and other natural appetites are worthy the divine hand which formed them ___ but the excess of all the natural impulses must die ___ so we pare these guards on the ends of our fingers, and this covering of the head when they grow luxuriant and troublesome.

Edwards' concern for his congregation is demonstrated in the sermon quoted in the preceding paragraph.

> And I hope God that, he means this day to inform us of its [the sermon text] utility. ___ This is what I look for pray for ___ and

labour for ___ And I hope you are working together with me herein; for what ever design you have in coming here on the Lord's day; I know that your profit, dearly beloved, is the constant companion of my coming to meet you here.

He also made it a practice to affirm his people in his sermons as on New Year's Day, January 1, 1764.[81]

> It rejoices my heart to think that so many were persuaded to this [i.e. practicing what he called positive holiness] last year. O let this [year] be as that, and much more abundant! Why should we be content with the outer court worship; when we may be planted in the inner court.

While he may have been pedantic and deliberate, Edwards's Welsh love of the dramatic also came out in a sermon on Revelation 3:17.[82]

> I come now to the cause of this tremendous deception viz. Ignorance ___ he knoweth not that he is wretched, miserable, poor, and blind and naked ___.
> And consummate ignorance this must be ___ What? be wretched and not know it? Be Miserable and not know it?" Be poor and not know it? Be blind and not know it? Be naked and not know it? Well; I never knew such a thing beside this! Never heard of such another instance of folly except in Morefields in London where all the mad people of the land are lodged. What a pass hath the Devil brought man to? How fearfully hath he practised upon him to hide man from himself? And to blow in his ear what he pleases?

The most dramatic sermon he delivered occurred in Philadelphia, on Sunday, October 31, 1763. In the middle of a sermon on repentance, the building began to shake as Philadelphia experienced an earthquake. The following Sunday, November 6, 1763, Edwards commended the congregation for showing "more presence of mind than the other congregations" during the quake.[83]

> You remember the subject I was upon at the time ___ It was repentance ___ And truly the earthquake of God came very opportunely to show you the necessity of it ___ the rumbling of the earth was an angry voice, that muttered out Repent ye ___ The tottering of this temple [the new meetinghouse] taught us repentance; for had the shock been greater we must all have been crushed to death with these walls; and the ponderous roof; without having time to say the Lord have mercy on us! ___ And had there been an impenitent sinner here he would have sunk to hell that moment.

Morgan Edwards is viewed by some as an austere, brilliant, doctrinaire preacher, but there is ample evidence in his extant sermon manuscripts that he was also vulnerable and self-disclosing. Few preachers in his day were as open about themselves as he was in a 1764 sermon.[84]

> My conduct from my youth up to the time of my conversion had been base and shameful. The thoughts of it make me drop the head and the eyes together. O that what I did had not been done! ___ that I had not been till I had been good! ___ I possess the sins of my youth ___ I cannot forget them.
> But they are not the chief cause of my dejection___I have at times vowed to God that I would sin no more ___ and that I would be no more a son of disobedience. Accordingly I went thru that rite which exhibts death and burial to sin; and a resurrection to newness of life ___ Thus I was born of water and entered into the kingdom of God, the church and thought all things were become new ___ and all old things over, dead, and buried. But alas! I have disobeyed God since that time ___ and have since that time committed sin: ___ I renewed my vows relative to sin and holiness ___ and again and again failed ___ And now the same vows to God are upon me ___ and I fear it will be the same in time to come. I am afraid of myself ___ I am afraid of the world ___ I am afraid of the devil ___ When I sin I am afraid of God ___ And when I have peace I am afraid to lose it ___ When I am

risen I fear a fall ___ When I am fallen I fear I shall not rise ___ When I have a respite from the working of corruption I fear that something will come to set my passions in a boil like Jeremiah's seething pot ___ And when in this torment and condition, I fear I have no holiness at all ___ and that I am not a vessel of honour fit for the masters use ___ And how can I forebear to bow the head & look down.

Of all the fine sermons Edwards preached throughout his ministry, none brought him greater notoriety than the one he preached in Philadelphia on January 1, 1770, entitled "A New Year's Gift," the so-called "Death Sermon." That sermon will be treated in detail in chapter eight but it is important to review the events of the last twenty-three months of his pastorate in Philadelphia to put that sermon in perspective.

August 1769 to July 1771--A Time of Anxiety
Following the death of his beloved Mary on August 16, 1769, the final twenty-three months of Morgan Edwards's pastorate in Philadelphia was a period of anxiety for both himself and the church. Contrary to common thought, there are no indications of a serious rupture in the relationship between the congregation and the pastor. Given the church's firm action to rid itself of Elhanan Winchester a few years after Edwards, it is clear it would have done the same with him had there been a major issue disrupting their relationship.

Edwards had returned from his European fund-raising tour by December 1768 to find the church had not suffered a statistical decline. Financial problems had developed by early 1769, and the church borrowed from trust funds to pay its bills. The receipts appear to have declined more from economic hard times than from lack of interest.

In July several members requested dismissal to form a new regular Baptist church in the newly created Northern Liberties section of Philadelphia.[85] The separation was friendly, and despite the transfer of members, there was a net gain in membership, with eleven new members coming by baptism.[86]

Mary Edwards died on August 16, 1769, during her eighth pregnancy. Until then, Edwards had been faithfully keeping the minute book, with a meticulously arranged index bearing the name and location of every person mentioned in the minutes. There are no minutes for the period July 1769 to January 1771.

It is assumed that records were kept during that period, but it is not known who kept them or what became of them. It is regrettable because the events of that period have been the subject of much speculation. The next extant churchbook is marked, "Book No. 2: January 8, 1771 to May 8, 1775." There is also a file of loose sheets marked "Minute Book No 2 1771." The original cover reads "No. 2 1769 to 1775," but there are no papers dated prior to 1771.

It is of interest to note the absence of dated sermon manuscripts of this twenty-three-month period. The one exception is the "Death Sermon," which was put into print. There are thirty undated and unmarked sermon manuscripts in the Crozer Collection and eight others marked Philadelphia, but the dates are missing or obscured. If any title were to be given to this period, it might be "The Silent Months," but Edwards was certainly not out of circulation.

Early in September 1769, Morgan Edwards enrolled Billy in Manning's academy in Rhode Island, and on September 17 he preached for Ezra Stiles at his Congregational church in Newport, Rhode Island.[87] By mid-

October he was in New York for the association meetings, where he served as clerk and was made receiver of funds from the Pennsylvania churches for Rhode Island College.[88] It was at this meeting that Edwards persuaded the delegates to print the association minutes on a yearly basis.[89]

Edwards served as clerk of the association again in 1770, and both he and Samuel Jones, now the moderator, collaborated on the circular letter to the churches.[90] Again, in 1770, the church enjoyed a small net gain, and there is no indication of disaffection over the "Death Sermon." The church had grown to be the second largest in the association, and Edwards was busily engaged in another project.

In 1770 Edwards published the first of what he intended to be a twelve volume history of Baptists in America. His role as a major Baptist historian will be treated later in more detail, but the first volume contains a hint of what he was planning for his own future.

In this volume Edwards set out five steps to promote Baptist unity. One step was the appointment of an evangelist by the Philadelphia Association. He had already proposed the establishment of a fund for such a purpose at the 1765 meeting of the Association. At the 1771 meeting, Edwards was appointed evangelist, three months after resigning his pastorate.[91]

On July 8, 1771, Morgan Edwards submitted his letter of resignation to the church.[92]

> Dear Brethren
> I have observed for some time that the interest does not thrive under my ministration as it was wont to do in years past, but is rather declining. This has given me trouble & trouble that I am less able to bear of any other trouble whatsoever. Accordingly I have the last year made this proposal to some of the Brethren. Viz

That they should look out for a popular Preacher; and that I should resign half my salary in order to enable the church to pay him. Things are still in the same situation, and my declining age and the present posture of Affairs forbid me to hope for a better time. I therefore now repeat to the Church what I before mentioned to Individuals. viz That you will seek for a minister suitable to the place; and a man of such talents as promise the revival of Interest. On this I am much in Earnest & being in earnest I do offer you my help to find such a Man either in America or in Europe and to bring him hither. I also propose to insist on no terms for myself which will hinder such an event from coming to pass; and in the mean time intend not to leave you destitute, because I seek your good, as a Church and the good of the Interest in general more than my own private Advantage; for the Credibility of this I appeal to my whole conduct Since I have been here and to my former and present proposal.

Edwards's letter states several reasons for his resignation. The church experienced a decline in 1771 when it dropped from 150 to 146 members with only three baptisms.[93] In addition, the church owed him over 390 pounds on his salary, but there is no indication his salary was withheld out of personal pique. The settlement he and the church negotiated defies such a suggestion.[94]

A committee of seven leaders and close friends arranged with Edwards that he would accept a little over two hundred and sixteen pounds, provided it was paid within six weeks. This action served as an incentive and a deadline, both of which were necessary.

The church frequently dragged its heels in decision-making, and the time frame would enable Edwards to clear his obligations to the church before the next associational meeting, October 15-17, 1771. The church minutes imply it was generally known he was to be appointed associational evangelist.[95]

The church was unable to raise the money by the October 1 deadline, and it was forced to borrow the balance from a trust fund and several individuals. The minutes of the October meeting indicate in length that the agreements were arrived at unanimously, in a friendly fashion and with good understanding, including Morgan Edwards.

The difficult financial straits in which the church found itself were in part a reflection of the adverse economic conditions then developing in the colonies as they moved toward independence from Great Britain. When Edwards referred to "the present posture of Affairs," in his letter of resignation, he was alluding to the economic stress in the colonies in the context of his own disagreement with the actions taken by colonial leaders.

The church followed Edwards's suggestion to seek a popular preacher as his replacement. At the August church meeting, a list of possible successors was prepared: six of the most famous Baptist pastors in America.[96] Since he felt free to assist in locating a new pastor, he was not in a strained relationship with them. It is clear the church had confidence he might persuade any one of the six to accept the post. In light the above it is safe to conclude a good relationship existed between the church and Edwards.

Edwards's appointment as the associational evangelist had been in the offing prior to the annual meetings on October 15-17, 1771. Such a ministry would not be new for him since he had been an itinerant preacher in his earlier years. The minutes state that his fellow ministers "expressed a readiness to supply Philadelphia" if he took the appointment.[97]

He did accept the call and left almost immediately. The minutes for the next year indicate a vote of appreciation for his services to the churches in the South.[98] Edwards' may have been anticipating the appointment when he placed Billy in Manning's academy.

A final review of Edwards's letter of resignation requires a pause at his statements about trouble that he is less able to bear and his declining age. His problems in caring for Billy and Joshua were no doubt behind his reference to "any other trouble." On the face of it, he would not have been much help to his wife because he was busy in his study preparing three weekly sermons, looking after the congregation, and fulfilling his myriad commitments in Baptist church life. By leaving Billy under Manning's care in Rhode Island and Joshua under Jones's care in Philadelphia, he was free to travel.

Edwards was certainly not old when he resigned, for he was only forty-nine years of age. He had periodic health problems, but the likelihood is he was exhausted from his frenetic pace, the grief over his wife's death, his anxieties about Billy and Joshua, and his own inclination to become engaged in some other form of ministry.

The separation of Morgan Edwards from the Baptist church of Philadelphia was friendly, so much so that he remained a member in good standing despite his frequent travels and living in Delaware. The matter of his loyalty to the crown was not yet as serious an issue as it would become later. Nor is there any clear evidence that Morgan's "Death Sermon" seriously impaired his relationship with the church. There was, however, widespread interest in the premonition of his death before he preached the sermon and considerable speculation about it afterward.

ENDNOTES

1. David Spencer, *The Early Baptists of Philadelphia*, (Philadelphia:William Sychelmore, 1877), 114-115.
2. Wiiliam W. Keen, *The Bi-Centennial Celebration of the Founding*

of the First Baptist Church of Philadelphia, (Philadelphia: The American Baptist Publication Society, 1899), 42.
3. Henry C. Vedder, *A Short History of the Baptists,* (Philadelphia: The American Baptist Publication Society, 1907), 314.
4. MS. Churchbook, First Baptist Church, Philadelphia, 12-13.
5. Ibid., 13.
6. Ibid.
7. William L. Lumpkin, *Baptist Confessions of Faith,* (Philadelphia: The Judson Press, 1959), 351.
8. There is a column of numbers adding up to forty at the end of a sermon by Edwards entitled, "Conversion to the Likeness of Children." There is no date or place indicated for the sermon, but when read aloud the sermon takes about forty minutes. The figures are in Edwards' hand, and imply he timed the sermon upon its completion. The manuscript is in the Crozer Collection at the Colgate Rochester Divinity School, Rochester, N.Y., No. 1738, Box 252, Ed. 9, V. 3, 30. Unless otherwise noted all manuscript sermons cited in the chapter are in that collection.
9. Churchbook, 28.
10. Ibid., 30.
11. Ibid., 32.
12. Ibid., 37.
13. Morgan Edwards, *The Customs of Primitive Churches,* (Philadelphia: 1774), 80-83.
14. A.D. Gillette, ed., *Minutes of The Philadelphia Baptist Association, A.D. 1707-1807,* (Philadelphia: The American Baptist Publication Society, 1851), 89.
15. Baptism certificate, made out to Miss Sarah Sallows and dated June 11, 1762. American Baptist Historical Society Archives, Rochester, N.Y.
16. Morgan Edwards, *Materials Towards a History of the Baptists,* (Philadelphia: James Crukshank and Isaac Collins, 1770), Frontispiece.
17. Ibid., 129.
18. Churchbook, 41.
19. Edwards, Customs, 83.
20. Churchbook, 22.
21. Ibid., 14.
22. Ibid., 14,15.

23. Gillette, 85.
24. Joseph J. Kelly, *Life and Times In Colonial Philadelphia*, (Harrisburg: Stackpole Books, 1973), 139.
25. Churchbook, 14.
26. Ibid., 57.
27. Ibid., 20.
28. Ibid., 19.
29. Ibid., 71.
30. Ibid., 78.
31. Spencer, 68.
32. William D. Thompson, *Philadelphia's First Baptists*, (Philadelphia: First Baptist Church, 1989), 8.
33. Keen, 37.
34. Churchbook, 21.
35. Ibid., 22.
36. Morgan Edwards, "I Magnify My Office," (Philadelphia: Andrew Stewart, 1763).
37. Churchbook, 23.
38. Ibid., 30.
39. Keen, 39.
40. Churchbook, 24.
41. Ibid., 26.
42. Ibid., 37.
43. Ibid., 47.
44. Ibid., 71-78.
45. MS. Letter from Morgan Edwards to Gardner Thurston, June 28, 1765. Manning Papers, (John Hay Library, Brown University, Providence, R.I.), OL 74-77 M.
46. Churchbook, Title Page.
47. Ibid., 17.
48. Ibid., 50.
49. Letter from Welsh Baptist historian, D. Hugh Matthews, Cardiff, to the author, Alhambra, 14 July 1994.
50. Ibid., 46.
51. Keen, 152.
52. Morgan Edwards, *Material Towards a History of the Baptists*, (Danielsville, Ga.: Heritage Papers, 1984), V. 2, 96.
53. Edwards, *Customs*, 12, 42, 44.
54. Churchbook, 14. Present-day American Baptists do not use the

A Dazzling Enigma   187

term "church meeting" or "congregational meeting," but refer to these meetings as "business meetings." For early Baptists, however, they took such meetings to be serious attempts to act as the Body of Christ in seeking the mind of the Lord. British and Welsh Baptists still use the term "church meeting."

55. Ibid., 14-15.
56. Ibid., 15-16.
57. Ibid., 41-42.
58. Ibid., 32.
59. MS Philadelphia Baptist Churchbook, No.2, Entry, July 8, 1771. n.p.
60. Churchbook, No. 1, 32,36,42.
61. Ibid., 69.
62. Ibid., 62.
63. Matthews, D. Hugh. "Datganiad Llantrisant (1654): Ymgais: Withio Presbyteraeth ar Fedyddwyr Cymore?" in *Agweddan ar Dwf Piwritaniaeth yng Nghyman yn ye Ail Ganrif ar Bywtheg.* ed. J. Gwynfor Jones. [The Declaration of Llantrisant (1654): An Attempt to Impose Presbyterianism on Welsh Baptists?" in Aspects On the Growth of Puritanism in Wales in the 17th Century.] (Edwin Mellen Press, 1992).
64. Ibid., 70,71,76-83.
65. Gillette, 88.
66. Churchbook, 19-20.
67. Ibid., 22.
68. MS. Letter from Frances Alison to James Moody, February 9, 1767.
69. MS. Minutes, Board of Trustees, College of Philadelphia, (University of Pennsylvania Archives, North Arcade, Franklin Field, Philadelphia: May 11, 1762), 168.
70. Ibid.
71. Catherine F. Byers, "More Than 150 Years Ago," *Focus,* (Newark Delaware: University of Delaware Archives), Vol. 3, No. 4, December 1983. 1.
72. Ibid.
73. Newcastle County Deed Book #2, Delaware State Archives, (Dover, Delaware), 638.
74. Morgan Edwards, "Through The Tender Mercies of our Lord," (MS. Sermon. July 17, 1763), V 17, No. 5, n.p.

75. Churchbook, 39.
76. John Rippon, ed. *Baptist Annual Register*, (London: 1796), 312.
75. MS. Letter from Oliver Hart to Hezekiah Smith, February 27, 1772, Manning Papers, (John Hay Library, Brown University, Providence, R.I.)
78. Churchbook, 32.
79. Morgan Edwards, "And Enoch Walked With God," (MS. Sermon, August 1, 1762), V. 10, No. 9, n.p.
80. Ibid., "This Is A Faithful Saying," (MS. Sermon, July 17, 1763), V.15, n.p.
81. Ibid., "He Spake Also This Parable, "(MS. Sermon, January 1, 1764), V. 27, No. 8, n.p.
82. Ibid., "Because Thou Sayest," (MS. Sermon, September 11, 1763), V. 33, No. 11, n.p.
83. Ibid., "When God Ariseth," (MS. Sermon, November 6, 1763), V 27, No. 3, n.p.
84. Ibid., "And When These Things Begin," (MS. Sermon, June 1764), V. 33, No. 7, n.p.
85. Churchbook, 92.
86. Gillette, 111.
87. F.B. Dexter, ed. *The Literary Diary of Ezra Stiles*, (New York: 1901), 24.
88. Ibid., 109.
89. Ibid., 111.
90. Ibid.
91. Ibid., 119.
92. Churchbook, No. 2, July 8, 1771, n.p.
93. Gillette, 122.
94. Churchbook, No. 2, August 20, 1771, n.p.
95. Ibid., January 16, 1772, n.p.
96. Ibid., Entry, August 5, 1771, n.p.
97. Gillette, 119.
98. Ibid., 124.

CHAPTER EIGHT

A TIME TO DIE

"The good man...preached his own funeral sermon."
John Rippon, 1795

Introduction

There were two very conspicuous sermons which emerged from eighteenth-century American Protestantism, and both were preached by men named Edwards. The first was preached by Jonathan Edwards in 1734 and was conspicuous because of its links to the "Great Awakening" and is entitled "Sinners In The Hands of An Angry God." The second was preached by Morgan Edwards, on January 1, 1770, and is entitled "A New Year's Gift." It was conspicuous because he predicted the time of his own death. The title of Jonathan Edwards's sermon crackles with the fire of God's judgment while that of Morgan Edwards's seems bland by comparison. It is not the title of the second sermon, however, which brought it such notoriety, but the way it has been perceived.

The event has been characterized as Morgan Edwards's preaching "his own funeral sermon." John Rippon was the first to describe it in print in 1796. He succeeded John Gill at the Carter Lane Baptist Church in London and served that church for sixty-three years; he was a composer of hymns and a Baptist historian. Rippon is best known in Great Britain and America for his publication of the *Baptist Annual Register* from 1790 to 1802.

In the January 1796 issue of the *Register,* Rippon printed William Rogers's memorial sermon preached for Morgan Edwards on February 22, 1795, three weeks after his death. Rippon added a footnote.[1]

> Led by a mere foolish impulse, and not by Scripture, the good man [Edwards] persuaded himself, that he should die on a certain day, and accordingly *preached his own funeral sermon* [italics mine].

Rippon printed what some others had been verbalizing since Morgan preached the sermon in 1770. That perception has been recycled in print by others up to the late twentieth century.

The earliest reference in the nineteenth century appears in David Benedict's 1813 history of the Baptists, in which he quotes Rippon's phrase.[2] This was followed by Babcock, Choules, and Peck in the *Baptist Memorials and Monthly Record* in 1844.[3] In 1865 there is a statement found in Sprague's *Annals of the American Pulpit.*[4]

> He had, for some unaccountable impulse, taken up the idea that he should die on a particular day, and this, it is said, was intended as his own Funeral Sermon.

David Spencer in 1877 stated that Edwards "became possessed of the idea that on a certain day of that year [1770] he would die, which,...had an injurious effect, and discouraged him in his pastorate."[5] In his 1881 *Baptist Encyclopedia,* Cathcart contends Edwards "was disappointed when the day of death dawned and departed, for instead of expiring he lived for nearly a quarter of a century after."[6] One is hard pressed to find sources for Cathcart's assertion that Morgan was disappointed because he did not die on March 9, 1770.

This perception of the sermon carried over into the twentieth century. It is implied in an article by David H. Ashton.[7]

> Another disturbing factor was his New Year's sermon of January 1, 1770, on the text, "This year thou shalt surely die" (Jer. 28:16), when he solemnly declared that he expected to meet his Maker before another year was born. Such prophecy was daring, to say the least, and must have undermined his good standing and reputation, particularly when next January found him still alive, indicating that his forebodings were the by-product of his own imagination.

The term is reiterated in McKibbens's and Smith's, *The Life and Works of Morgan Edwards* in 1980 which reads, "It is generally believed that Edwards was preaching his own funeral sermon."[8] While writers and historians have used such expressions as "it is said," or "it is generally believed," the fact remains that no solid primary evidence is known to demonstrate that Morgan Edwards intended the sermon as his funeral sermon. Indeed, the sermon must be viewed through the eyes of the man who wrote it and preached it.

A careful review of the sermon will demonstrate that Morgan Edwards did not preach the sermon as his funeral oration. It did not result in a serious breach between himself and his people. To review the sermon, one should examine the premonitions of both Morgan and Mary Edwards and the effect of her death on him, look closely at the relevant sections of the sermon to see what he did say and did not say, and finally, delve into any possible connection between the sermon and his resignation.

The Premonitions

On March 9, 1755, Morgan Edwards was sitting quietly, meditating in his home in Cork, Ireland, when

> the Notion or Tho't instantly rushed into his Mind with distinct and vivid clearness, in a singular manner, he knew not how, but giving him a fixt indubitable Persuassion of the future fact, the year when he should die, viz., 1770 and the very day of the year.[9]

Edwards made continual efforts to rid his mind of what he knew to be a "chimerical Notion," but without success. It stayed with him, off and on, with the same clarity as when he first experienced it. He told Ezra Stiles on September 17, 1769, that he did not dwell on it, but when it came to mind the notion was vivid.[10]

He did not talk about the experience until four years later when he probably related it to his mentor at Cork, Ebenezer Gibbons.[11] Gibbons thought to rid him of the idea by telling others about it, but that only exacerbated the situation for Edwards. Shortly before he left England for America Edwards confided the experience to two friends, and these in turn communicated it to Philadelphia from whence it spread through the colonies.[12]

Morgan Edwards was very precise in his description of the experience. He said it was "not a revelation or a dream," and thus he distanced himself from those who might attach an other-worldly quality to the experience. He always referred to it as a notion, i.e., a conception or vague thought, but never referred to it as a clairvoyant or extra-sensory experience. One must place his wife's premonition alongside his.

Edwards related to James Manning in September, 1769, that soon after he and Mary were married "she had a persuassion that she should have six children, and dye [sic] in child-bed of her seventh child undelivered."[13] Ezra Stiles reported Edwards' conversation with Manning in his diary for September 22, 1769, but there is a contradiction. Stiles said it was during Mary's seventh pregnancy that she died whereas Morgan reported it to be the eighth.[14] Edwards's information is first hand, so his is the accurate figure. The data in Stiles's diary, however, helps in outlining a sequence of events.

Morgan and Mary Edwards were married in late 1754 or early 1755. Shortly after the wedding, she had a premonition which she related to her husband. In March 1755 he experienced his "indubitable Persuassion." It is very possible, on hearing the unsettling news from his bride, he may have become psychologically predisposed to have such an experience himself. One other factor may have had a more subtle influence.

The Edwardses both came from a Celtic lineage where superstition had its place. Geraint Jenkins reports, for example, that many primitive beliefs in the Celtic culture were not easily eliminated even by the Protestant Reformation.[15] Edwards would not consciously have given room to superstition, but his cultural heritage may have inclined him to be more susceptible to such a conception.

Mary Edwards was more prone to talk of her premonition than was her husband, especially to other women. Following the delivery of her seventh child, who died in childbirth, she reported it again to the women who attended her. When she died in August 1769, these same women recalled her speaking of it.[16]

There are records of only five persons to whom Edwards spoke of his premonition. These were Gibbons, two friends in England, Stiles, and James Manning. Stiles reported Edwards "seemed rather to avoid discoursing on it." Manning told Stiles, "He was rather averse to conversing about it," and he "declined to tell Mr. Manning the day he should die: which s[ai]d he had imparted to none."[17]

Stiles, however, reported in his diary on December 26, 1769, that Edwards was moving out of his house in Philadelphia on March 9, 1770, because he expected to die at that time.[18] This report came to Stiles from Nicholas Tillinghast who dined with Edwards on December 12, 1769. Edwards said nothing about his death on that occasion. At that time, a Mr. Sullivan was living in the house with Edwards, and he told Tillinghast that he jokingly offered to rent the house from Edwards after the ninth or eleventh of March.[19]

By late 1769, the issue of Edwards's premonition was the subject of widespread public conversation, no doubt because of the talk circulating about his wife's premonition and death. For this reason, Edwards intended to "publish it [i.e., the facts about his premonition] to the world the beginning of the year [1770], when he purposed to print all his Expectation, and send it [to] his Friends as a new year's gift."[20] He divulged more about his sermon plans in his conversations with Manning.

Manning reported the conversations as taking place in September 1769.[21]

> [H]e constantly refers his Inquirers to an acc[ount] he intends to print next New Year's day. He told Mr. Manning the Text he intended to preach from on New Year's day, and the plan of his Discourse which was to contain this narrative. Previous to preach-

ing it he intended to print the sermon (to be secret between him and the printer as to the contents) & have it ready to deliver & send to his friends [as] a New Year's gift.

Morgan Edwards did not take his premonition too seriously prior to his wife's death. Neither did they take hers too seriously either, as she continued to conceive children up to her eighth pregnancy. Following her death, his attitude about his own premonition appears to have changed. Did he blame himself for her death? Certainly the conversations with Stiles and Manning only one month after her death indicate he had been forced to deal with the issue more seriously and with the runaway gossip, which confront him everywhere. He chose to handle it in a sermon.

The Sermon: "A New Year's Gift"
The printed edition of Morgan Edwards's sermon "A New Year's Gift" has a statement by Edwards on the title page.[22]

> A New Year's - Gift Being A Sermon Delivered at Philadelphia On January 1, 1770 And published for rectifying some wrong reports and preventing others of the like sort; but chiefly for giving it another Chance of doing Good to them who heard it.

Edwards stated clearly the sermon was published to correct erroneous reports and to prevent such reports in the future. The primary reason for its printing, however, was to bring more good to those who heard it. There is no hint of it being his funeral sermon. Indeed, Sprague reports that "some of Mr. Edwards' friends have denied that this was designed as his Funeral Sermon, and a perusal of the Sermon itself would seem to leave the case somewhat doubtful."[23] The sermon seems to support the view of Edwards' friends.

The text for the sermon is Jeremiah 28:16 where Hananiah, the false prophet, is told by Jeremiah, "Thus says the Lord; ...This year you shall die." After giving his text, Edwards cited three maxims which are generally true: (1) All must die; (2) No one knows the time of his or her death; and (3) A person is better off not knowing the time of death.

Edwards then laid the groundwork for the rest of the sermon by outlining the exceptions to all three maxims. The first maxim is that all must die because all have sinned. His exceptions to this maxim were Enoch and Elijah and the saints living on earth at the return of Christ. He then used the device of a diatribe to help his hearers see that these exceptions are not unjust to other believers who do die.

Edwards's point was that Christ died for those who were the exceptions, and death for believers who do die has no sting. He used the New Testament figure of "fallen asleep" as an illustration. He then cited examples of people who had what he calls "fits," and what today are called "near-death" or "out-of-body" experiences. Apparently these were very negative out-of-body experiences, and were denials that death was an "usher to glory." He then told of his wife having had a positive near-death experience three days before her death. When she came out of it, she comforted her husband with her description of it.[24]

In his exceptions to the second maxim-that no one knows the time of his or her death-Edwards pointed to Hananiah, Hezekiah and Dives in the Bible as people who did know. Then he listed many others from what he defined as "profane history." These include Justyn Martyr,

Cyprian, Hale, Usher, Jewell, Tyro, Peden, and people he had known personally. In each specific case he described how they came by that knowledge, and how each death occurred as predicted.

Coming to the cases he had known personally, he related the experience of his wife, who told of her premonition of dying in her eighth pregnancy, and her death occurred as she said predicted.[25]

> I myself knew a man [Morgan used this Pauline device to refer to himself] who, on the Ninth of March, in the year 1755, was seized with an impression, *'That at the end of a full fifteen years, from that time, he should be dead.'* About four years after he told a friend of it; that friend endeavouring to rally him out of the notion, made the thing known abroad, which was presently spoken of in various ways. But the above is the state of the case. Whether a premonition or a deception, time will show, and that time is at hand; If the first, the thing will claim no praise, because involuntary; if the last, others have been deceived the same way without blame, and that for the same reason.

It is important that Edwards did not linger long on either his wife's or his own premonition but used both situations as personal illustrations to make a point.

When Edwards spoke of the third maxim and its exceptions, he made no claim to know why God chose to make known to some and not to others the time of their deaths. For evil people, he suggested it may be to give time for repentance. In the case of believers, it may have been to produce "either a brighter display of his piety...Or for exciting him to greater obedience."[26]

At this point, in dramatic fashion, Edwards applied his text to his hearers. The following extended quotation provides a sample of his sermonic abilities, and near the close, contains the explicit statement concerning his own death. It is critical to understanding his purpose in the sermon to take note of his positive retrospect on the year past (1769) despite the loss of his wife, the loss of another child, and his separation from Billy, then in Rhode Island.[27]

IV. I proceed to the second thing I promised, viz. to address you in a manner that may suit the text, and the time; and that will, by the blessing of God, be of benefit to each of you.

1. The time, you know, is the first day of the *new year,* and that which connects it with the *old*; on which account, it, like Janus, casts a double aspect, the one on the year past; and the other on the year begun. It will be suitable to the time, therefore, to say something to it, both in its retrospection, and in its prospect. If, with the day we look back to the year it pushes from us, we shall see cause for thanksgiving for a year's bounties; and sorrow for a year's sins. Every day and every night of the last year yielded us some favours. God's mercy was new every morning, and his faithfulness repeated every night. He gave us food and raiment, and health and liberty. He gave us his sabbaths, his gospel, and his means of grace. He gave us hope, and supported it by tokens of his love. He hath born with us and spared us a year longer. He hath crowned the year with goodness.

Thanks therefore be to his holy name. But these thanks are to be mingled with sorrows. We have a year's sins to bewail. -How many these have been, God only knows; but we easily know the number of them to be great. Not a day nor a night passed without producing some wants of conformity to, or transgressions of, the law and the gospel. O Lord, we look back with shame from the beginning of this year; we judge and condemn ourselves, and most humbly ask forgiveness of the past year's sins! But if, with the day, we look forward to the year commenced, we have a prospect big with instructions. It meets us with calls to resolve, to pray and to strive. To resolve, That in the name and strength of God, we will spend this year better than the past. To pray that God will be bountiful and kind to us, as he hath been the last year; and to strive to offend him less, to please him better; to love him more. Such resolutions, prayers and strivings, suit the time well, but suit our own character and interest much better.

2. Having said so much to the time, I will add somewhat that may be suitable to the peculiar nature of the text. It is a very alarming one to wicked men; but pleasing, highly pleasing to the righteous. *This year thou shalt die!* What, die? And that, this year? Alarming indeed! Every syllable sounds like the ticking of a death watch! Observe! Death is in the text! And a specification of *this year,* for the time of death to someone or other! But who is the one? I answer, possibly everyone here-probably many a one-and certainly some one or other! It is possible that every one of us will be dead before the end of the year; for the world is grown old. And where is the man, or the angel, that will insure its continuance for a month, a week, or a day longer? Or if the end of all things be at hand, who can say, that neither the sword, nor famine, nor pestilence, nor Indians, nor earthquake, shall put an end to us, all in three hundred sixty-five days? May I repeat my text therefore to express a possibility of what may befall *everyone* of us this year? But possibilities are light things. Therefore, I add, that the text will *probably* be verified this year in the case of *many a one* here. The congregation consists now of an hundred and forty-nine communicants; and as many hearers besides, as will augment the number to about four hundred. If we suppose that five in a hundred will die, (and the bills of mortality for the years past justify the supposition) a score will never see another new-year's day. Shall I then repeat the text to express the probability, that this year twenty of us shall die? And shall not this affect us? I am sure the thought affects me; for some of the twenty may be the best friends which the society has! But I may proceed to *certainty* in applying the text. It is *certain,* morally *certain,* that *some one* of us will die this year. To suppose the contrary, were to suppose such a thing as never happened in any other society of equal number. -There stands among you one who firmly believes that he is the man. But let not that draw attention of any other from himself, for probably several more will never see the end of this year.

Clearly, the sermon was not funereal in its purpose. The

burden of Edwards's message was that any one or all of his hearers could die before the new year had run its course. He urged them to receive God's grace immediately. To make his point he brought into play the three maxims about death and cited exceptions to each with biblical, classical, historical and personal examples. He used his wife and himself as examples of exceptions to the second maxim, that no one knows the time of his or her demise.

He described his wife's premonition in only one sentence. He described her as a gentlewoman, and he made no dogmatic claims with reference to her premonition. He simply described it as "something of this premonition or foreboding impression on her mind for a considerable time."[28] The only other mention of his wife's premonition was when he told of her near-death experience.[29] He used two sentences to describe both her premonition and her death, and not much more to relate his own.

Edwards spoke of his own premonition in the same paragraph in which he spoke of those of Hananiah, Hezekiah, Saul, Tyro, Polycarp, Cyprian, Usher, and others. He devoted one sentence to relate his wife's experience and four the details of his own. The details suited the purpose he stated on the title page "rectifying wrong reports." It is obvious that he included the personal experiences in the sermon as examples used to illustrate his points.

Edwards graphically highlighted with statistics the possibility that everyone in the congregation could be dead by the end of the new year, the probability that some would die, and the certainty of at least one death, his own.[30] Though he was very specific and clear in his prediction, he did not use it as a preaching device, but as a single small piece of the overall message he hoped would impel his hearers to an act of faith and commitment.

Balancing Edwards's prediction of his own death was his anticipation of God's being "bountiful and kind" to him and his people in the new year.[31] As further evidence that he recognized the possibility his prediction could be wrong, he made the following statement in the sermon.[32]

> Whether a premonition or a deception time will show, and that time is at hand: If the first [i.e. a premonition], the thing will claim no praise, because [it was] involuntary [i.e. it will not be to Edwards's credit if his prediction comes true]; if the last [i.e. a deception], others have been deceived the same way without blame, and that for the same reason.

In speaking of others who had similar experiences, Edwards no doubt had in mind the great evangelist George Whitefield. He knew Whitefield and also knew he had a premonition about one of his children. Whitefield believed that premonition until events disproved it.

When Whitefield's wife was pregnant, he had a premonition that the born child would be a boy, would be named John, and would become a great preacher of the Gospel. The child was a boy, and he was named John. Whitefield made no secret of the premonition, and thousands came to the tabernacle for the christening of the child. But within four months, the little boy was dead. In hindsight, Whitefield saw his experience as a delusion of the devil and an important lesson in his life.[33] The experience in no way sullied his reputation.

Edwards's reputation among Baptists has suffered because of his "notion" and the New Year's Day sermon. Any fair assessment of the treatment he has received, however, must be compared with that received by other Baptist leaders in other times who had similar experiences. Augustus Hopkins Strong, a major contributor to Baptist life and thought in the late nineteenth and early twentieth centuries was one such person. Strong probably is the most scholarly of all Baptist systematic theologians. His autobiography records an experience similar to Edwards's premonition which has not diminished his stature among Baptists.[34]

> When I was twenty-one years old, life seemed sad and mysterious; I had no desire to live; I expected soon to die. Though my view of life brightened as I went on, I never quite got rid of the idea [Edwards called it a notion] of an early death, until after a curious experience in Cleveland. There I began one of the years with a premonition that I should never live to see its end. Month after month, however, passed by, and I was still in the land of the living. December came, and the last week in December, and I still lived. In the middle of that last week a farmer called with a buggy to take me to the quarterly meeting of the Association with his church. All the way into the country and all the way home I was waiting for the horse to run away, throw me out, and break my neck. But I reached home in safety. When I came down stairs on the first morning of the new year, my wife said that my countenance wore a look of disappointment. It taught me not to trust in premonitions.

Like Whitefield and Strong, Edwards acknowledged that "he was mistaken in his impulses."[35] One of these impulses may have been to spell out the details of his premonition in a sermon, with the hope it would silence the gossip and correct the misinformation. While acknowledgment worked for Whitefield and Strong, it did not for Edwards.

The Sermon and the Philadelphia Church

There has been a long-held understanding that there was an adverse reaction to the sermon, and it was a major factor in his resignation. This view has been expressed as recently as 1971 in an article on Edwards by John S. Moore. Writing of the sermon, he said, "The sermon was printed and passed through four editions in a few months time. This along with other personal eccentricities had a damaging effect."[36] There are, however, no primary resource materials which affirm a serious break in Edwards's relationship with his congregation. Discomfort, no doubt, but not a serious disruption, since he continued his pastorate for another eighteen months.

Further evidence of his continued good standing is found in an entry in the church minutes for July 6, 1772, one year after his resignation.[37] While Edwards was on his evangelistic tour of the South, he requested the opportunity to purchase the collection of window shutters left from the old meeting house which had been torn down in 1761. This request was made through Isaac Moulder, a member of the church. The church voted unanimously to give him the shutters.

It was discovered in February, 1774, that the church still owed Morgan over one hundred forty pounds back-salary, which it voted to pay him. Then, in October of that year he was appointed a messenger of the church to the Philadelphia Association's meeting.[38] By this time Edwards had moved to Pencader, Delaware. He apparently wanted the shutters for his new home, one the British army would subsequently burn down.

Edwards remained a member in good standing until after the Revolutionary War despite his avowed loyalty to the Crown. The esteem in which he was held may also be seen in the protection he received when threatened by a mob of patriots. There is evidence, however, that some of his fellow ministers perceived that the relationship had been damaged.

This is evident in a letter from Francis Pelot, a friend of Edwards,s and pastor of the Baptist church in Euhaw, South Carolina, to Hezekiah Smith in Haverhill, Massachusetts.[39]

> I then wish they [the Baptist church in Philadelphia] could agree with Mr. Edwards again: Thus [I] argue to myself: if he may preach occasionally and the mantles [of] Christ easily cover small Imperfections; beside this present disatisfaction [sic] _____ could make him more cautious, for the future. & might be the means of preserving the usefulness of a talented man - a man who has serve[d] his Fellows in a warm attachment to our Baptist interest- Some people are so blinded by Self-partiality; that they can by no means bear that in a minister, they freely allow themselves in-it may indeed not be so in Philadelphia; but I have often seen it elsewhere.

Any effort to assess the reaction to Edwards's sermon must also include his standing in the Philadelphia Association which was unchanged by it. There was no diminution of his leadership or of the esteem in which he was held by his fellow ministers. He continued to be trusted with leading roles on that important stage of national Baptist life, the Philadelphia Baptist Association.

ENDNOTES

1. John Rippon, ed., *Baptist Annual Register,* (London: 1796), 311.
2. David Benedict, *A General History of the Baptist Denomination In America* (Boston: Manning & Loring, 1813), II, 298-299.
3. R. Babcock, J.D. Choules, J.M. Peck, eds., *The Baptist Memorials and the Monthly Record* (New York: John R. Bigelow, 1844),

III, 342.
4. William B. Sprague, *Annals of the American Pulpit* (New York: Robert Carter & Brothers, 1865), VI, 83.
5. David Spencer, *The Early Baptists of Philadelphia*, (Philadelphia: William Sychelmoore, 1877), 104.
6. William Cathcart, ed. *The Baptist Encyclopedia*, (Philadelphia: Louis H. Everts, 1881), 362.
7. David H. Ashton, "First Historian of American Baptists," *The Chronicle*, XIV, 2 (April 1951), 74.
8. Thomas McKibbens and Kenneth L. Smith, *The Life and Works of Morgan Edwards*, (New York: Arno Press, 1980), 23.
9. F.B. Dexter, ed., *The Literary Diary of Ezra Stiles*, (New York: 1901), 3 Vols., 24,25.
10. Ibid.
11. Morgan Edwards, *A New Year's Gift*, (Newport: Solomon Southwick, 1770), 8.
12. Dexter, 25.
13. Ibid.
14. Edwards, 8.
15. Geraint H. Jenkins, *Literature, Religion and Society in Wales, 1660-1730.* (Cardiff: University of Wales Press, 1978), 49.
16. Dexter, 25.
17. Ibid., 24,25.
18. Ibid., 30.
19. Ibid.
20. Ibid.
21. Ibid., 25.
22. Edwards, Title Page.
23. Sprague, 83.
24. Edwards, 8.
25. Ibid.
26. Ibid.
27. Ibid., 10-13.
28. Ibid., 8.
29. Ibid., 6.
30. Ibid., 12.
31. Ibid.
32. Ibid., 11.

33. Rippon. 311.
34. Crerar Douglas, ed. *Autobiography of Augustus Hopkins Strong,* (Valley Forge: Judson Press, 1981), 332.
35. Benedict, 299.
36. John S. Moore, "Writers of Early Virginia Baptist History," *Baptist History and Hertitage,* VI, 2. (January 1971), 29.
37. MS. Churchbook, First Baptist Church, Philadelphia, Entry July 6, 1772, n.p., (American Baptist Historical Society, Valley Forge, PA.).
38. Ibid., Entries for February 17 and 21, 1774; March 14, 1774; October 3, 1774.
39. MS Letter from Francis Pelot to Hezekiah Smith, October 27, 1771, Manning Papers, (John Hay Library, Brown University, Providence).

CHAPTER NINE

A LEADER OF LEADERS

> "Among Baptist leaders...of the
> Philadelphia Association,...he had
> been a central and commanding figure."[1]
> James A. Rogers, 1985

A Major Figure

Morgan Edwards was a "central and commanding figure" in the Philadelphia Association during the second half of the eighteenth century and thereby impacted the whole of American Baptist life. A memorial to Edwards is included at the end of the minutes for the 1795 meeting of the Philadelphia Association. The statement is enclosed in a black border.[2]

> Rev. Morgan Edwards, formerly of the Philadelphia Church, resigned his place in the church militant in the year past. "Blessed are the dead who die in the Lord."

That memorial came at the close of a thirty-four year period of active involvement in the leadership of the Association.

Historian David Spencer has described Edwards's activism.[3]

> Morgan Edwards at once took a preeminent position, because of his talents, energy and piety. Accordingly at the meeting of the Association [1761], succeeding his arrival, he was placed in a position of prominence, trust and work.

In 1898 it was said of Edwards, "No sooner did Mr. Edwards arrive in this country than the denomination showed the results of his restless intellectual activity."[4] That view of Edwards's leadership role was echoed by James Rogers almost one hundred years later. He wrote, "Edwards was the statesman among Baptist leaders of the colonial period."[5] In describing his leadership role in the Association, twentieth century Baptist historian H. Leon McBeth wrote, "Morgan Edwards...lent doctrinal and spiritual stability to Baptists."[6]

The historical importance of the Philadelphia Association afforded Edwards an appropriate stage to perform his leadership roles in the offices in which he served. It also allowed him to circulate his *Customs of the Primitive Churches*, to put forward his plan for a national body of Baptists, to fulfill his various miscellaneous responsibilities, and, above all, to launch his proposal for a Baptist college in Rhode Island.

The Philadelphia Baptist Association

The importance of the Philadelphia Baptist Association lies in the fact that "it was the parent stem from which all the major cooperative bodies in America have sprung."[7] The earliest efforts of Baptists in America to form an association were by General Baptists in New England who began holding yearly meetings by 1670. By 1690, however, four Particular Baptist churches in the middle colonies began meeting together for "fellowship, administering baptism, observing the Lord's Supper, and ordaining ministers."[8] These churches were the Pennepeck church in Pennsylvania, and the Middletown, Piscataway, and Cohansey churches in New Jersey. Within a few years, they were joined by the Welsh Tract church, in what is now Delaware, and in 1707 they formed the Philadelphia Baptist Association.

Until the second half of the eighteenth century, the Philadelphia Association was the only association for Particular Baptists in America, and churches from Virginia to New England joined it. The Great Awakening, which began in the 1730s, had by the 1740s touched Baptist churches. They began to multiply more rapidly, and soon they were forming new associations. The Charleston Baptist Association, which was organized in 1751 was the second. As these and other associations were formed, they were patterned after the Philadelphia Association to which numbers of these churches had formerly belonged. What must not be forgotten as the new associations came into being was that they maintained a close linkage with the "mother association" and adopted its Confession of Faith.

The Philadelphia Confession was formally adopted by the Philadelphia Baptist Association on September 25, 1742, and was printed by Benjamin Franklin in 1743.[9] The Philadelphia Confession was the Second London Baptist Confession of 1689, with the addition of two articles favoring the singing of hymns and laying on of hands on newly baptized believers.

The first confession was produced by seven Particular Baptist churches in London in 1644 to distinguish themselves from the sixteenth century Anabaptists and the seventeenth century General Baptists.[10] The Baptist confession of 1644 underwent two revisions in 1677 and

1689, and the final product was the Second London Confession of 1689. The Baptists had borrowed heavily from the 1658 Savoy Declaration of the Congregationalists who had relied on the 1646 Westminster Confession of the Presbyterians.[11]

The Philadelphia Confession of 1742 strongly influenced Particular Baptist church life in America well into the nineteenth century. For example, when Deism and Universalism became popular religious movements in the latter part of the eighteenth century, the Philadelphia Association utilized its annual circular letter to give an exposition on some facet of the confession related to both of these movements.[12] Indeed, the annual sermons at the association meetings usually were on some assigned topic of Calvinistic theology.

There are two reasons why the Philadelphia Baptist Association became a national arena for the leadership role of Morgan Edwards. The first is that the Particular or Regular Baptists became the largest group of Baptists in eighteenth-century America; the second is the newly emerging associations patterned themselves after the Philadelphia body. The result was the Philadelphia Baptist Association had become a quasi-national Baptist body by the time Morgan Edwards arrived on the scene in 1761.

LEADERSHIP ROLES
Association Clerk
Morgan Edwards's first meeting with the Philadelphia Association was in 1761, the year he arrived from England. He was immediately elected as clerk along with Peter Peterson VanHorn of the Pennypeck Church.[13] He filled that office numerous times during his many years in the association, including the year his wife died and the

year he preached the "Death Sermon." As clerk, Edwards was responsible for numerous innovations and improvements, including tighter control of the minute book.

Edwards and VanHorn were "appointed to take care of the association book of records, and insert therein the minutes of our proceedings; the said book to be kept in the city of Philadelphia, and not to be removed thence without the order of the Association."[14] If one reads between the lines, it is possible to imagine that word had reached the other churches of what Edwards had done with the Minutes of the Philadelphia church. VanHorn lived outside the city, and if the book had to stay in Philadelphia, he would not have immediate access to it. It would be the only time two persons would occupy the clerk's office, and Edwards was the more assertive of the two. Under his immediate care, the association's records would be kept in better condition and so maintained.

One of the improvements Edwards made was to print the 1766 association minutes, at his own expense. Gillette reports that they were "probably published by Morgan Edwards at his own expense, and for his own convenience, it being in folio size, and about equal to the newspapers of the province."[15] This simple improvement was still influencing other Baptists to do the same thing seventy years later.[16] The association began to pay the cost of printing the minutes in 1769. At the 1794 meeting of the association, only three months before Edwards's death, he presented the association with a bound copy of the minutes "from the beginning thereof to the year 1793." Edwards was given a unanimous vote of thanks by the association. All of the minutes were written in his own hand.

With his election as clerk in 1761, and much to the

bane of Baptist church clerks ever since, Morgan Edwards persuaded the association to begin the practice of receiving annual statistical reports from all the churches. As clerk, Edwards was authorized to have the Confession of Faith reprinted because the demand for it by the churches had exhausted the supply.

One of the responsibilities of the clerk was to write the associational letter to the sister associations throughout the colonies. It was sometimes done by Edwards alone or in collaboration with the moderator. Consequently, Edwards's name became known to Baptists in the other colonies. He and VanHorn also cosigned the letter which revived correspondence with the Particular Baptist Fund Board in London. There had been no correspondence between the groups since 1734, and it was no doubt rekindled at the behest of Morgan Edwards.

The letter to the board in London told of many new churches since the last letter and the inability of the American Baptists to find pastors for all of them. They asked for help in that area, and also for their fledgling academy at Hopewell, New Jersey. Specifically the school needed books and scientific apparatus. In addition they asked for financial help to buy books for a new ministers'library and expressed a wish for continued correspondence to be conducted through Morgan Edwards.

Moderator

The second major office to which Morgan Edwards was elected was as moderator in 1762. The association held its annual meeting in the Lutheran church of Philadelphia because of the construction at the Baptist meeting house. It was at the 1762 meeting that Edwards proposed the establishment a Baptist college in Rhode Island. At that meeting he also introduced the practice of the association issuing an ordination certificate.[17]

The wording on the certificate is obviously Edwards's and four were issued that year to David Thomas, David Sutton, Samuel Jones, and Isaac Jones in testimony of their ordination. Samuel Jones and Isaac Jones both were from the Baptist church in Philadelphia, and the latter was a prominent attorney in the city. The certificates were not intended to usurp the role of the local church in the ordination process but to provide a credible evidence of ordination. The certificates bore the seal of the city, as a validation of their authenticity. Whenever feasible, Morgan Edwards took steps to enhance the status of Baptists in the public eye.

Preacher of the Annual Sermon
Another leadership role accorded to Edwards at his first associational meeting was his selection as the back-up preacher to Benjamin Griffith at the 1762 meeting on the "Doctrine of the Trinity." He became the preacher of the annual sermon at the 1763 meeting on the subject of the "State of Man Before the Fall." The next occasion at which Edwards was to be the annual preacher was ten years later at the 1773 meeting. He used Numbers 23:10 as his text; the sermon was so well received that a solicitation was made to pay for its printing. At that time Edwards received a warm welcome home after his three-thousand-mile tour as the associational evangelist.

Associational Evangelist
At the suggestion of Morgan Edwards, a fund for a traveling evangelist was established in 1765, and three months after he had resigned his pastorate in 1771, he

was selected to fill that office. The other pastors in the association offered to fill the pulpit at the Philadelphia church which he still occupied. At the 1772 meeting the association expressed its gratitude and voted to pay him a bonus. It was on his tour that Edwards garnered extensive historical data about Baptist churches in the South. His turn-around point was Savannah, Georgia, where he visited with George Whitefield at his orphanage.[18] Through the association, Edwards maintained a pulpit supply ministry for the rest of his life.

Associational Librarian
Morgan Edwards's convictions about an educated ministry motivated him to offer himself and attorney Isaac Jones to operate a ministers lending library from Philadelphia. A collection of books had been donated earlier by a wealthy Baptist layman in London named Thomas Hollis, but it had never been organized and made available. Edwards, however, had another conviction which prompted him to act for the improvement of Baptist church life.

A BOOK ON BAPTIST POLITY

Morgan Edwards's background in the Anglican Church spilled over into his life as a Baptist. It was his conviction that Baptists would benefit from having an ordered set of principles by which to conduct church life and which would be compatible with their confessions. Early in his ministry he drew up an organized set of principles which could serve as a manual on Baptist polity and practice for his own ministry. He wrote about this project in a letter dated June 28, 1765 to Gardner Thurston of the Farewell Street Baptist Church in Newport, Rhode Island.[19]

A Dazzling Enigma   215

> If you remember, I mentioned to you that I had many years ago, formed offices for my own direction in performing the several branches of a ministers work, I have lately incorporated these offices with a set of propositions relative to the nature, constitution, officers, and government of a gospel church. The book in quarto manuscript makes 192 pages--I wish I could send a copy of it to every baptist [sic] minister for his correction, alteration, addition, or retrenchment. Oh But how can this be done? I will tell you--If I could get my brother ministers to join me in the expence we would get it printed and then every minister would have a copy, and I would take care that no more would be printed than are bespoke. By this means we should be able to make something of it that would bear to make public to the churches. If you think well of this proposal I desire you will privately speak of it to our brother ministers in Providence and Newport, or elsewhere as soon as you can--I intend to do the same hereabout--I am persuaded that something of this sort is necessary towards *doing everything decently and in order;* and would be exceeding useful especially to young ministers, if it could be well executed-We profess to make the word of God our rule, to profess to *work by the same rules;* and yet our walk is not uniform--The diversity of our practices bespeaks that we walk by different rules.

At the 1774 associational meeting inquiries from the Welsh Tract church in Delaware concerning this quarto publication of Edwards were the subject of much discussion. By this time he was living in Delaware, and attending the services at the Welsh Tract church, though still a member of the Philadelphia church. The book in quarto form was titled *The Customs of the Primitive Churches and* the church wanted to know if the book was an association publication.

Edwards stated in the introduction that the copies were printed for circulation among his fellow pastors for their review and suggestions.[20] The Welsh Tract congregation regarded the printing of the book and its limited distribution at least ten years before as another of the association's printed materials.

The association appointed a committee of four men, all friends of Morgan Edwards, to respond to the church's inquiry.[21]

> Whereas, a book was published, entitled, 'The Customs of the Primitive Churches', which the author proposed should be altered, amended, and corrected, by his ministering brethren, and then reprinted for the use of the churches, which was never done; and whereas, we have reason to think, that it is understood by many abroad to have been adopted by us in its present form, as our custom and mode of church discipline and practice; it is therefore thought meet, that we should thus publicly testify to the contrary, as it is not, nor ever has been adopted by us, or by any of the churches belonging to the Association.

The committee did not disagree with the publication; it simply stated that it was never adopted by the association in its present form. In fact, the association already had an authorized, published discipline.

By the early 1740s, there was a growing awareness that a discipline was needed because of the rapid growth in the number of churches brought on by the Great Awakening. Jenkin Jones and Benjamin Griffith were asked to prepare one, but Jones was unable to help. By using a tract by Elias Keach and seeking the counsel of others, Griffith was able to design a discipline which was adopted by the association, attached to the confession, and printed with it in 1743.[22]

It soon became clear that more was needed and Griffith wrote an "Essay on the Power and Duty of an Association of Churches," which was inserted in the 1749 minutes.[23] That material was later revised and further expanded by Samuel Jones and finally published in 1798 as *A Treatise of Church Discipline, and a Directory.*[24]

There has been a lingering misperception that the association's communication to the Welsh Tract church was a repudiation of Edwards and his book. The communication itself dispels such a notion, but some historians have been wary of Edwards's publication. For example, Robert Handy cites a sermon by Oliver Hart in 1791 as another source of church discipline for the period.[25] He also refers to Edwards' *Customs of the Primitive Churches*, but cautions that it "must be used with care."[26]

Hart's sermon was entitled "A Gospel Church Portrayed and Her Orderly Service Pointed Out." Handy opines that though Hart's sermon lacked official endorsement, his words must have carried "considerable weight," because he had been moderator of the association four times since 1749 when he became pastor of the Baptist church in Charlotte, South Carolina.

Oliver Hart was one year younger than Morgan Edwards.[27] Though they were close friends they were very different persons. Edwards remained loyal to the British Crown until August 1775, whereas Hart actively promoted the patriot cause throughout the South Carolina countryside.[28] Hart was never a prolific writer, but Edwards wrote out all his sermons and published several works. Oliver Hart was well read but not formally educated.[29] Edwards, on the other hand, was both well read and well schooled. Hart had been pastor of the Charleston church for thirty-one years before fleeing the city in 1780 under threat of the advancing British General Cornwallis.[30] Edwards's longest pastorate was at Philadelphia where he spent ten years. Despite their differences, their sons were classmates at Rhode Island College,[31] and Edwards was quick to recommend Hart for a vacant New England pulpit in 1764.[32] Both men were very prominent in the life of the Philadelphia Association, but it is evident that Morgan was the more influential of the two.

Though Hart was elected moderator four times, Edwards was elected clerk many more times. A review of the association minutes reveals that a number of men served as moderator several times, whereas the office of clerk was filled by fewer men. Edwards served a term as moderator, but his greater value to the association was as clerk, and in the other offices he filled. In addition, Edwards's name appears in the minutes many more times than does that of Hart's. Without question his book exerted a greater influence than did Hart's sermon.

Baptist historian Norman Maring has described the *Customs of the Primitive Churches* as "the first manual on Baptist polity produced in America."[33] Morgan Edwards "gave an elaborate account of each of the offices and their functions." His stated intention was to print it in quarto (four pages to a sheet and folded), send copies to fellow ministers in the association, and ask them to make corrections, emendations, etc. Next, he intended to call a meeting of those ministers to compare notes and set out the best way to issue the book just as had been done with the Confession of Faith.[34] Edwards's manual was one-hundred-ten pages in length, and went into more depth and detail than did Hart's single sermon. Furthermore, the book was listed among the Association's printed resources for the churches.

Among the printed materials provided to the churches, were the Confession of Faith, the Treatise of Discipline, a catechism, a hymnal, the minutes and the circular letter. Two other publications listed for sale were Stennett's *Sermons* and Edwards' *Customs of the Primitive Chur-*

ches. The 1774 communication to the Welsh Tract church makes it clear that Edwards' book was not an authorized publication, since he had never submitted it to the association for examination and approval.[35]

There is not the slightest hint of hostility toward Edwards in the 1774 action. In fact at that same meeting, the Association appointed him to the Grievance Committee, which was to meet with several members of the Continental Congress over the sensitive issue of religious liberty in New England. This appointment occurred less than one year before Edwards would disavow his loyalty to the English Crown on August 7, 1775. Contrary to some popular thought, Edwards's Toryism did not play a role in the nonacceptance of the plan he proposed for a national union of Baptists.

A PLAN FOR A NATIONAL BODY OF BAPTISTS

Morgan Edwards published his first volume on the history of American Baptists in 1770, and it would be fascinating to learn when it was published--before or after March 9. Recalling his prediction of his death on that date, we must assume the book was published after the ominous date. The book, among other things, was his vehicle to propose a plan for a national body of Baptists, however, others were talking about such a possibility even before Edwards published his plan.

One such leader was Samuel Jones who wrote to James Manning, on September 8, 1767, the occasion of the organization of the Warren Baptist Association.[36]

> For, as particular members are collected together and united in one body, which we call a particular Church to answer those ends and purposes which could not be accomplished by any single member, so a collection and union of churches into one asso-

ciational body may easily be conceived capable of answering those still greater purposes which any particular Church could not be equal to. And, by the same reason, a union of associations will still increase the body in weight and strength and make good that a threefold cord is not easily broken.

While the concept of a national body may not have originated with Edwards, he was the first to develop a plan for its accomplishment. As historian Robert Torbet has said, "In 1770, the Reverend Morgan Edwards, an older man than either Jones or Manning, but also a progressive spirit who was the leading founder of Rhode Island College, actually proposed a plan for such a national union of Baptists."[37] There is little question, however, that not all Baptists were of the same mind.

Baptist leaders in Philadelphia and in the South were not unfriendly to what has been called "a general church view" in contrast to the "local church only view" of New England Baptists. Some Baptists deemed a national organization of their congregations more desirable than the very loose type of associational union in which the local churches enjoyed so much autonomy as to nullify the value of associations with sister churches.

Edwards, on the other hand, believed an association like the Philadelphia Association "recommend such a combination of churches, were there no divine precept or precedent for it."[38] He cited three ways in which an association was beneficial. First, Edwards saw it giving respectability to Baptists in the eyes of other denominations and the civil authorities. This respect was important at a time when Baptists were still subject to persecution by established churches and government agents. Second, he believed the association brought stability to the pastoral ministry among the churches by setting up procedures for licensing, ordaining, and issuing credentials to authorized ministers; practices that would protect the churches from ministerial charlatans. Third, churches could help each other in practical ways, such as a fund to aid in building programs, for legal costs in fighting persecution, or in disputes between church members, and relieving privation caused by some natural or man-made disaster. Beyond these three benefits Edwards saw a more important spiritual reason for an association. He believed an association "introduces into the visible church what are called joints and bands whereby the whole body is knit together and compacted for increase."[39] He was a Baptist who gave equal weight to both the universal church and the local church.

His work in compiling materials for a history of the Baptists was related to his plan for a national body for three reasons. First, his own personal "desire to know the american [sic] Baptists." Second, he had an "equal desire to make them known to one another." Finally, his overall desire "to unite them together and to settle some useful means of intercourse and familiarity beteeen the churches."[40] He then defined his use of the term "union."

Morgan Edwards believed all individual Baptist believers should be united in local churches, and all churches united in associations. He believed there should be an association "in every province" and that they should link together in the Philadelphia Association. His reasons for so designating the Philadelphia Association was its geographic centrality to the provinces, and the fact that it was already performing that function.[41]

The links he envisioned uniting the associations were the sharing of mutual knowledge and advice and the exchange of correspondence and representatives. He noted that such a relationship had already been established among the Ketockton Association in Virginia, the Warren Association in New England, and the Philadelphia Association. Edwards saw his proposed union as already in existence and needing only five more steps for its accomplishment.[42]

First, a legal charter would be obtained for the Philadelphia Association and one delegate elected from each association to form the corporation. The experience of Caleb Evans at Trosnant Academy had taught Edwards the importance of having legal status. Second, a capable preacher would be appointed to travel among the churches as an evangelist. A fund for such a project had already been established in 1766. When the associational leaders appointed Edwards as evangelist in 1771, they were aware that the establishing of the fund in 1766 and the publication of his plan for a national body in 1770 were related to his selection as the associational evangelist in 1771.

Third, the association would have no power or authority over the churches, but would be advisory only. Fourth, all Baptist churches from Nova Scotia to Georgia would be included in the proposed body. The final step was that the principles governing the creation of such a national body would be general enough to include "any baptist church of fair character, though differing from others in unessential points of faith or order. Practicing believer's baptism is our denominating article."[43]

The question now posed is, What became of that plan? To suggest, as some have, that Edwards's plan was rejected because of his Tory leanings is to misread the facts and the chronology of events. The plan was published in his first book in 1770 while he was still pastor the the

Baptist church in Philadelphia. His loyalty to the Crown was well known at the time and he was continually given other responsibilities by the Association, with no hint that his Tory convictions were an issue.

The fact is that Edwards's plan was not supported by others because the time was not right. Edwards himself never lost sight of it, but he led no crusade to implement it. Rather, he would allow time for a favorable climate to be created as Baptists became more understanding of each other through his historical writings.[44] Meanwhile, he would take yet another step to encourage a union of Baptists.

After his resignation from the Philadelphia church, he was appointed the evangelist of the Philadelphia Association. That ministry lasted over a year and required riding horseback over some three thousand miles.[45]

The association leaders were very intentional in their appointment of Edwards. They were aware of the connection between his proposal for a national body and his plan for a twelve-volume history of the Baptists, as well as his desire to see all the churches more closely tied to the Philadelphia Association. As discussed in chapter seven, his appointment appeared assured before it became a fact. Despite these steps, however, the plan never gained momentum during Edwards's lifetime. There is, however, an opinion among Baptist historians which holds that his plan did influence later Baptist organizations.

Dean H. Ashton's study of Morgan Edwards published in 1951, credits him with anticipating the creation of the General Missionary Convention of the Baptist Denomination in the United States of America, for Foreign Missions, formed in 1814,[46] and known as the Triennial Convention.

It is unlikely Edwards would have seen that organization as fulfilling his dream for a national body. It was not a general convention of Baptist churches, but a coalition of persons, churches, and societies devoted at first to foreign missionary work. Ashton may have been right, however, when he said the creation of the Southern Baptist Convention would have been more in accord with Edwards's hopes.

It was toward the end of converting the Philadelphia Association into a general convention of Baptist churches that Edwards ended his proposal by saying, "that I am anxious to render the said combination of baptist churches universal upon this continent. And should God give me success therein, as in the affair of the baptist college [sic], I shall deem myself the happiest man on earth."[47] It is possible to trace an historic connection between Edwards's proposal and the plan for the organization of the Southern Baptist Convention in 1845.

Edwards wrote *Materials Towards a History of the Baptists in the Provinces of Maryland, Virginia, North Carolina, South Carolina, and Georgia* in 1772 from the notes he made on his southern tour. He loaned the material to Richard Furman and it is now in the Baptist Collection at Furman University in Greenville, South Carolina.[48] Though Furman was much younger than Edwards, they knew each other and corresponded. Furman had succeeded Oliver Hart as pastor of the Baptist Church in Charleston in 1787, but Edwards had met the Furman family on his tour during his 1772 visits to the South Carolina Baptist churches.

Richard Furman's father, Wood Furman, settled his family in South Carolina in 1770 at the fork of the Congaree and Wateree rivers, which formed the Santee

River.[49] Because of its elevation, the area was known as High Hills and was settled mostly by Anglican familes, of which the Furmans were one. A Baptist witness began in the area in 1769 with Jeremiah Dargan, who soon left and was replaced by Joseph Reese.

Reese had converted from Anglicanism in 1760 and became an unordained Separate Baptist minister upon his baptism. Separate Baptists were converts during the Great Awakening, but they lacked the New England and Middle Atlantic traditions of Baptists from the British Isles. Their experience of the Christian faith was simple, direct, emotional, and void of liturgical rite or ceremony.

When Reese came to High hills about two months after the return of the Furmans, young Richard attended his meeting and fell under conviction but made no public response. For several months he spent long periods in Bible study and prayer meditating about the whole matter of conversion and believer baptism. When Reese returned, Richard Furman and his mother, both professed faith and were baptized. Their names appear on Morgan Edwards's list of people converted under Reese and making up the membership of the High Hills church.

The Baptist church at High Hills called Furman to the ministry in April of 1772, and he was ordained in May of 1774. In November he was called as pastor of the High Hills Baptist Church where he remained until becoming pastor of the Charleston Church in 1787.[50] Sometime between 1787 and August 1795, Edwards sent the manuscript notes of his history of the Baptists in the South to Furman. These notes now state that the church at High Hills was without a pastor as of August 1795, but Edwards died in January 1795. Thus, Furman had added notes to Edwards's materials, and he became the medium by which Edwards's plan for a general convention of Baptist churches influenced the formation of the Southern Baptist Convention in 1845.

The first convention of the South Carolina Baptists was organized in 1821 and it bore the mark of Richard Furman. He had drawn up a set of constitutional principles in which he held that Baptists should form a voluntary association, centrally organized from the local church to the association, to the state convention to the national level. The constitution adopted by the South Carolina Baptist Convention in 1822 would pass to other state conventions in the South and ultimately be the basic pattern for the Southern Baptist Convention.

Furman believed the associational principle should be extended nationally. This was a break from the society method which had been employed in 1814 for the organization of the Triennial Convention. The idea of extending the associational principle nationally was at the heart of Morgan Edwards' proposal.

Baptist historian H. Leon McBeth has said of Edwards's proposal, "I am fascinated by his proposal for a national body, and I notice that when a national organization came [the Triennial Convention] it was not on that basis, but in the twentieth century the various restructurings we now actually follow more of Morgan Edwards' proposal than many people realize in the interlinking of Baptist associations, state conventions and general bodies."[51]

RHODE ISLAND COLLEGE

Morgan Edwards stated that the creation of a national body of Baptists and his success in creating Rhode Island College would make him the "happiest man on earth."

We turn now to the leadership role in which he left his most enduring mark, the founding of Rhode Island College (now Brown University). That part of the story is so full and dramatic that it requires a chapter of its own.

ENDNOTES

1. James A. Rogers, *Richard Furman, Life and Legacy* (Macon: Mercer University Press, 1985), 170.
2. A.D. Gillette, ed., *Minutes of the Philadelphia Baptist Association from A.D. 1707 to A.D. 1807* (Philadelphia: The American Baptist Historical Society, 1851), 313.
3. David Spencer, *The Early Baptists of Philadelphia* (Philadelphia: William Sychelmore, 1877), 84.
4. William W. Keen, *The Bi-Centennial Celebration of the Founding of the First Baptist Church of Philadelphia, 1898* (Philadelphia: The American Baptist Publication Society, 1899), 45.
5. Rogers, 170.
6. H. Leon McBeth, *The Baptist Heritage* (Nashville: Broadman Press, 1987), 212.
7. Norman H. Maring and Winthrop S. Hudson, *A Baptist Manual of Polity and Practice*, rev. ed (Valley Forge: Judson Press, 1991), 175.
8. Ibid.
9. William L. Lumpkin, *Baptist Confessions of Faith* (Philadelphia: Judson Press, 1959), 349.
10. Ibid., 145.
11. Winthrop S. Hudson, ed., *Baptist Concepts of the Church*. "The Philadelphia Tradition," Robert T. Handy (Philadelphia: The Judson Press, 1959), 30.
12. Ibid., 31.
13. Gillette, 82.
14. Ibid.
15. Ibid., 98.
16. *Southern Baptist and General Intelligencer*, September 9, 1836, 1. Baptist Collection, Furman University, Greenville, South Carolina.
17. Gillette, 86-87.
18. Morgan Edwards, *Materials Towards a History of the Baptists*. (Danielsville, Georgia: Heritage Papers, 1984), Vol. 2, 62.

19. MS Letter from Morgan Edwards to Gardner Thurston, June 28, 1765. Manning Papers. (John Hay Library, Brown University, Providence).
20. Morgan Edwards, *Customs of the Primitive Churches*. n.p. 1774, 4.
21. Gillette, 131.
22. Hudson, 32.
23. Gillette, 60-63
24. Hudson, 33.
25. Oliver Hart, *A Gospel Church Portrayed and Her Orderly Service Pointed Out*. (Trenton: no publisher named, 1791).
26. Hudson, 226.
27. William Cathcart, ed. *The Baptist Encyclopedia*. (Philadelphia: Louis H. Everts, 1881), 505.
28. Rogers, 28.
29. McBeth, 219.
30. Rogers, 39.
31. Reuben A. Guild, *Early History of Brown University, Including the Life, Times, and Correspondence of President Manning*. (Providence: Snow and Farnham, 1897), 288.
32. MS. Letter from Morgan Edwards to Gardner Thurston, November 9, 1764. Manning Papers, (John Hay Library, Brown University, Providence).
33. Norman H. Maring, *Baptists in New Jersey*. (Valley Forge: The Judson Press, 1964), 22.
34. Edwards, 4.
35. Winthrop S. Hudson, *Baptists In Transition; Individualism and Christian Responsibility*. (Valley Forge: Judson Press, 1979), 44.
36. William W. Barnes, *The Southern Baptist Convention, 1845-1953*. (Nashville: Broadman Press, 1954), 2.
37. Robert G. Torbet, *A Social History of the Philadelphia Baptist Association: 1707-1940*. (Philadelphia: Westbrook Book Publishing, 1944). 21.
38. Morgan Edwards, *Materials*. V. 1, 58 ff.
39. Ibid.
40. Ibid., 2.
41. Ibid.
42. Ibid., 2,3.

43. Ibid., 4.
44. Ibid., 2.
45. Morgan Edwards, *Materials Towards a History of the Baptists.* (Philadelphia: Thomas Dolson, 1790), 1.
46. David H. Ashton, "First Historian of American Baptists," *The Chronicle,* XIV, 2., (April 1951), 78.
47. Edwards, *Materials.* V. I, Appendix III, 130.
48. Letter from Alester G. Furman to Mrs. Lorraine Whitehead, September 10, 1951, Baptist Collection, (Furman University, Greenville, South Carolina).
49. Rogers, 11-18.
50. Morgan Edwards, *Materials Towards a History of the Baptists.* (Danielsville, Georgia: Heritage Papers, 1984), V 2, 150.
51. Personal Interview, November 15, 1990, Fort Worth, Texas.

CHAPTER TEN

A PRIME MOVER IN EDUCATION

"The credit of establishing the University [Brown]
in the State belongs to Morgan Edwards."[1]
Samuel Arnold Greene, 1874

Morgan Edwards's Greatest Service

When Morgan Edwards described his role in the founding of Rhode Island College (Brown University), he wrote,

> He laboured hard to settle a baptist college in Rhodeisland [sic] government and to raise money to endow it; which he deems the greatest service he has done or hopes to do for the honour of the baptist interest."[2]

Indeed, William Rogers, Edwards's successor in Philadelphia, reported that Edwards held that conviction until his last days. Rogers further stated, "The College of Rhode Island is also greatly beholden to him."[3] Now, two hundred years after Rogers's tribute, how have historians viewed Edwards's role in the founding of that school? They are almost unanimous in describing him as the primary mover in that accomplishment.

Barnas Sears, the mid-nineteenth century president of Brown University, said in his *Centennial Discourse*, "The

Rev. Morgan Edwards was undoubtedly the first projector of the College."[4] William Cathcart was even more specific in 1881, in his *Baptist Encyclopedia*, when he said, "He was the founder of Brown University, at first called Rhode Island College."[5] In 1885, Horatio Gates Jones stated, "The college which he was the means of founding is now known as Brown University."[6] After lauding the work of James Manning in the start of the Warren Association and Rhode Island College, Baptist historian Thomas Armitage, in 1887, said of Morgan Edwards, "Justice, however, demands as high a tribute to Morgan Edwards as to James Manning, for his zeal and ability in establishing the college."[7]

The most familiar portrayal of Edwards' role, i.e., "prime mover," is from the pen of Reuben A. Guild, longtime librarian of Brown University. He said, "The great enterprise in which Mr. Edwards engaged, and the one with which his name will be forever associated, was the founding of Rhode Island College. In this he appears to have been the prime mover."[8] Two years later, in 1898, A. H. Newman said, "In 1762...members of the Association, under the inspiration of Morgan Edwards, began a plan for the establishment of a Baptist College."[9] The historian of the First Baptist Church in Philadelphia, William W. Keen, who said of Edwards in 1898, "He has been truthfully called the founder of Brown University."[10]

In the twentieth century, Welsh Baptist historian E.K. Jones, in 1902, described Morgan Edwards as "one of the foremost workers on behalf of Brown University."[11] In comparing the roles of Manning, Hezekiah Smith, and Edwards, Henry C. Vedder wrote, "He [Edwards] took hold of the project with his usual ardor, and the success of the project was no less due to him than to Manning and Smith. He was the most influential of the three in

A Dazzling Enigma

enlisting the sympathies of Baptists generally in favor of the college and obtaining funds for its endowment."[12]

An unpublished and undated tribute is found in a paper written by Robert W. Kenny, Professor Emeritus in the Department of English of Brown University, in which he said, "The college had been founded largely through the vision and energy of Morgan Edwards."[13] Famed Baptist historian Robert A. Baker simply stated, "It was his [Edwards'] suggestion in 1762 that led to the establishment of what is now Brown University.'[14]

The only contemporary deviation from the solid historical support for Edwards is found in Katherine W. Johnson's 1975 book, *Rhode Island Baptists,* in which she inferred that Edwards became interested after Manning had started the school. She said of Edwards, "The Reverend Morgan Edwards, pastor of the Philadelphia Baptist Church, became interested in the new college."[15]

As recently as 1984, however, historical accuracy prevailed when McKibbens and Smith wrote of Edwards, "His leadership in the founding of Rhode Island college had earned him a preeminent place in the history of the school."[16] Then, in 1987, H. Leon McBeth stated, "Morgan Edwards...conceived the idea of forming a Baptist college in America."[16] Any review of the sweep of his participation in the founding of the college should include his initial proposal, the charter controversy, his fundraising activity, and his various other efforts on behalf of the college.

The Perceptive Proposal

The Philadelphia Baptist Association was unable to hold its 1762 meeting in the meetinghouse of the Baptist church of that city, as was their usual custom. The building had been razed and a new and larger facility was under construction in its place. Instead they "met at the Lutheran church, in Fifth Street, between Arch street and Race street where the sound of the organ was heard in Baptist worship."[18]

The moderator was Morgan Edwards, only eighteen months in America, and he used that opportunity to put forward a very simple but perceptive proposal. The simplicity of Edwards' proposal was his calling on the Baptists to establish their own college. It was perceptive because it suggested the school be in Rhode Island, with no religious tests for students, and with representatives from other Christian bodies on its board. The proposal came at both the right time and the right place because of the Great Awakening and because of Baptist strength in the government of Rhode Island.

During the seventeenth and early eighteenth centuries, Baptists were not a major Protestant body in America. Beginning at Providence and Newport in the 1630s, they spread throughout New England and southward to the Middle Atlantic and Southern states. By 1740 there were only thirty-six churches in all of New England, and fourteen of these were in Rhode Island. A dozen more could be found in Pennsylvania and New Jersey, but the Great Awakening would change all of that.[20]

The Great Awakening was an extended religious event which profoundly affected the history of America between 1728 and 1776 through a series of spiritual revivals.[21] By 1739, the movement began to coalesce around the ministry of George Whitefield in the middle and southern colonies, and in New England by 1740. Early in the revival it was the Congregationalists, Dutch Reformed and Presbyterians, who were most involved and most directly affected.

The Baptists, on the other hand, stayed on the side

lines in its early stages. It was not until the coming of George Whitefield with his Calvinistic theology that they began to get caught up in it. As it was they gained the most from it. In 1700 there were only 839 members in 24 Baptist churches, but by 1790 they numbered 67,857 in 987 churches.[22] By the end of the eighteenth century they were the largest denomination in America.[23] With this numerical growth came a greater prestige and self-confidence and a desire for a better educated ministry among the Regular Baptist churches.

Among the Separate Baptists, however, the Great Awakening created a pietistic climate in which the emphasis was on one's spiritual call and gifts for ministry, while the importance of classical learning was downplayed. Furthermore, Baptists in general were wary of an educated clergy because numbers of them had suffered persecution at the hands of the educated ministers in the established churches of other denominations. New England Baptist leader, Isaac Backus, expressed Baptist apprehensions in a public debate in 1768 with Joseph Fish, a Congregational minister.[25]

> And the Baptists in general have been so much abused by those who boast of their *Learning,* that it is not strange if many were prejudiced against such men... .

In 1765 or 1766, Backus wrote to a friend in England about the perception people had of Baptists as unlearned people.[26]

> One grand objection made use of against Believer's Baptism, has been that none but ignorant and illiterate men have embraced the Baptist sentiments. And there was so much color for it as this, namely, that ten years ago there were but two Baptist ministers in all New England who had what is called a liberal education; and

they were not clear in the doctrines of grace.

There were schools which Baptists could attend before the founding of Rhode Island College in 1764, but most were controlled by other religious bodies. These included Harvard (1636) and Yale (1701) by the Congregationalists; William and Mary (1693) by the Anglicans; the College of New Jersey (1746, now Princeton University) by the Presbyterians; King's College (1754, now Columbia University) by the Anglicans, and the College of Philadelphia (1755, now the University of Pennsylvania) by the Anglicans. The problem facing Baptists, however, was not the absence of schools but prejudice and proselyting.

In the main, Protestant sectarian tests were not officially applied at the existing colleges in America. Harvard had no tests. Indeed some scholarships which gave preference to Baptist students, were provided by the wealthy English Baptist benefactor, Thomas Hollis. In 1766, the President of Yale was on record that "sons of all Denominations of Protestants are allowed the Advantage of an Education here."[27] The charter of King's College forbade any discrimination in matters of religion, and the College of Philadelphia was open to all. The College of New Jersey granted open entrance in its second charter in 1748. Given the character of human prejudice, however, what public statements proclaim and what private actions produce may be opposites.

Baptists at that time were discriminated against in public life by the Anglicans, Congregationalists, and Presbyterians. This extended to college admissions. Barnas Sears, speaking in the nineteenth century, described the situation at Harvard and Yale at that time.[28]

> Both [Harvard and Yale] were exclusively under the government of the Congregationalists, and wholly devoted to the maintenance and advocacy of their creed and church polity. Both colleges were founded by good men; and nobly have these venerable, and now magnificent, seats of learning answered the purposes of their being. But, by some strange fatality, it was not given to those otherwise excellent men, to recognize, as do their descendants, the good qualities of the Roger Williams Baptists. At any rate, they did not extend to this class of men a very cordial welcome, but treated them as disorderly brethren, if not heretics.

The more visible problem, however, was the proselyting of Baptist students and their subsequent loss to the Baptist ministry. Isaac Backus addressed this issue in his 1768 public debate with Joseph Fish cited above.

> Several [Separatists] who have formerly sent their sons to college have been disappointed, as the clergy have found means to draw them over to their party; which has discouraged others from sending their sons."

Indeed, even Ezra Stiles acknowledged the existence of such conversions in relating the story of George Wheaton. He was from a Baptist family in Norton, Massachusetts, and went to Harvard in 1765. After graduation, he became a Congregationalist minister.[29] In light of such prejudice and proselyting, Morgan Edwards called on Baptists to go beyond the preparatory school level of the Hopewell Academy to create their own college.

The Baptists who crossed the Atlantic Ocean from the British Isles brought with them a commitment to academies. The first established by Baptists in America was at Hopewell, New Jersey, in 1756, by the pastor, Isaac Eaton. He became pastor of the Hopewell church in April 1748, and was ordained the following November. It was his only pastorate, and he died July 4, 1772, at forty-seven years of age. Eaton founded the academy to train young men for the ministry, and because he was a very learned man he was well suited for the task.[30]

Morgan Edwards described the subject matter of the classes at the Hopewell Academy as "the first rudiments of learning,"[31] and several of its graduates became doctors and lawyers as well as clergymen. The Philadelphia Association raised four hundred pounds for the school, and appointed a general oversight committee.

The Hopewell Academy never developed beyond the preparatory level and closed in 1767, with the endowment money put into a general education fund.[32] Though the school was short-lived several of its graduates rose to leadership roles in American Baptist church life. Among these was James Manning, who became the first president of Rhode Island College and the on-site developer of the school.

Edwards's proposal had within it the discerning stroke of establishing the college in Rhode Island. At that time charters for colleges were seen as "monopoly grants by those who held them."[33] The Congregationalists had a lock on Massachusetts and Connecticut with Harvard and Yale respectively. The Anglicans had preempted New York and Virginia with Kings College, and William and Mary. New Jersey was Presbyterian territory, and Pennsylvania was occupied by the Anglicans. None of these groups would have tolerated a rival, least of all the Baptists, and the Baptists eventually faced the same issue in Rhode Island.

When there was a threat that the Baptists in the Newport area might apply for a charter for a second college and thus threaten the charter of Rhode Island College, a protest was lodged with the Assembly. The board of Rhode Island College protested in May 1770.[34]

> That, the granting of our charter, being for erecting and endowing a College in the Colony of Rhode Island, must, rational and justly, be considered as exclusive of any other college being erected therein.

Morgan Edwards was astute enough to realize the best place for Baptists to obtain a college charter was in Rhode Island for four very good reasons: One, the province had been founded by Baptists; second, they had created a climate of religious freedom in the colony; third, the Baptists controlled the Provincial Assembly; and fourth, there was no other college in the province. Edwards was candid as to why Rhode Island was his choice.[35]

> The reason of his attempt in this province was (as has been observed) that the legislature is here chiefly in the hands of the baptists [sic], and therefore the likeliest place to have a baptist college established by law.

Edwards's focus on Rhode Island is made clearer in his later brief history of Rhode Island.[36] He described it as "the Land of the Baptists," and stated why. First, they were the first people to settle at Providence, beginning with Roger Williams and Thomas Olney. Second, the Baptists have remained "more numerous than any other sect of Christians which dwell therein." Third, "the baptists in this government have always had much power in their hands," including the executive, legislative, and judicial branches. The fourth reason he gave is "that their college is a baptist college." He explained that the Baptists alone began the school, paid for it, and gathered the money for its endowment, though each of the last two claims may be a bit of an overstatement.

As discussed earlier, Edwards was at Trosnant Academy in Wales when Caleb Evans was summoned before an Anglican bishop for operating an illegal school. Though it came to nothing, that action did convince Edwards of the importance of a legally chartered school. Furthermore, while they might have sought a charter in another province through a long, drawn-out legal process, Rhode Island offered a pathway with fewer obstacles. There were, however, some hurdles to be leaped over at that 1762 associational meeting.

Edwards's proposal was greeted with guffaws of disbelief, howls of hostility, yawns of apathy, and nods of approval.[37] The laughter was heard from those who saw the idea as totally impractical. In their minds the Baptists did not have enough money for such a project, and they were no doubt right. As one historian stated, "Poverty was probably the basic reason for the Baptists' failure to found a college sooner."[38] Edwards was to find out how poor the Baptists were when he sought to raise money for the school.

The reality is that the Baptists of New England never did support the school alone, but Edwards had a higher view. He believed the unique circumstances accompanying the founding of Rhode Island College "infer the interposition of Providence, and bespeak it to be a thing of God and not of man only."[39]

Many at the association meeting on that fall day in 1762 voiced outright opposition to establishing a school of higher learning. They vowed to strive against it because they were opposed to an educated ministry. Still others neither supported it nor opposed it. Fortunately there were enough to approve it, and to send James Manning to Rhode Island to begin the process of starting the college.

Standing with Morgan Edwards were such strong leaders as Samuel Jones, Isaac Sutton, Abel Morgan, John

Gano, Isaac Eaton, Hezekiah Smith, and others. Isaac Backus reported what resulted from some men from the Philadelphia Association having travelled through New England.[40]

> ...obtained such an acquaintance with our affairs, as to bring them to an apprehension that it was practicable and expedient to erect a college in the colony of Rhode Island, under the chief direction of the Baptists, wherein education might be promoted, and superior learning obtained, free from any sectarian religious tests. Mr. James Manning, who took his first degree in New Jersey College in September, 1762, was esteemed a suitable leader in this important work.

James Manning was born in Piscataway, New Jersey, on October 22, 1738. His father James, a prosperous farmer, and his mother Grace reared their seven children by Christian principles. Young James became "an accomplished reader, an excellent penman and a good speller,"[41] and at eighteen entered Hopewell Academy as its first pupil. After two years under the influence of Isaac Eaton, he professed faith in Jesus Christ. His baptism took place at the Scotch Plains Baptist Church before he entered the College of New Jersey at twenty-two years of age.

At the Presbyterian college, Manning excelled in rhetoric, eloquence, moral philosophy, and the classics, in addition to maintaining an athletic discipline. He has been desribed as "remarkable for his dexterity in athletic exercises, for the symmetry of his body, and gracefulness of his person."[42] Even though a large man of up to three hundred pounds, he was portrayed as "easy and graceful in his motions and gestures."[43] Manning graduated with second honors in his class of twenty-one on September 29, 1762, two weeks before Edwards presented his proposal to found a Baptist college.

On February 6, 1763, Manning was licensed to preach by the Scotch Plains Baptist Church, and on March 23, married Margaret Stites, the daughter of John Stites, a prominent Baptist layman. John Stites was a wealthy farmer and land owner who supported Edwards's proposal for the college. Margaret did not make a public profession of faith until twelve years later during a revival in which her husband was the evangelist.

Another major event in Manning's life during that busy year following his graduation was his ordination on April 19, 1763. Some have questioned why Manning did not arrive in Rhode Island until July 1763, nine months after his appointment.[44] The delay is understandable given the time required to prepare for the mission, his marriage, his ordination, and the travel time involved.

The Controversy Over The Charter
The process of obtaining the charter for the college was mired in controversy. Edwards was important in this process because he recorded the narratives of it by James Manning and Daniel Jenckes, his sharply worded observations reveal the tensions involved, and because of the judgments of others on his observations. It should not be forgotten that Edwards, Manning, and Ezra Stiles remained friends during this entire period.

The minutes of the Philadelphia Baptist Association meeting of 1762 contain no record approving the establishment of a college, but approval is implied in the dispatch of Manning to Rhode Island. Nor is there a record of where in Rhode Island the college was to be established, but Newport is implied by Manning meeting with the Baptists of that city in July 1763. At first glance, that appeared to be a sagacious move on the part of the Baptists because Newport was "one of the most wealthy and sophisticated cities in colonial America."[45]

Newport's wealth came from its ships, which captured rich prizes from the enemies of England. Further, a lucrative trade flourished between New England and the West Indies in rum, slaves, and molasses, and a still broader trade with the mother country and the nations bordering the Mediterranean Sea.

Newport's wealthy merchants had created a cosmopolitan atmosphere in the city. Added to the native born were people from the Indies, Ireland, Scotland, Germany, France, and Jews from Spain and Portugal.[46] All gave Newport an ambience of comfort, elegance, and sophistication. One would not expect to find too many Baptists in such an environment, but there were three Baptist churches in the city.

Newport was also the first choice for the site of the new college because the First Baptist Church in Providence was officially a Six-Principle Baptist Church (General Baptist) while the Philadelphia Association was Particular Baptist. In addition the Providence church was weak and subject to frequent theological disputes.[47]

Edwards recorded Manning's version of the charter dispute which began in the summer of 1763 over the college charter. In June of that year, Oliver Hart extended a call to James Manning to be his assistant at the Baptist church in Charleston, South Carolina, but the call was declined.[48] Soon after, Manning and his wife set sail for Halifax, accompanied by John Sutton, a minister and a member of the Scotch Plains church. Sutton had been to Nova Scotia several years earlier on a preaching mission where he baptized a number of converts.[49] He and Manning were to deliver a letter from a Reverend Simpson, answering a call from the people of Halifax.[50] En route the ship called at Newport, Rhode Island.

In Newport, Manning convened a meeting of fifteen Baptists at the home of Deputy Governor John Gardner to present the proposal for the college. Manning was asked to draft a rough plan for a meeting the next day.

Other Baptists joined in the second meeting, when Manning presented his rough draft for "the institution was to be a baptist one; but that as many of other denominations should be in as was consistent with the said design."[51] The design was approved, and lawyers Josias Lyndon and Job Bennet, were appointed to prepare a charter for the next General Assembly. However, at that point, a problem developed.

Both Lyndon and Bennet pleaded inadequate skills for the assignment and suggested that Ezra Stiles be asked to help them. Manning objected to annoying Congregationalist Stiles with Baptist business. The two lawyers assured the others that Stiles had a great love of learning and a generous ecumenical spirit, and would be glad to help. With that incentive the proposal was approved.

Stiles did help or, as Manning put it, "the draughting of the charter was left entirely to him, after being told that the baptists were to have the lead in the institution and the government thereof forever."[52] The numbers from the other denominations were to be "consistent with that." When Stiles finished his work a third meeting was set to review his plan, but there was a problem.

On the day of the meeting with Stiles, Manning's ship was scheduled to sail for Halifax, so it was a hurried session. As Manning heard Stiles's proposed charter, it read "the corporation was made to consist of two branches, trustees and fellows, and those branches to sit and act by distinct and separate powers, it was not easy to determine by a transient hearing what those powers might be."[53] There were to be thirty-five trustees, nineteen of whom

A Dazzling Enigma 245

were to be Baptists. That sounded good to the Baptists, but Manning believed the fellows, with a Congregationalist majority, had been vested with too much authority.[54] Despite Manning's misgivings, the group voted to present their petition and the proposed charter to the Assembly.

When the petition and charter were read before the Assembly in August, 1763, many were ready to quickly enact it into law. Some objected, however, and the most vocal of these was a Baptist lawyer from Providence named Daniel Jenckes. He asked the governor (who was also a Baptist) for permission to make a more thorough reading of the document during the noon dinner break. Against the wishes of some, permission was granted.

After dinner Jenckes took Governor Lyndon aside to ask which denomination would have control of the college, and he was assured the Baptists would. With that Jenckes indicated to the governor that the charter had been so "artfully constructed" that eight of the twelve fellows would be Congregationalists, and there was nothing in the charter to prevent the other four from also being Congregationalists.

The Governor met with Stiles and asked why "he had perverted the design of the charter." Manning reported his answer as, "I gave you timely warning to take care of yourselves, for that we have done so with regard to our society." He did not see himself as a culprit because he had warned the Baptists of his intentions. In Manning's eyes, Stiles's design would put control of the college under the Board of Fellows with a Congregationalist majority.[55]

When the Assembly reconvened, Jenckes managed to delay the charter issue until the next session to give the Baptists time to redesign it according to their original intentions. The delay would also allow time to update

Baptists in other parts of the province. To facilitate this Jenckes asked for and received permission to distribute the copy of the charter to Baptists around the colony for reading and study.

In the meantime, the Philadelphia Association was notified of the Assembly's action. They sent Samuel Jones, pastor of the Pennypeck church in Pennsylvania, and lawyer Robert Strettle Jones to Newport to assist the Rhode Island Baptists.[56] In Newport they joined Newport physician Dr. Thomas Eyres and the members of the committee to draft a revised charter and petition.

When completed these were filed with the provincial government. The new charter equalized the number of Baptists on the Board of Fellows, with the Congregationalists. The office of president was permanently placed in the hands of the Baptists, and five Baptists were added to the Board of Trustees, and the number of Anglicans and Congregationalists in the corporation was equalized.

At the end of Manning's report Morgan Edwards paused in his writing to insert a personal comment. He said, "Thus the Baptists narrowly escaped being jockied out of their college by a set of men in whom they reposed entire confidence. How that same party in general have acted since, will appear hereafter."[57] Though it repeats much of Manning's account, Edwards recorded Jenckes's account.

Judge Daniel Jenckes, Chief Justice of the Inferior Court of Common Pleas for the County of Providence, represented the city of Providence in the General Assembly for thirty years. He was an original trustee of the college. At the Assembly meeting in August 1763, when Stiles's original plan was presented, Jenckes had been requested by Captain William Rogers to sign it. Rogers was a Baptist, a merchant in the city of Newport, and the father of William Rogers, first graduate of Rhode Island College and Morgan Edwards's successor as pastor of the Baptist church in Philadelphia.

Before Jenckes could study the documents, the speaker called for action by the Assembly. Jenckes opposed any action and was able to obtain a delay. He informed both Governor Lyndon and Colonel Bennet of what appeared to be a deception in the proposed charter. It took some convincing since Ezra Stiles was held in high honor. As they read the proposal, however, they agreed with Jenckes. Of their conversation, Jenckes said, "What reflections followed may be better concealed than published."

They managed a postponement until the next session in spite of the efforts of the Congregationalists in the Assembly to act on it. Jenckes was given permission to hold the charter, on his promise to deliver it to the next session of the Assembly. He carried the charter back to Providence, from whence it was circulated among Rhode Island Baptists. Meanwhile, Samuel Jones and Robert Strettle Jones from the Philadelphia Association arrived in Newport, and when search was made for the charter it could not be found.

When the Assembly reconvened in October 1763, a second charter was presented, which was criticized and opposed by those who wanted the previous one. When demand was made for the first charter Jenckes explained what had happened, but the Congregationalists charged him with deception and a heated altercation broke out. The Baptists tried diligently to locate the missing charter, but it was nowhere to be found. For the sake of peace they voted to table the matter until the next session which would meet in February 1764.

At the February session, the acrimonious dispute was

renewed. Following "much and warm debate," the charter was approved by a solid majority. After that episode, Morgan Edwards described the charter as "a brand plucked from the burning."[58] At the eye of the storm over the charter was Ezra Stiles, a man of impeccable moral reputation and great learning.

Few men in eighteenth century America were more respected and trusted than Ezra Stiles, and that is why the Baptists entrusted him with the writing of the charter for their college. He was born at North-Haven, Connecticut, on November 29, 1727, graduated from Yale College in 1746, and by 1749 was a tutor at his alma mater. In 1755 he became pastor of the Second Congregational Church at Newport, Rhode Island, and remained in that position until 1776, when he fled to New Hampshire because of the Revolutionary War.

Stiles was installed as president of Yale in 1778, and for the rest of his life served that institution as its head. He was not only a profound theological scholar but also well versed in a number of scientific fields. The breadth and depth of his learning gave him a preeminent place in the ecclesiastical and academic arenas of early America.

Stiles' name was synonymous with ability and integrity, and despite the dispute over the charter he remained friends with both James Manning and Morgan Edwards.[59] But, Stiles's own words seem to confirm an attempt to piggy-back his dream of a college on the shoulders of the Baptists' efforts to found a school.

When Ezra Stiles responded to Governor Lyndon by saying, "I gave you timely warning to take care of yourselves, for that we have done so with regard to our society,"[61] he was telling the Baptists, "You put in what you want done in regard to the role you want Baptists to play in this college."

A Dazzling Enigma 249

The Baptists, however, simply surrendered the entire project to Stiles, assuming he understood their intendions. The end product put the Baptists in control of the physical and fiscal operations of the school through the trustees, and the Congregationalists in control of academic operations. Stiles's statement to the Governor shows he was not trying to hoodwink the Baptists, but it should have been an indication to them that he would do what he thought was right.

On the other hand, Stiles seemed to harbor the common perception that Baptist ministers were an ignorant and unlearned lot. This is implied in a letter he wrote August 26, 1768.[62]

> We had lately a catholic plan for a College in Rhode Island, but it turned out Supremacy & Monopoly in the hands of the Baptists, whose Influence in our Assembly was such that they obtained a most ample Charter to their purpose....However I heartily wish the College prosperity, as it is the only Means of introducing Learning among our protestant Brethren the Baptists, I mean among their Ministers.

From the foregoing it appears the Baptists were not specific enough in what it was they wanted Stiles to do. It is also apparent he believed the Congregationalists were better suited to control the academic life of the new college. The unfortunate part of the drama was that Manning could not remain in Newport to work with Stiles and Ellery. Morgan Edwards did rightly perceive that they would have been "jockied out of their college," but the Baptists should not have left the whole task to Stiles. When the lost copy of the charter was found in the nineteenth century, Stiles's view was clearer.

One hundred years after the charter was granted, the missing copy from the August 1763 session of the General Assembly was found among old papers at the Second Congregational Church of Newport, Rhode Island. Also found was a memorandum of Stiles's record of the events.[63]

> A Charter draughted by a committee of Baptists and Presbyterians [Congregationalists], for a College in Rhode Island, was preferred to the Assembly, August, 1763, read and continued. After this the Baptists deserted the Presbyterians, and prepared the same Charter, with the alteration of the proportions of the denominations in the Corporation. This passed the Assembly at their session at Greenwich, by adjournment last Thursday, February, 1764.

This terse summary of the events confirms those of Manning and Jenckes as recorded by Edwards. It also cleared Jenckes of the false charges of deception lodged against him by some Congregationalists in the Assembly. How it ended up in Stiles's hands is not known. His comments are written on the back of that charter and they reveal his reactions to the steps the Baptists took to protect their original intentions.

Stiles's remarks were addressed to the Rev. Dr. Charles Chauncy of Boston; three of the four remarks are relevant.[64]

> 2. The Baptists have shown a greater affection for all other denominations than for the Congregationalists.
> 3. Instead of eight or a majority of Congregationalists in the branch of the Fellowship, according to the original agreement, they have inserted eight Baptists; thus assuming a majority of two-thirds in both branches, hereby absorbing the whole power and government of the College, and thus by the immutability of the numbers, establishing it a party College more explicitly and effectually than any college upon the continent. This is the most material alteration.
> 4. Most of what is contained between the original crotchets in

A Dazzling Enigma 251

page six is omitted; and the whole paragraph for securing the freedom of education with respect to religion, so mutilated as effectually to enable and empower the Baptists to practice the arts of insinuation and proselyting upon the youth by private instruction, without the request of the parents.

Stiles acknowledged that the one alteration which materially affected his design was the change in denominational representation cited above.

Another problem with the Stiles's plan was that there were no Baptists on the boards from outside of Rhode Island, thus cutting off all representation from the Philadelphia Association, including Morgan Edwards. The Baptists did not want the Congregationalists to control the college's destiny and they revised the charter accordingly. They maintained their original intention to have multidenominational representation on the governing boards of the college, but the majority were to be Baptists.

The continuing Congregational hostility to the college after 1764, is described in a letter from Manning to John Ryland in Northhampton, England dated June 1, 1771.[65]

> The Institution calls for the vigorous Exertions of all its friends with on Account of the smallness of its Funds; as the unreasonable Opposition made against it by Paedobaptists; especially the New Light Presbyterians [Congregationalists] in general, who express the greatest Bitterness on every occasion.

One last word must be said about Morgan Edwards's act of publishing the Manning and Jenckes's accounts of the controversy. David Howell was the first tutor of the college and a classmate of Manning's at Hopewell and Princeton. He later became a judge and a member of Congress. In a letter to Isaac Backus, he cautioned him against putting an account of the controversy in his impending publication of his history of the Baptists.⁶⁶

> I think what is taken from Mr. Edwards' Book about the Quarrel in geting [sic] the Charter ought to be buried in oblivion if ever we wish to engage the Presbyterians [Congregationalists] in the Interest of the College & in it [is] nothing to our honor or advantage but rather disgraceful to Mr. Manning, and altogether respects the Conduct Surmises Suspicions, & c. of Individuals whom it is not in our Interest to offend for nothing....I would by no means have Mr. Mannings & Mr. Jenckes injudicious ill-natured reflections in your History.

Because Backus was a historian, he did not follow Howell's advice in either the 1784 or 1796 volumes of his history. Furthermore, Howell seemed not to perceive Manning's efforts to put the whole business behind him, and as the letter demonstrates, the Congregationalists were not yet ready to let bygones be bygones.

In a letter to James Manning, Morgan Edwards reviewed the history of Congregational opposition. While Manning was trying to win their support for the college, the New England Baptists had pubished complaints in the newspapers about the ill-treatment of Baptists by the Standing Order (Congregationalists). The letter is vintage Morgan Edwards.⁶⁷

> I should not have thus ventured to oppose my opinion to yours had not the facts, recent facts, decided the matter in my favor, and shown that the goodness and candor of the President have imposed on his judgment. Remember you not the first charter? While the baptist college was yet in embryo, they very disingenuously opposed it, though courted again and again to accept even a fellowship therein, and when the present charter was presented to the Assembly, at South Kingston, remember you not what clamor they raised against it there? and what stout opposition they made to the passing of it, insomuch that its friends thought it best to desist? and how they triumphed afterwards? And when the af-

A Dazzling Enigma 253

fair was brought on again at East Greenwich, the next session, you can never forget with what heat and coarse expressions the same oppositions were renewed; nor the mortification and murmurings which the passing of it occasioned.

It is true, while the charter lay dormant they remained easy, and (as you say) appeared well pleased when you had set it on foot at Warren. But the reason of that is obvious; they knew that while the college stood friendless and moneyless, (as it then did) they should have the pleasure to see it fall, and to mock them who began to build a tower and were not able to finish it. But seemed they good humored when the money came thither from Europe? Or did they not look as the man of Bristol did at your first commencement; and put the same invidious construction upon everything that he did on the complaisance you showed him that day?

Their good affection towards the college edifice was but varnish; for while with specious arguments they would have it here, and anon there, and then in another place, they were only working to prevent its being anywhere; and as it had a locality, and the beginning of existence at Providence, did they not (with some misled baptists) attempt to get another college to destroy ours? and actually carried their design through the lower house. This also failing, what remains but to prevent youth from resorting to it?

Their slandering the officers of instruction, as insufficient, the town where it is as a lawless place; the college as wanting government, their representing it as a nest of anti-pedobaptists calculated to make proselytes; their visiting grammar schools and tampering with masters and parents; their scolding Presbyterian [Congregational] youth when they enter with you (as your neighbor Rowley did, who is capable of nothing but what is gross and indelicate); their refusing to pay their subscriptions, etc., are all intended to hurt what they could neither prevent nor destroy.

Think you that their present opposition to the college is the effect of those newspaper complaints and threatnings of Presbyterian [Congregational] opposition in New England? Why then did they oppose it before those complaints and threatnings had existence? Think you that they will be friends should we desist from those complaints and court their favor? It cannot except God should once teach them to love their neighbors as themselves, and do as

they should be done by.
Destroying the Baptist college will pacify them, and nothing else; the existence of that on the hill of Providence is a Mordecai in the gate. I told you long ago that if you could not do without the Presbyterians [Congregationalists], you could not do it at all. I need not inform you that while I deal in generals I expect the honest, the trusty, and the good; and some such Presbyterians [Congregationalists] I met in their connexions with this college. God send us more such and mend the rest.

The letter was written shortly after the college moved from Warren to Providence. Edwards has been accused of referring to Ezra Stiles as a trickster who tried to cheat the Baptists out of their school when he said, "...the Baptists narrowly escaped being jockied out of their college."[68]

There is no direct evidence that Edwards meant Stiles personally in that remark, and he used only one person's name (Rowley) in the letter. He did, however, write positively about those Congregationalists who wished the best for the college and supported it. Indeed, at the time he wrote the letter (1771), he was on the best of terms with Stiles, preaching in his church and sharing confidences with him.

There is no known original source where either Edwards, Jenckes, or Manning spoke in a negative manner about Stiles. In fact Stiles was listed on the original charter as an incorporator and fellow of the school, but on September 3, 1766, he wrote to the corporation to decline the offer to serve because he did not wish to offend his fellow Congregational ministers.[69] The two Congregational leaders who are referred to most often as hostile are William Ellery of Newport and Rev. Charles Chauncy of Boston. Chauncy was a Congregational leader in New England and was the focal point for oppressive

A Dazzling Enigma

actions against Baptists.[70]

It is noteworthy that only twelve Baptist ministers graduated from Rhode Island College between 1764 and 1791, whereas twenty-six Congregational ministers did.[71]

To conclude the matter of the charter controversy, it is enough to say that one's opinion about it depends on whether one views it through Congregational or Baptist lenses. The tenor of the times was such that the best of intentions could be misread. Such seems to be true for both factions in the controversy.

The Congregationalists, were accustomed to controlling such decision-making in the politics of New England, but could not do so in Rhode Island. The frustration may have distorted their perceptions. The Baptists were buffeted in other parts of New England, so their perceptions may have been clouded by a tint of paranoia when they had the opportunity to control their own destiny.

Morgan Edwards's role in the charter controversy is not as visible as that of Stiles, Jenckes, or Manning. His importance lies in the historical records he has provided and his straightforward counsel to James Manning. As a result of his candor, Edwards's reputation has suffered.

The Trip to Europe to Raise Funds

After the charter had been granted in February 1764, Morgan Edwards reported that it "lay dormant for about two years, except that some nominated in it, did qualify themselves in order to become a corporation; and did open a subscription among themselves and choose Rev. James Manning to be President."[72] Instruction began in September 1766, but several events transpired before tutoring began at Warren, Rhode Island.

Warren was located about ten miles southeast of Providence, and there were in the town fifty-six persons who were Baptists. Of these, twenty-four had migrated from Swansea, Massachusetts, and had begun the church in Warren by 1762. The original church at Swansea traced its origins to the first Particular Baptist church in Wales, founded in 1649 at Ilston by John Miles. By 1763 the Warren Baptists had erected a meeting house, and ministers would occasionally visit the town to preach and baptize converts.

Warren's representatives in the Provincial Assembly were Baptists, and when the charter was approved in February 1764, the congregation must have sensed the opportunity to call a pastor. On February 17, 1764, a pulpit committee wrote to Manning inviting him to become pastor.[73] James Manning accepted the call, and with his wife arrived in Warren on Saturday, April 21, 1764. A church was formally organized on November 15, 1764, with the original twenty-six members from the Swansea church being dismissed to join. Thus by 1765, Manning, twenty-seven years old, was the first pastor of a new church with an ancestry of one hundred and sixteen years, and the first president of a newly founded college that was yet to open.

As soon as Manning was settled in Warren, he began a Latin School which would channel students into the college. The school was eminently successful and, in the nineteenth century, became the University Grammar School. The first meeting of the corporation was held in Newport on the first Wednesday of November in 1764, when organizational matters were cared for, and arrangements made to handle money. At the second corporation meeting in 1765. also at Newport, Manning was elected President, "with full power to act immediately...at Warren, or elsewhere."[74] The members of the Corporation, Fellows and Trustees alike, pledged nineteen hundred and ninety-two pounds for building and endowing the school.[75] But the need for greater sums of money was evident if the college were to move from a dream to a reality.

At the same meeting, two other actions were taken to strengthen the finances of the school. Subscription books were distributed to the corporation members so that they in turn might induce others to pledge money to the college and Jeremiah Condy was appointed to travel to Europe to raise money there.[76]

Condy was pastor of the First Baptist Church in Boston and had opposed Whitefield when he preached there in 1740. In 1743 a group of his members broke with him to form the Second Baptist Church because they regarded him as too cold and formal.[77] Since Condy was one of two New England Baptist ministers with a liberal education, some assumed he would be president of the new school.[78] He was not, of course, and neither was he destined to make the trip to Europe.

There were several reasons why Condy was not elected president and why he declined to make the trip to Europe. A Congregationalist minister named Andrew Eliot offers an explanation.[79]

> It was supposed Mr. Condy, a Baptist minister of great candor, learning and ingenuity would be the first President. He would have been an honor to that or any other seminary. Mr. Condy did not approve the alteration that was made to the plan and the charter.... When he saw that he could do no good, he silently withdrew as did all the Presbyterian or Congregational ministers, who had been nominated to be Trustees.

Condy attended only the Corporation meeting in 1765 after retiring from his Boston pastorate in 1764, and then resigned from the Board of Fellows. Furthermore, Condy was a General Baptist and General Baptists were fading more and more into obscurity, not only with the college but also in Baptist life as a whole. He was replaced at the Boston church by Samuel Stillman, a Particular Baptist and a close friend of Edwards's and Manning's. A letter from Oliver Hart to Samuel Jones on December 1, 1763, reveals that he too was ready to make the trip.[80]

> And I hope with you, that all the Baptists on the Continent will work in promoting so laudable a design. I had some thought of paying a visit to my native land next Spring, but am advised by many, rather to go to London; as yet I am undetermined, but suppose I should go, do you think I could thereby serve the new college? You might speak to Mr. Edwards of Philada. on this stead, and let me know your thoughts as soon as you can.

As it was, however, Edwards thought Condy a good choice. On November 9, 1764, Edwards wrote to Gardner Thurston in Newport, "Their choice of Mr. Condy to go to great [sic] Britain pleases me much." So neither Condy's theology or his patronizing attitude to his less educated fellow Baptists affected Edwards's respect for the learned Condy.

Nonetheless, Edwards told Thurston in that same letter, that the visit ought to be delayed for a couple of years to allow time to develop support for the school in America.[81] He thought the fund-raising ground in England had been overworked in 1763 by the Anglicans for their colleges in New York and Philadelphia. In addition, large sums had been raised earlier for Harvard and the College of New Jersey.

Edwards then suggested that a waiting period might be profitably used. He proposed that at least three grammar schools (academies) be established in Rhode Island, ostensibly to feed Baptist students into the college. He also proposed that a solicitation be made first in America, and then a "crie for help to our mother country."[82] He said the emissary for the college should take two items with him. First, letters from several denominations and "half a dozen diplomas," to grant honorary degrees. In Edwards's mind the school's authority to grant such degrees would be highly regarded in England and Ireland and would cost the school nothing while creating much goodwill.

Following Condy's selection for the trip in September 1764, Edwards assumed he would leave as soon as possible. Hence, at the 1764 meeting of the Philadelphia Asssociation, he tried without success to get the association to write the Particular Baptist Fund Board in London and outline the design for the college. In this way Morgan thought they could make the most of a "bad market."

The association assigned the matter to a committee. Edwards drew up the letter, but was unable to get it signed for the association. He seemed, however, to have developed a sense of what the school needed financially to succeed as he stated in a letter to Thurston dated, June 28, 1765.[83]

> When the subscription books come I shall do that in me lies to have them filled___If we can raise 2000 pounds between America and Europe we shall set our institution agoing___The interest of one will pay a master___the interest of the other will pay the expensions of two students for the ministry, who shall be able at the time to pay for their education, but may be able afterwards to do which they shall stand bound.

James Manning had a similar appraisal. He shared it in a letter to Samuel Stennett in London.[84]

> The Beneficence of the Baptists here, their fortunes considered

is almost unparalleled. I would rejoice to find many also were like-minded. We should then soon see it properly endowed, as well as founded, this we must expect from abroad; and added to the Sum collected by Mr. Edwards in Europe, our Brother Hezekiah Smith of haverhill [sic] has collected & obtained Subscriptions in South Carolina and Georgia, from whence he has just returned, to the amount of about 500 sterling.

Meantime, Edwards had developed his own plan for soliciting money in America. When he approached a person for a pledge, he took someone with him to attest to the signature on the commitment. In 1769, for example, he and Isaac Duncan met with Samuel Jones, who pledged sixty pounds to the school. Jones completed payment by October 25, 1771.[85] Edwards's most demanding commitment, however, was his own offer to go to the British Isles.

At some point after his 1765 letter to Thurston, Morgan Edwards made the decision to offer himself to the college for the trip to the British Isles. There can be little question that he believed himself most qualified for the task because of his close connection with Baptist leaders in Great Britain, his wide connections with pastors of other denominations, and his recently acquired relationships with leading Philadelphians then in London, such as Benjamin Franklin, Thomas Penn, and Benjamin West. Thus, on November 20, 1766, at a special meeting, the Corporation approved the appointment of Edwards.[86]

> Voted That Rev. Morgan Edwards be requested and duly authoriz'd to go to Europe & solicit Benefactions for this Insititution & that the Thanks of this Corporation be returned Him for his generous offers.

The authorization also reflected the confidence of the board in Edwards.[87]

A Dazzling Enigma   261

And whereas, the Corporation of said College or University, reposing special trust and confidence in your abilities and integrity, and convinced of your disinterested zeal and ardor in promoting and completing the design of the General Assembly, did at their meeting held by authority of, and agreeable to their charter, at Newport, in the said Colony, on the day of the date hereof (Nov. 20, 1766) unanimously resolve, that you, the aforesaid Morgan Edwards, should be requested to proceed with all convenient speed to Europe to solicit and receive donations for the aforesaid purpose:

So, on February 16, 1767, Morgan Edwards left his family and sailed down the Delaware River from Philadelphia on a mission which was to put a solid fiscal foundation under the new college. His own assessment of that mission was that he, "succeeded pretty well considering how angry the mother country then was with the colonies for opposing the stamp act."[88] Edwards's mission was sharply focused, well planned and broadly based.

The focus of the mission was to raise money to be placed in an endowment fund from which the president's salary was to be paid. There was, at that time, no fund for the president's salary, and by 1769, the school was in arrears to him. As a result he was experiencing considerable privation because his salary from the church at Warren was inadequate.[89] Edwards carried with him a signed certificate stating the single purpose of the funding campaign.[90] The action to so direct the funds had been approved on July 6, 1768, by the committee appointed to transact business between corporation meetings for the college. Printed certificates were prepared and sent to Great Britain to the donors.[91]

Not only did Morgan Edwards keep his mission sharply focused, but he planned it well. He operated in the areas of his strength. First he approached leaders of both the

Particular and General Baptists among whom he had a positive reputation. Second, he carried letters of endorsement from the leaders of other denominations in America to their leaders in the British Isles. Third, he visited prominent people from Philadelphia who were then in England, and fourth, he called in places where he had many acquaintances, such as Cork, Ireland.

In each solicitation, Edwards presented his credentials, the college charter, and the design. He first visited an assembly of General Baptists who gave him an official endorsement.[92] Two days later, on May 27, 1768, Edwards was able to add another endorsement from major Particular Baptist leaders.[93]

One of the very useful pieces of literature Edwards carried with him was a printed booklet consisting of two parts. The first part contained the act of the General Assembly of Rhode Island by which the college was established, and the second part was a report entitled, "The State of the College in Rhode Island." In it is presented a brief history of the college, the number of members on its governing boards, and their multidenominational character, the liberal and catholic character of the student body, a financial report on the building fund and operating expenses, an update on the Edwards campaign, and notice that a printed list of all subscribers would be made available.[94]

All of Edwards' efforts in fund raising were carried out in a first-class manner, and the printed lists were distributed to the donors "to let every one of them see that I gave true credit for what I have received."[95] Such accountability was important at that time because two of the earlier campaigns for American colleges had invited criticism for failure to publish such a list. The printed lists of donors differed from his original handwritten lists in that important persons were listed first for leadership purposes.

Because of the publicly stated catholic character of the college, Edwards friends in other denominations supported his efforts to solicit funds. One of these friends was Dr. Francis Alison, pastor of the Presbyterian church in Philadelphia and a professor at the College of Philadelphia. Alison wrote a letter to Rev. James Moody, a Presbyterian minister in Newry, Ireland, which contained a glowing endorsement of Edwards and the Baptists.[96]

Alison's recommendation yielded good results--two Presbyterian churches in Belfast and one in Ballymony donated over thirty pounds.[97] In addition, James Manning and Stephen Hopkins, Governor of Rhode Island and Chancellor of the college, gave Edwards a memorial to present to the General Assembly of the Church of Scotland so he might solicit among their people.[98]

Another component of Morgan Edwards's plan was to approach Philadelphians who were in the British Isles during the period of his tour. No doubt the most prominent of these was Benjamin Franklin, who was then living in London as the agent for the Pennsylvania Assembly to the British government. Edwards knew Franklin from their ties with the College of Philadelphia.

Franklin was a thoroughly secular man but had outgrown his anticlericalism. The sectarianism, traditions, and doctrines of most of the churches were too confining for him. He used Sunday as a day for study and rarely went to church. While he had been brought up a Presbyterian, he could not abide the heavy emphasis on doctrine so prevalent at that time. After his marriage the family rented a pew at Christ Church, Anglican, but Franklin would visit other churches when there was a particular preacher he wanted to hear.[99] Given the crowds that were flocking to hear Edwards preach at the Baptist meeting-house, located next to Christ Church, it is likely that Franklin heard Edwards preach.

Franklin and Edwards found more common ground in their ardor for education, and it was because of their acquaintance through the College of Philadelphia that Edwards could appeal to Franklin. The canny statesman would today be classified as a "leadership" or "advance giver."

The first name on the London printed list is John Gill's and included in the first twenty are some of the major Baptist leaders in Great Britain, along with Benjamin Franklin, Thomas Penn, and Samuel Roffey.[100] Roffey was a major banker in London, and had been severely criticized for his generosity to such causes.[101] Despite the larger donations he received from notable people, however, Edwards plugged away, street after street, to garner all gifts, large and small, for the college.

Morgan Edwards pursued his mission in the face of stiff competition, harassment, adverse weather conditions, loneliness, and ill health. The most memorable description of his experience is in a letter to James Manning.[102]

> If I were to stay in London ever so long I believe I should get money, but it comes so slowly and by such small sums that I cannot spare the time____However, I may depend on the friendship of two or three when I leave the kingdom, who have promised to solicit for us____and do not doubt but what they will do more than I shall be able to accomplish, as they may watch convenient seasons___There have been no less than six cases of charity pushed about town this winter viz two from Germany, two from the country of England, and two from America___The unwearied beneficence of the city of London is amazing!
> Your newspapers, and letters from your government, published in other papers, have hurt me much___You boast of the many yards of cloth you manufacture & This raises the indignation of

the merchants and manufacturers___I have been not only denied by hundreds, but also abused on that score___My patience, my feet, and my assurance are much impaired___I took a cold in November, which stuck to me all winter, owing to my transpoosing [walking heavily] the streets in all weathers___Pray let me hear from you by every opportunity___.

Edwards made two trips to Ireland, where he received a donation from his brother James in Waterford, and from two of his wife's relatives in Dublin, Benjamin and Joseph Nun. Her parents are not listed among the fifty-two donors from Cork, so it is possible they may have died by the time of his visits. Most of the donations, literally hundreds of them, were from five shillings, five pence down to the one shilling of a Benjamin Boon of Taunton, England.

Edwards's plan was not only broadly based financially, but he also arranged for donations of books. One source of books was Edwards's alma mater, Bristol College, which sent duplicates in their library to Rhode Island College.[103] Armitage reports that he so stirred the sympathies of Dr. William Richards of Lynn, England, that he bequeathed his library of over thirteen hundred books to the college.[104] This is hardly likely since Richards did not begin his pastoral ministry until 1776, eight years after Edwards returned home to America. It is possible, however, that others who were moved by Edwards's visit influenced Richards at a later date.

Another book donation of considerable importance which resulted from Edwards's visit was a complete set of John Gill's works.[105] Edwards's former continuing-education mentor, Thomas Llewelyn, gave two gifts. The first gift of twenty-one pounds was for the endowment, and the second of ten pounds, ten shillings, for the purchase of books.[106] There is an interesting sidelight to

Llewelyn's donation.

Not all went well with book donations, however, as seen in a letter to Samuel Jones on December 25, 1784.[107]

> Mr. Timothy Thomas tells me that Dr. Gifford is dead, and has left his fine library to the Academy of Bristol___Also that Dr. Llewelyn left his to the same Academy, consisting of upwards of 7000 vol. all valuable books___Our college had the promise of them___How it has happened I know not, except our political conduct has disobliged them___.

Edwards was referring to the books of both Gifford and Llewelyn, since both had told him they would donate their libraries to Rhode Island College.

Andrew Gifford's name appears only three below that of John Gill on Edwards's printed subscriber list, and that for a larger gift than Gill.[108] It may be remembered that Andrew Gifford worked as Bernard Foskett's assistant in Bristol beginning in 1728, but stayed less than two years before going to the Wild Street Baptist Church in London in 1729. Unfortunately that church became embroiled in a violent quarrel over a long past repented sin in Gifford's life which had become public. Some of the congregation called for him to resign, and he left with a considerable number of members to form the Eagle Street Church. His fellow ministers expelled him from their Society, and refused to supply his pulpit.

Meanwhile, Gifford, in addition to his pastorate, became family chaplain to Sir Richard Ellys and a personal friend of the Speaker of Parliament, the Lord Chancellor, and the Archbishop of Canterbury. He collected ancient objects and his coin collection was puchased by George II. Later he was appointed assistant librarian of the British Museum. Among the books donated to Bristol Academy was the only complete copy of William Tyndale's New Testament, which was recently sold to the British Museum.[109] While this precious volume belongs where it is today, one must pause at the thought of it almost coming to America.

Though an eminent scholar, Thomas Llewelyn was not a preacher and never became pastor of a local church. He married into wealth and did some guest preaching. His great contributions were in the evangelization of North Wales, and his fervent support of the Particular Baptist Fund. Both he and Gifford never lost their lively interest in Bristol College, an indication of the influence Morgan Edwards had with both men in that they at first consented to leave their libraries to Rhode Island College. Perhaps Edwards was correct eight years later when he ascertained that the American Revolution brought a change in their plans.

To sum up Morgan Edwards's activity in the British Isles, his report indicates he visited twenty-four towns and cities, twelve each in England and Ireland, while making at least four hundred and ninety-five successful calls. Allowing a minimum of sixty days for the two voyages across the Atlantic Ocean he would have traveled some nineteen months in Great Britain to make his nearly five hundred productive calls.

There are no records of the unsuccessful calls he made, receiving no donations, which he said in his letter were in the hundreds. There are no entries of gifts from Scotland or Wales. Realistically, Edwards would have received donations in Wales had he sought them, but he never mentioned Wales. Trosnant Academy closed in 1761, so he may have deemed it better not to solicit in his home country.

Edwards had returned home from Europe by December 1768 and was present for the first commencement in

Warren on September 7, 1769. One of the seven young men receiving his bachelor of arts degree was Richard Stites, James Manning's brother-in-law. He delivered the salutatory address in Latin and then expressed the gratitude of the College to Morgan Edwards, "who encountered so many difficulties in going to Europe to collect donations for the Institution, and has lately returned."[110] At the same commencement Edwards was awarded his second master of arts degree. A number of others were so honored, including his brother James. On the evening of that same day, Morgan Edwards delivered the first commencement sermon.[111]

Morgan Edwards's Commitment to the College

To see the full scope of Edwards's commitment to Rhode Island College it is necessary to step back and view the whole picture. Edwards spoke of his role in the founding of the school as his "greatest service."[112] "It grieved me much," he wrote to Gardner Thurston when the Philadelphia Association refused to send Jeremiah Condy on a fund-raising trip to Europe in 1764.[113] There are several other references in other correspondence which make it clear that Edwards was firmly committed to Baptist-sponsored education in general, and to Rhode Island College in particular.

It was Edwards who took the primary action to start the college and define it as a catholic institution in the fullest sense of the word. If Brown University today is open to students of all persuasions, it is because that evangelical, Calvinistic Baptist minister in eighteenth-century Philadelphia took the first steps to make it so before its birth. Reuben Guild reported the action in his biography of Hezekiah Smith.[114]

> The Philadelphia Association,...urged on by the zeal and enthusiasm of Morgan Edwards, had resolved, in the words of Isaac Backus, "to erect a College in the Colony of Rhode Island, under the chief direction of the Baptists, where education might be promoted and superior learning obtained, free from any sectarian tests."

Morgan Edwards continued his commitment to the college after resigning his pastorate in Philadelphia. He maintained his membership on the Board of Fellows until 1789, lectured at the college, continued to raise funds, and never lost interest in the school.

When Robert W. Kenny wrote his unpublished paper on Morgan Edwards' place in the history of Brown University, he closed his work with this statement, "Certainly his [Morgan Edwards'] efforts for our Alma Mater should endear this little man to the family of Brown."[115]

Morgan Edwards was not little in stature, nor was he little in his importance to Brown University. It would be pure speculation to suggest there would not have been a Brown University without Morgan Edwards because there were also people like James Manning and Hezekiah Smith, among many. As the "first projector" of the school and as the first major fund raiser, he does deserve full and lasting recognition as "the prime mover" of the University.

With the completion of Edwards's role as associational evangelist in 1772, the locus of his life changed from Philadelphia to Delaware. It was following his move to Delaware that three major problems arose to bedevil him the rest of his days and haunt his memory down through history. These were his loyalty to the crown, his brief period of intemperance, and the charge of universalism.

ENDNOTES

1. Samuel Arnold Greene, *History of the State of Rhode Island*, (New York: D. Appleon & Company, 1874), 2 Vols., II, 248.
2. Morgan Edwards, *Materials Toward A History of the Baptists*, (Danielsville, GA.: Heritage Papers, 1984), 2 Vols., I, 23.
3. John Rippon, ed. *Baptist Annual Register*, London: 1796, 310. Memorial Sermon, William Rogers, February 22, 1795.
4. Barnas Sears, *Centennial Discourse in Celebration of the One Hundredth Anniversary of the Founding of Brown University*, (Providence: Sidney S. Rider & Bro., 1865), 12-21.
5. William Cathcart, *The Baptist Encyclopedia*, (Philadelphia: Louis H. Everts, 1881), 362.
6. Morgan Edwards, *Materials*, II, 2.
7. Thomas Armitage, *A History of the Baptists*, (New York: Bryan, Taylor & Co., 1887), 722.
8. Reuben A. Guild, *Early History of Brown University, Including the Life, Times, and Correspondence of President Manning*, (Providence: Snow & Farnham, 1896), 12.
9. A.H. Newman, *A History of the Baptist Churches in the United States*, (Philadelphia: The American Baptist Publication Society, 1898), 278.
10. William W. Keen, *The Bi-Centennial Celebration of the Founding of the First Baptist Church of the City of Philadelphia*. (Philadelphia: American Baptist Publication Society, 1899), 226.
11. E.K. Jones, *The Baptists of Wales and Ministerial Education*, (Wrexham: Hughes and Sons, 1902), 13.
12. Henry C. Vedder, *A Short History of the Baptists*. (Philadelphia: American Baptist Publication Society, 1907), 315.
13. Robert W. Kenny, Unpublished Paper, (Providence: John Hay Library Brown University, n.d.), 7.
14. Robert A. Baker, "Profile of a Baptist Historian," *Baptist History and Heritage*, I, 1. (August 1965), 5.
15. Katherine W. Johnson, *Rhode Island Baptists*, (Valley Forge: Judson Press, 1975), 32.
16. Thomas R. McKibbens, Jr.; and Kenneth L. Smith, *The Life and Works of Morgan Edwards*, (New York: Arno Press, 1980), 201.
17. H. Leon McBeth, *The Baptist Heritage*, (Nashville:Broadman Press, 1987), 237.
18. A.D. Gillette, ed. *Minutes of the Philadelphia Baptist Asso-*

ciation, From A.D. 1707, to A.D. 1807. (Philadelphia: American Baptist Publication Society, 1851), 86.
19. Edwards, V. I, 191.
20. Robert G. Gardner, *Baptist of Early America: A Statistical Study, 1639-1790* (Atlanta:Georgia Baptist Historical Society, 1983), 65-84.
21. Robert G. Torbet, *A History of the Baptists,* 3rd. ed. (Valley Forge: Judson Press, 1963), 221.
22. Gardner, 62-63.
23. Winthrop S. Hudson, *Religion in America,* 3rd. ed. (New York: Charles Scribner's Sons, 1981), 218.
24. William G. McLoughlin, *New England Dissent, 1630-1833,* (Cambridge: Harvard University Press, 1971), 492.
25. Isaac Backus, *A Fish Caught in His Own Net,* (Boston: n.p., 1768), 109.
26. Walter C. Bronson, *The History of Brown University,* (Providence: Brown University, 1914), 6
27. Ibid., 4.
28. Sears, 5.
29. F. B. Dexter, ed. *The Literary Diary of Ezra Stiles,* 3 Vols., (New York: n.p., 1901), 492.
30. Edwards, I, 97.
31. Ibid.
32. Ibid., 153.
33. McLoughlin, 492.
34. Guild, 134.
35. Edwards, I, 191.
36. Ibid., 159-160.
37. Ibid., 191.
38. McLoughlin, 492.
39. Edwards, I, 191.
40. Isaac Backus, *A History of New England With Particular Reference to the Denomination of Christians Called Baptists.* 2 vols., (Newton:, n.p., 1871), II, 137, 347.
41. Guild, 24.
42. Ibid., 31.
43. Ibid.
44. Edwards, I, 191.
45. McLoughlin, 493.
46. Bronson, 11.

47. J. Stanley Lemons, *The First Baptist Church in America*, (Providence: Charitable Baptist Society, 1988), 20-21.
48. Guild, 37.
49. Ibid., 42.
50. Sears, Appen. B., 63-64.
51. Edwards, I, 191.
52. Ibid., 192.
53. Ibid.
54. Ibid.
55. McLoughlin, 494.
56. Edwards, I, 193, 211.
57. Ibid., 193
58. Ibid.
59. Ibid., 195.
60. Bronson, 20.
61. Edwards, I, 192.
62. Bronson, 21.
63. Guild, 61ff.
64. Ibid.
65. MS. Letter from James Manning to John Ryland, June 1, 1771. Manning Papers, (John Hay Library, Brown University, Providence).
66. Bronson, 26.
67. Edwards, I, 198-199.
68. Bronson, 19.
69. MS. Letter from Ezra Stiles to Rhode Island College, September 3, 1771. Manning Papers.
70. MS. Letter from James Manning to Samuel Stennett, November 13, 1772. Manning Papers.
71. Norman Maring, *Baptists In New Jersey* (Valley Forge: The Judson Press, 1964), 89; Quoting W.W. Sweet, *Religion in the Development of American Culture*, 6.
72. Edwards, I, 195.
73. Guild, 48.
74. MS. Corporation Minutes, Manning Papers.
75. MS. Record of Subscriptions, Manning Papers.
76. Corporation Papers, 2.
77. David Benedict, *A General History of the Baptist Denomination in America and Other Parts of the World*. (New York: Sheldon, Lamport and Blakeman, 1855), 392f.

78. McLoughlin, 495-496.
79. Ibid., 496
80. MS. Letter from Oliver Hart to Samuel Jones, December 1, 1763, McKesson Collection, Jones Section. (Historical Society of Pennsylvania, Philadelphia).
81. MS. Letter from Morgan Edwards to Gardner Thurston, November 9, 1764. Manning Papers.
82. Ibid.
83. MS. Letter from Morgan Edwards to Gardner Thurston, June 28, 1765. Manning Papers.
84. MS. Letter from James Manning to Samuel Stennett, June 7, 1770. Manning Papers.
85. MS. Subscription by Samuel Jones, October 30, 1769, Manning Papers.
86. MS. Corporation Minutes, November 20, 1766. Manning Papers.
87. MS. Authorization, Manning Papers.
88. Edwards, I., 195.
89. Ibid.
90. MS. Certificate, Manning Papers, I 39.
91. MS. Certificate, Manning Papers, I 35.
92. Certificate of Endorsement, Manning Papers, I 35.
93. Ibid.
94. Morgan Edwards, *The State of the College* (Newport: Samuel Hall, 1767).
95. MS. Letter from Morgan Edwards to James Manning, April 26, 1768. Manning Papers, I 33.
96. MS. Letter from Francis Alison to James Moody, February 9, 1767, Manning Collection, (John Carter Brown Library, Brown University, Providence).
97. Morgan Edwards, Subscription Lists, Manning Papers, I 37, 4, 5. In addition to the printed lists are the original manuscript lists kept by Edwards and signed by the donors.
98. MS. Memorial, James Manning and Stephen Hopkins to the Moderator of the Church of Scotland, n.d. Manning Papers, I, 65.
99. Carl Van Doren, *Benjamin Franklin*, (New York: Penquin Books, 1938), 131-132.
100. Edwards, Subscription Lists, 158
101. Edwards Letter, 2.
102. Ibid., 3.

103. Frank E. Robinson, "Reviews: (A Baptist Bibliography)," *Baptist Quarterly,* (London: Baptist Union Publication Department, V. I, 1922-1923), 46.
104. Armitage, 722.
105. MS. Letter from James Manning to Benjamin Wallin, May 10, 1773, Manning Papers.
106. Edwards, Subscription Lists, 158.
107. MS. Letter from Morgan Edwards to Samuel Jones, December 25, 1784, McKesson Collection.
108. Subscription Lists, 158.
109. Personal letter from the Reverend D. Hugh Matthews, dated July 13, 1994.
110. Guild, 83.
111. Ibid., 84-85.
112. Edwards, I., 23.
113. MS. Letter, November 9, 1764.
114. Reuben A. Guild, *Chaplain Smith and the Baptists.* (Philadelphia: American Baptist Publication Society, n.d.), 49.
115. Kenny, 14.

SECTION THREE

The Story in Delaware

CHAPTER ELEVEN

THE MATTER OF LOYALTY

"In the beginnings of the Revolutionary
War he showed attachment to the Royal Family
of Great Britain...and was classed a Tory."[1]
G.W. Paschal, 1930

THE HISTORIC SETTING

Without a doubt the most dramatic and threatening crisis in the life of Morgan Edwards was triggered by his loyalty to the British Crown. History has not been kind to him in this matter because his motives have been misunderstood and because of the inaccuracies which have been handed down. Cathcart's appraisal is a case in point.[2]

> In his brief biography of 3,200 Tories given by Sabine in his "History of American Loyalists," we find forty-six clergymen of one denomination, six of another, three of another, and but one of the Baptist faith. This minister was Morgan Edwards, a man of great ability and general worth, but eccentric. He had a son, an officer in the British service, whose position is charged with helping to blind his father's eyes to the glories of patriotism. He gave up the public duties of the ministry while the war lasted, and conducted himself with so much moderation as to save himself

from exile during and after the Revolutionary struggle. Edwards was about to be arrested by Colonel Miles, a member of the First Baptist Church of Philadelphia, but he was notified of his danger and left this city immediately.

Inaccuracies in Cathcart's statements include the one that Edwards was the only Baptist minister who was a Tory. As will be shown later, he was not. Secondly, his son did not influence him. William was only thirteen at the time of his father's recantation on August 7, 1775, and still a student at Rhode Island College. Another error is that Edwards gave up public ministry, but it is more accurate to say he did not serve in another pastorate. Finally, Colonel Miles was not bent on arresting Edwards. Rather he protected his former pastor and friend from a mob until he formally renounced his loyalty to the Crown. Understanding the basis for Morgan Edwards's loyalty to the King requires an examination of the Tory movement in the American colonies.

About Tories in General

John Adams believed Americans were divided in their loyalties to England. He estimated that one-third were totally patriotic, one-third indifferent, and one-third Tories.[3] Those loyal to the King were tagged Tories by the Patriots after their English counterparts who supported the despised Lord North. Tories called themselves Loyalists and, in the main, displayed snobbery toward the Patriots.

This aloofness was because the Tories included some of the best political, diplomatic, and financial talent in the colonies. Edwards, like many Tories, preferred the orderly procedures of the British government moreso than did the more democratic elements of American society who came from the laboring and agrarian classes.[4] The Loyalists of the second half of the eighteenth century included the richer American farmers, businessmen angered by the loss of trade, high ranking judges, and some eminent lawyers and physicians. Obviously, the tensions between Tories and Patriots were not just over political differences, but were expressions of class distinctions as well.[5]

Most of the Tories were not militant and wanted only to keep a political system which they saw no reason to overthrow. As one historian has described it,[6]

> This was the mission of the Tories: to make the British constitution work in the American wilderness....these conservatives are believed to have been largely responsible for perpetuating in a raw, new country much of the best heritage of the old.

In March 1765 the term "Loyalist" came into use for those who supported the Stamp Act and opposed popular uprisings against the Crown.[7] In reality, Americans were more united against the Stamp Act than they were for independence, and many Loyalists disapproved of British policies even as late as the sixth decade.

It was not until the Boston Tea Party December 16, 1773, that serious division began to develop. Most people were still loyal to George III and blamed his ministers and Parliament for the problems. In fact, many Loyalists were actively involved in the illegal provincial congresses of the 1770s.[8]

The First Continental Congress created the Association (militia) in 1774, and this action hardened the lines between Loyalists and Patriots.[9] Persons who did not support the Patriots were blackballed and their names were published in the newspapers. Strangely, many Loyalists enllisted in the Association because they were opposed to British actions, but they were also opposed to separation.

By early 1775 the associations or militias were ready to use force against the British. The Battle of Lexington on April 15, 1775, was the start of an undeclared war. In June 1775, the Congress declared that all colonists who were sympathetic with Great Britain or fought for it were guilty of treason. To enforce this edict, local "Committees of Safety" were established to search out Tories.

Finally, the Declaration of Independence on July 4, 1776, made clear the issue of loyalty. Approve the Declaration of Independence and you were a Whig or a Patriot. Deny it and you were a Tory or a Loyalist. Many who stayed with the Patriot cause until then sided with the British.

The above chronology illustrates the pattern of loyalty of many Americans. Like them, Edwards maintained his loyalty to the Crown only until it was clear that a final break was inevitable. His retraction on August 7, 1775, came eleven months before the Declaration of Independence was signed. The question is, what was the basis for his loyalty?

WHY EDWARDS REMAINED LOYAL

To understand the reasons behind Morgan Edwards's loyalty to the King, we must examine four mitigating factors. First, his experience was little different from other notable Americans. Second, he felt compassion for poor, struggling Baptist churches which had lost much of the value of their meager assets with the change from the British pound sterling to congressional script. Third, contrary to the opinion of some later writers, he cared deeply about religious liberty, and fourth, there is the drama of the relatively early retraction of his loyalty.

Edwards' Loyalty Was Not Uncommon

Not every American, including Benjamin Franklin, became a Patriot with the passage of the Stamp Act in 1765. The Stamp Act was repulsive to most Americans when it was passed, but Franklin approved the proposal to let Americans administer it even though he was opposed to the Act itself. In London at the time, he was later caught off-guard by the angry reaction at home.[10] On August 9, 1765, he counselled loyalty to the Crown:[11]

> A firm loyalty to the Crown and faithful adherence to the government of this nation, which it is the safety as well as honour of the colonies to be connected with, will always be the wisest course....

By the end of 1765 Franklin was being accused of framing the Stamp Act and profiting from it. Rebellious Philadelphians were so incensed at him that they threatened to set fire to his new house,[12] but Franklin continued working for years to keep the colonies and the mother country united.

Even as late as September 30, 1769, in response to French hopes for the American colonies to be separated from England, he wrote to Pierre du Pont de Nemours, "Our [American] prudence will, I hope, long postpone the satisfaction our enemies expect from our dissensions."[13] Like Morgan Edwards, Franklin believed the blame for the ill-treatment of the American colonies belonged on the doorstep of the King's ministers and Parliament. Franklin and Edwards both believed George III had the best interest of the colonies at heart.

It was not until July 1773, that Franklin finally began to see that the King's attitude and actions toward the American colonies were changing.[14] This was only two years before Morgan Edwards renounced his loyalty, and Franklin, because of his governmental position and because he lived in London, was privy to more accurate knowledge of events than Edwards.

Another case demonstrating loyalty akin to that of Edwards' was that of American naval hero, John Paul Jones. A quote from the award winning biography of Jones by naval historian Samuel Eliot Morison will illustrate the point.[15]

> Thus when John Paul Jones accepted his commission on 7 December 1775-*a date when only a few radicals wanted a complete separation from England* [italics mine]-he well and truly believed that he was fighting not for American independence but for the principle of Liberty-the right of a free people to determine their destiny without coercion by a misguided king and corrupt ministry. And the flag he raised with his own hands on the jackstaff of his first temporary command, the ALFRED, on 3 December 1775, was not the Stars and Stripes of an independent republic, but the "Grand Union Flag," the Union Jack and Stripes, which symbolized a united resistance to tyranny, but loyalty to the English King.

Morison went on to point out that many Americans at that time believed that a firm resistance by them would force George III to back down and matters would return to what they had been earlier. This was four months after Morgan Edwards had recanted his loyalty, and seven months before the Declaration of Independence would be signed. Edwards's loyalty, then, was not unlike that of a majority of his fellow Americans at that time.

Care for the Churches
A second mitigating factor in Edwards's loyalty was the devaluation of Baptist church assets when Congressional

script was used in place of the pound sterling. He consistently expressed his disgust over this matter in a context of concern for furthering the Baptist cause.

Because Britain did not supply hard currency for its profitable trade with America, the Americans created their own solutions to the problem. First, in 1652, in Massachusetts they began to mint their own coins. The shortage of sound money continued, and the colonies began to issue paper money in 1690. No provision was made for the redemption of the paper money. When it dropped too low in value it was withdrawn from circulation at a small percentage of its worth. The colonial governments then issued new money causing great distress among the people.[16]

In the colonial period silverware served in place of money. It was "beautiful, interesting, distinctly individual, and was abundant in the American colonies all through the first three-quarters of the eighteenth century."[17] The colonists also bartered and used the currency of their native lands in their local areas, such as the Dutch guilder in New Amsterdam and the British pound sterling in Pennsylvania. In addition, as the economy grew, the local commodities became mediums of exchange. It was tobacco in Virginia, rice in South Carolina, wool in Rhode Island. In some areas the Indian wampum was used. Finally, there was the "land bank," which was basically a loan office for farmers who normally would not be able to obtain money from other sources.[18]

The Restraining Act of 1764 prevented the colonies from making legal tender. They, in turn, attempted to repeal it but failed. By 1774 the First Continental Congress was calling the act a violation of colonial rights. Paper money, then, occupied an important place in the life of the colonies because of the service it rendered to the communities.[19] The available gold and silver was used primarily in trade with Britain, and when used in the colonies it was limited to business between merchants.

In his historical materials, Morgan Edwards made an effort to portray the comparative value of what he described as "Congress Money."[20]

> The pecuniary terms, pounds, shillings, pence, having been used in the foregoing sheets, it may be proper to observe, that in Pennsylvania the sums they express are less in value by one third than the sums which the same terms express in Greatbritain. Subtract the third from any sum and the remainder will be sterling.

Edwards made specific references to the value of money in the other colonies as he wrote the history of each one. The list included New Jersey, Delaware, Maryland, and South Carolina. It was not these statements, however, which got him into trouble, but rather his caustic comments about the currency for which many colonists were willing to take risks in the cause of independence.

He frequently referred to "Congress-money" as sacrilegious because he saw it robbing the churches of important resources, as with the case of the church in Middletown, New Jersey:[21]

> (2) Half a plantation, the gift of Hannah Chesterman; her will is dated May 10, 1769; this plantation was sold for 712 pounds; but the 365 pounds which belonged to the church was reduced to a pittance by that sacriligious thing, Congress money.

In writing about the Upper Freehold Church of New Jersey, he charged that "'congress-money' hath committed sacrilege in this church also."[22] He reported on a legacy left by one John Manners to the Hopewell church in New Jersey, as "all lost in 'Congress-money.'"[23] In the same paragraph he described a legacy of 350 pounds left to the Philadelphia Association for needy ministerial students by a Mrs. Elizabeth Hobbs as losing two-thirds of its value because of "Congress-money." Edwards's passion for prosperous churches and an educated ministry made him feel strongly about such losses.

Morgan Edwards's outspoken comments against colonial script ran counter to the popular feelings of the time. These feelings have been captured in an anonymous statement written in 1874.[24]

> The patriotism of the Jerseymen was evinced in the fact that most of them placed their church money, as well as their own, in Continental funds, thereby losing largely during the war of the Revolution.

On the other hand, Edwards's fervency for the Baptist cause was equally intense, as may be seen in his comment on legacies left to the Baptist church at Scotch Plains, New Jersey:[25]

> The forementioned parsonage with its appendages, values at 20 pounds per year. Twenty-five pounds, the gift of Richard Runyon: ditto, the gift of John Lambert: ditto, the gift of Peter Wilcox: ditto, a collection of the church; but all reduced to nothing. O thou robber of churches, and of the fatherless and widows, what hast thou to answer for? Can an end gained by such means prosper? The widow Micah cursed him that robbed her (Judg. xvii.2); but when it was restored, she blessed. And cannot a certain revolution do as much to reverse a curse into the blessing of the widow and fatherless and churches?

There are no extant reports that Edwards ever condemned

the Revolution, per se, only the monetary devastation brought on by it. His plea was for the Revolution to reverse these ill effects. As will be seen, Edwards had no difficulty renouncing loyalty to the Crown and adopting the cause of independence as his own. His argument with the movement toward independence was very practical and twofold, namely the damage to the cause of Christ by the monetary chaos and the denial of religious liberty to Baptists by some of the very people who were in the vanguard of the independence movement.

The Cause of Religious Liberty
The religious liberty component in Morgan Edwards' loyalty to the Crown was demonstrated in two specific instances--the Regulator Movement in North Carolina and the oppression of Baptists in Massachusetts.

The Regulator Movement in North Carolina began in 1765 when Presbyterians and Baptists protested restrictions that kept them from performing legal marriage ceremonies. They contended that the Act of Toleration of 1689 allowed them to do so. The protest later expanded to include taxation for the support of the Established Church in North Carolina (Anglican). Much of the turmoil occurred in the Western counties where there was little money and the taxes were more keenly felt. In one county violence broke out.[26]

When Governor William Tryon summoned the militia to suppress the violence in Orange County, the people did not respond. It was an area heavily populated with Baptists. Baptist leaders urged moderation, and pastors cautioned their people not to take up arms against legal authority. In addition, the Sandy Creek Association in 1769, forbade member churches from participating in the movement under threat of losing fellowship in the association.[27] They did not, however, forbid individual Baptists from joining the Regulator Movement. The consequence was that many Baptists did participate, in the hope of gaining relief from the oppressive measures of the provincial government.

Governor Tryon's troops soundly defeated the Regulators in the Battle of Alamance on May 16, 1771. Following the battle, Baptists fled in great numbers from North Carolina to Tennessee, South Carolina, and Georgia. While the exodus resulted in the spread of Baptist doctrine, it also left many of the churches in North Carolina in a weakened condition.

Within a year after the Battle of Alamance, Morgan Edwards rode into North Carolina as the evangelist of the Philadelphia Baptist Association. While there he also collected historical data for his history of the Baptists. Many who were involved in the uprising, for or against it, were still there. As he was wont to do, Edwards interviewed them for his records. Later historians, however, had a different perspective of the incident than did Edwards.

He said that he "made it his business to enquire into the matter; and can aver that among 4000 regulators there were but seven of the denomination of Baptists."[28] But scholarly North Carolina Baptist historian George W. Paschal has demonstrated that there were many more Baptists in the Regulators.[29] In refuting Edwards, he cited evidences which clearly indicated virtually the entire Baptist population was in the Regulator camp. Even Edwards acknowledged that a large exodus had occurred because of the uprising.[30]

McKibbens and Smith have seen in Edwards's material

a distortion of the facts in order to show that the Baptists were not disloyal to the British Crown.[31] Such judgments appear to bypass several factors about Edwards's report.

Because Edwards gathered his material less than a year after the Battle of Alamance and while Governor Tryon's troops might still be in the area, the responses from the Baptists he interviewed would be tainted by fears of reprisal. Small wonder he found that only seven Baptists were known members of the Regulators, and these seven were disciplined by their churches.[32] Indeed, one of the seven, Captain Benjamin Merrill, was executed for his part in the disturbance.

Furthermore, Edwards reported the seven persons were excommunicated because of the action taken by the Sandy Creek Association. Edwards indicated that word of their action had leaked out of the association meeting, and an armed group of Regulators invaded the room demanding to know if they had so acted. In that climate of fear and intimidation, they gave an ambiguous answer and the whole intent of the motion was offset.[33]

In his report on the Regulator episode, Edwards took the side, not of the Royal Governor and the Provincial government, but of the oppressed Baptists. In addition, Edwards believed that the non-Baptist leadership of the Regulators had misled the Baptists and others into violent confrontations with the Governor's forces. He feared there might be a repeat of the Munster tragedy in Germany in the 1530s.

Munster was a city in Germany where some radical reformers flocked, gaining control of the city in 1534. They once had been Anabaptists, but no longer. Polygamy was established, as was a form of communism, and all who disagreed were slaughtered. The city was recaptured by Catholic and Lutheran troops in June 1535, and the leaders of the rebellion were executed by extreme torture. The incident triggered a violent persecution against authentic Anabaptists. The onus of that terrible event hung over Anabaptists and later Baptists even up to Morgan Edwards's day.

Edwards blamed abuse of power for the dispersion of the Baptists after Alamance. He defended their action in taking up arms as justified because of severe oppression, burdensome taxes, and corrupt government officials. He also claimed that the four principal leaders of the Regulator Movement were members of churches in other denominations, but did not state which. Finally, he reported that Baptists were leaving North Carolina in droves because "they despaired of seeing better times."[34]

In summary, it can been seen that Morgan Edwards opposed the actions of the Royal Governor of North Carolina and supported the Baptists and others whom the Governor's administration was exploiting. Edwards did so because he wanted to defend religious liberty and avoid Baptists being tarred with the Munster brush. His figures were inaccurate, not because of his loyalty to the King, but because his information came from those still cowering in fear for their lives.

There is another instance in which historians have seen Edwards's loyalty to King George III compromise his zeal for religious liberty. That case was the oppression of the Massachusetts Baptists.

The Massachusetts case began at Huntstown (later Ashfield) when nine Congregationalists became Baptists in 1761 and formed a church with one Ebenezer Smith as their elder. Soon there were twenty-four members. Fourteen out of the nineteen families in town attended Baptist services, and eventually they decided to build a meeting house. Meanwhile, the Congregationalists began to move into town, and along with others soon outnumbered the Baptists.

The Baptists were forced to drop their plan for a meeting house, and were required to pay taxes for a Congregational meeting house. At that time the Congregational Church was the Established Church of Massachusetts. Those Baptists who resisted had their lands seized in 1763. Eventually the Congregationalists called to be their pastor a Yale graduate who was hostile toward Baptists. The Baptists were required to pay for his settlement and his support.

When the incorporation of the town was proposed in 1767, the Baptists (now numbering ninety) filed a petition asking to be relieved of paying for a minister and church which was not their own. The incorporation act technically gave the Baptists an exemption from the taxes, but the town proprietors thought otherwise.

A new tax was levied on all the inhabitants, but the Baptists refused to pay. Their lands were confiscated, and sold to pay their taxes. They tried without success to reclaim their property and to be exempted from further taxes. The lands involved were extensive tracts of well-cultivated farms. By 1770 the Baptists were no better off, and all the lands confiscated for taxes were sold for a pittance of their real value.

Meanwhile, the Grievance Committee of the Warren Baptist Association began to petition the Assembly for redress, but their persistent efforts so annoyed the legislators that they were told no action would be taken. The Grievance Committee and the Warren Association voted to appeal directly to King George III. This threat

A Dazzling Enigma 291

appeared to evoke a softer tone toward the Baptists, but the nature of the decisions being made against them did not change.

With the help of Baptists in England, a petition was presented to the King on July 31, 1771, and he ruled in favor of the Baptists of Ashfield. Five American Baptist leaders were responsible for persuading British Baptist leaders Samuel Stennett and Thomas Llewellyn to carry their petition to the King. The five were James Manning, John Davis, Hezekiah Smith, Isaac Backus and Morgan Edwards. The properties of the Ashfield Baptists were restored, and they were exempted from further taxation to support the Congregational church and ministry. But it was a Pyrrhic victory.[35]

The eight-year running battle of the Ashfield Baptists to obtain their rights convinced them an effort was being made to force them out of the town. The decision to petition the King stirred up suspicions of their commitment to the cause of the colonies against Britain on the eve of the Revolution. In the minds of their countrymen, the appeal to the King marked them as Tories. Hence, the harassment of Massachusetts Baptists continued.

The Continental Congress was to begin meeting in Philadelphia on September 5, 1774, and New England Baptist leaders urged Isaac Backus, the leader among Baptists in the cause of religious liberty, to go there and plead the case of the Massachusetts Baptists.

The Warren Association collected money for his expenses, and on September 26 Backus rode off toward Philadelphia. Backus and Baptist leaders from other colonies arrived in the city for the annual meetings of the Philadelphia Baptist Association by October 11. That same day they met with three Quaker leaders and Robert Strettle

Jones, a Baptist and prominent Philadelphia attorney.

Robert Strettle Jones was a member of the Philadelphia Baptist Church and served on the Grievance Committee of the Philadelphia Baptist Association. He was neutral in the cause for independence, and some thought him a Loyalist.[36] At that meeting he urged Backus not to do anything that might prejudice the King against the Baptists.

The three Quakers at the meeting were Israel and James Pemberton and Joseph Fox. Israel Pemberton was friend enough to Morgan Edwards to be blunt with him. Sometime after Edwards had preached the sermon in which he predicted his own death Pemberton said to him, "Thy dream will come true--this year is the death of thy ministry."[37] Pemberton's prediction, of course, was no more accurate than Edwards's, but such a remark indicates that the two men enjoyed a close relationship.

Pemberton was a wealthy merchant, a politician and philanthropist. He was opposed to the Continental Congress and later opposed the Revolution. Ultimately, he was imprisoned in 1777 and died there a year later. His brother John held similar views and also was imprisoned, but managed to survive his imprisonment. After the Revolution he became a well-known preacher.[38] Fox was also a Loyalist.

Jones erred when he invited the Quakers to the meeting. The New England delegates to the Congress were not open minded on anything involving Israel Pemberton. In fact, John Adams once accused him of trying "to break up the Congress, or at least to withdraw the Quakers and the Governing Part of Pennsylvania from Us."[39]

Backus, in his diary, stated that the meeting included several other gentlemen. Morgan Edwards had to be among those gentlemen because two days later he was

A Dazzling Enigma 293

named to the Grievance Committee appointed to meet with the Congressional delegation.

Jones and the Quakers had previously advised the Baptists not to address the Congress as a whole, but to obtain an audience with the Massachusetts delegates and others who were recognized as friends of religious liberty. This was a flawed strategy.

The whole Congress involved many delegates from other colonies who would have sided with the Baptists. Furthermore, given the negative attitude of the Pennsylvania Quakers toward the Continental Congress, the Baptist plea to the New England delegates was doomed before it could be made because Pemberton was present at the meeting.

Meantime, the association meeting opened on Wednesday, October 12, 1774; on Friday, October 14, the Grievance Committee was appointed. It was to work with the Warren Association Committee to present its case.

On Friday evening, the joint Baptist Grievance Committee met with the Congressional delegates from Massachusetts and other delegates at Carpenter's Hall in Philadelphia. The conference opened with Manning reading a memorial written earlier by Backus and Jones.

John and Samuel Adams responded to the memorial by saying, "There is indeed an ecclesiastical establishment in our province but a very slender one, hardly to be called an establishment."[40] Isaac Backus's record of the exchange which followed is important for two reasons. First, Backus alone carried on the exchange for the Baptists; second, Edwards's silence was no more indicative of his loyalty to the Crown, than it would have been for any other Baptist present.

The exchanges between Backus and John and Samuel

Adams and Robert Treat Paine were very pointed and neither relented. Paine was a lawyer, political leader, and a signer of the Declaration of Independence. A Bostonian by birth, he saw himself as the leader in the fight against the Baptists in their struggle for religious liberty. He and Samuel Adams tried unsuccessfully to refute the facts Backus presented. The meeting lasted four hours, with John Adams saying, "We might as well expect a change in the solar systim [sic], as to expect they would give up their establishment."[41]

In the folklore surrounding Edwards there is the suggestion that he was silent at the Carpenter's Hall meeting because of his loyalty to the Crown.[42] Isaac Backus's report of the conference makes it clear that he alone spoke for the Baptists, who were a mixture of Loyalists and Patriots. The Baptists from the Middle Colonies deferred to the Massachusetts Baptists because it was their meeting with their Congressional delegates. In any case the mission failed to achieve its objective, but certainly not because Morgan Edwards failed to speak out. Backus recorded a comment by Edwards as they left the meeting, indicating that Edwards wanted to confront the Massachusetts delegates.

In his remarks Backus appealed the issue as a matter of conscience. Robert Treat Paine responded that conscience had nothing to do with it. He continued, "They [the Baptists] plead for liberty of conscience and yet deny it; for we believe in our consciences that we ought to support our ministers in that way [i.e. by taxing the people in the community], and they will not allow us to do it."[43]

After they came out of the building Edwards said to Backus, that "he [Edwards] wanted to have asked Mr. Paine, how far they must get over the river before conscience operated? for no such thing [i.e. taxing to support churches] was done in Boston, where their laws were made."[44] Thus we know Edwards wanted to speak out on the issue of religious liberty, but he held his tongue. So did the others.

It appears that Morgan Edwards's loyalty to the Crown was not political in nature, but practical. At its heart was his commitment to religious liberty. A reading of his *Materials Towards a History of the Baptists,* reveals repeated incidents of oppression of Baptists and his convictions on religious liberty. He believed the Baptists must appeal to the King if they were to have religious liberty. This was demonstrated in the Ashfield case. Further, the drama and character of his retraction both indicate his loyalty to the Crown was not a life and death commitment.

The Retraction of Loyalty
By the summer of 1775 Morgan Edwards was rethinking his stand as a Tory. He had been a Tory "more in principle than in action,"[45] and now he could see that his principles must be recast in a new arena of action.

Events were moving toward a break with the mother country, and his life was now in America. On May 20, 1771, he married Elizabeth Singleton of Newark, Delaware, the widow of John Singleton, a land holder in the colony.[46] Sometime after 1776, she had passed away. He later married the widow of a Nathaniel Evans, a member of the Welsh Tract Baptist Church in Delaware. Edwards listed him as one who had helped start the Peedee Baptist church in South Carolina in 1736.[47] We know nothing about his third wife, whom Edwards outlived by many years.

With each passing day, Edwards knew his life and

property were in increasing danger from overzealous bands of Patriots. In fact, they were seeking him in Philadelphia. Officers from the Committee of Safety in that city questioned young Joshua concerning his father's whereabouts. Joshua was unable to tell them where he was, and the lad was warned not to leave the city. There was one man who could help Morgan Edwards, and he was Colonel Samuel Miles.

Samuel Miles was a merchant and capitalist in Philadelphia, who with a number of other merchants established the Bank of Pennsylvania in 1780. He was born in 1739 of Welsh ancestry, was a member of the Baptist church in Philadelphia, became a deacon during Morgan Edwards's tenure and died in 1805. At sixteen years of age he enlisted in the First City Troop, a militia formed earlier by Benjamin Franklin. He rose quickly to the rank of sergeant and fought in the frontier Indian wars. In 1760 he was given a captain's commission, and one year later, on January 26, 1761, was honorably discharged from the service.

On February 16, 1761, he married Catherine Wister, a Quaker lady of Germantown, at the Baptist church in Philadelphia. Miles was elected City Warden in 1766 and later that year Commissioner for the City and the County of Philadelphia. The Quakers were still in solid control of the politics of both Philadelphia and Pennsylvania, and his election to the General Assembly of Pennsylvania in 1772 says much about the esteem in which he was held. Two years after being elected to the Assembly, he moved outside the city to a country plantation at Spring Mills.

Miles became an early opponent of Parliament's onerous actions. When a militia was formed he was given command with the rank of colonel. He was also given a seat on the Committees of Safety for both Philadelphia and Pennsylvania, and became chairman of the Philadelphia Committee. Miles fought valiantly in the Revolutionary War and was captured by the British. He spent twenty-one months as a prisoner of war before being exchanged in April 1778. The conditions of his exchange prohibited his returning to combat, so he became Deputy Quartermaster for the Army of the State of Pennsylvania for the balance of the War.

In 1782 Miles went into the sugar refining business and later became Mayor of the City of Philadelphia. In that post he led a parade through the city on July 4, 1788, marking the ratification of the U.S. Constitution. Later he moved to Cheltenham where he became a Justice of the Peace in 1793. He maintained his captain's rank in the First City troop throughout his life. It is obvious why Morgan Edwards would turn to Samuel Miles for help when his life and property were being threatened by the Patriots.[48]

Though no doubt rethinking his position as a Tory, Morgan Edwards could not refrain from his satirical or perhaps sarcastic public comments about the state of affairs. These were too much for the Patriots of Delaware, and a directive was issued for his arrest. Ironically, the order for Edwards's arrest was prepared by Colonel Miles.[49]

Before Miles drew up the order for Edwards's arrest, he took the precaution of secretly moving him to his own home. As a cover for his clandestine action, Miles "raised a hue and cry for his apprehension."[50] When officers came to inquire of Miles about Edwards's location he assured them he himself would deliver Edwards to the Committee of Safety in Delaware.

On August 7, 1775, a meeting of the White Clay Creek Committee of Safety (New Castle County) was held at the home of Henry Darby in Newark, Delaware, with William Patterson presiding. Morgan Edwards presented himself (not brought in by force) before the group which was made up of people who were no doubt his neighbors. He read the following retraction of his loyalty to the Crown:[51]

> Whereas, I have some time since, frequently, made use of rash and imprudent expressions with respect to the conduct of my fellow-countrymen, who are now engaged in a noble and patriotick struggle for the liberties of America against the arbitrary measures of the British ministry, which conduct has justly raised their resentment against me. I now confess that I have spoken wrong, for which I am sorry and ask forgiveness of the publick; and I do promise that for the future I will conduct myself in such a manner as to avoid giving offense, and at the same time, in justice to myself, declare that I am a friend to the present measures pursued by the friends of American liberty and do heartily approve of them, and as far as in my power, will endeavor to promote them.

Morgan Edwards's recantation follows the pattern of others and indicates that certain matters were required to be in the statement. These included confessions of improper conduct and speech concerning the patriot cause, asking for the forgiveness of the public, a pledge of correct future conduct, and a promise to support the cause of independence. He was not placed under house arrest as some have alleged, but continued to preach in churches. The only restrictions placed were on his speaking out about political issues.

Was his recantation sincere? There is a division of opinion. Those who believe that Morgan Edwards never really renounced his loyalty to the Crown present no factual evidence to demonstrate it. The political climate remained emotionally charged for so many years after the Revolution that many who were true Patriots, up to and during the Revolution, came under suspicion of both the Tories and the Whigs after it. A case in point was Thomas Rodney of Delaware.

Thomas Rodney, was a major figure in Delaware during the drive towards independence. He commanded the militia and was an officer in the Kent County Committee of Safety.[52] More importantly he and Morgan Edwards had developed a close friendship.

There is an inkling of the post-Revolution political climate, and the nature of Rodney's friendship with Edwards in a letter to a Dr. Evans in North Carolina, written March 20, 1791.[53]

> The Reverend Mr. Edwards did me the honor of spending an Evening at my house on his way to the lower Baptist Churches. I felt myself highly pleased and Entertained by his company and conversation___He possesses a degree of pleasantry and humour which is so happily adapted to his age, that it enables him to communicate the knowledge of years [of] study and experience in a most agreeable manner. I endeavoured to make him happy while he stayed, and he left in very good health except the Complaint of Sore Eyes___I pressed him to call on me on his Return, but where he may find me is uncertain....
>
> I have unfortunately acted a part that seems to have Equally offended both the friends of the American revolution and its Enemies, so Egregiously that the heads of each in this state have combined together and make it a common cause to destroy both my reputation and property.

Rodney went on to describe in detail his problems with both his Patriot friends and his Tory detractors. Whether his association with Edwards was part of that problem cannot be ascertained, but Edwards was still moving about freely inside and outside the state only four years before his death.

Thomas Rodney and Morgan Edwards maintained a correspondence which covered many subjects related to the biblical accounts of creation, and the laws of God.[54] Edwards felt free to stop at Rodney's home near Dover in central Delaware whenever his preaching assignments took him in that direction. What their association demonstrates, however, is that Morgan Edwards had renounced his loyalty to the English Crown years before and had found acceptance among those who had been leaders of the American Revolution.

A story which is part of the folklore purporting to demonstrate the insincerity of Edwards's retraction surfaced in the nineteenth century. The only known evidence to support it is the Webster letter of 1853.

It relates to John Gano's travel through Delaware as a chaplain with his army unit during the Revolution. He stopped to pay his respects to Morgan Edwards, but "the servant was sent out to say that Mr. E. had once known a Mr. Gano that preached the gospel, but never knew any by that name that followed the drum."[55] Sharp responses were sometimes characteristic of Edwards, but the spirit behind that one would not. Gano would have noted it in his biography, since he and Edwards were good friends. The crowning proof of Edwards's sincerity, however, was the burning of his house by the British army.

The Burning of Morgan Edwards' House
There are many gaps in what is known of Morgan Edwards's personal life in Delaware because so many personal possessions and records were lost in the house

burning. Edwards married Elizabeth Singleton of Newark, shortly after the death of her first husband, John Singleton. His will was not filed until June 16, 1771, and it was probated August 20, 1771, with both Morgan and Elizabeth listed as executors.[56] Singleton had owned several parcels of land in the area, and it was one of these which Edwards later sold to the Newark Academy. How much land Edwards inherited from his third wife is not known. Suffice to say, however, the Patriot cause reigned supreme in that part of Delaware.

In 1780 John Adams said of Delaware, "There were in this little State, from various causes, more tories in proportion than in any other."[57] The population at that time was about thirty-seven thousand, including approximately two-thousand slaves and bonded servants. The largest population was in the northern county of Newcastle, and the major group there was Scottish-Irish Presbyterians.[58]

The Presbyterian churches in Delaware numbered more than twice their nearest competitors, the Episcopalians and Methodists. Seventeen of the twenty-nine Presbyterian churches in Delaware were in Newcastle County. The only Baptist church in Delaware in 1775 was the Welsh Tract church in Pencader, Newcastle County, the church Morgan Edwards attended. Citizens of Newcastle County were predominantly patriotic, while Kent and Sussex County's were largely Loyalists.

Edwards was in good standing with the Presbyterians. The Academy at Newark was Presbyterian, and its founder, Francis Alison, was a friend of Edwards. Edwards had sold to the school the land that was adjacent to the campus. His fund-raising efforts for Rhode Island College were supported by Presbyterians in both Ireland and Scotland. Presbyterians also controlled the White Clay Creek Committee of Safety.

Colonel Samuel Miles of Philadelphia and the Presbyterians of northern Delaware, protected Edwards from hostile actions by vigilante Patriots. Not so the British military, which had a stern policy for dealing with turncoat Tories.

With the beginning of the Revolution, all of the state governments required oaths of allegiance and renunciations of fealty to the King. Likewise the British. In the areas they controlled, they administered oaths and issued certificates to erstwhile rebels who recanted. Thus the house of a Loyalist might be burned by the Patriots, and the hose of a Loyalist turned Patriot might be burned by the British. That is why Morgan Edwards's house was set afire by the British Army after the Battle of Cooches Bridge.

In the summer of 1777, Sir William Howe, Commander of the British Army in America, planned a campaign to capture Philadelphia, rout the Congress, defeat Washington and end the Revolution. On July 23, his brother, Admiral Sir Richard Howe, anchored two hundred ships bearing seveteen thousand men in Chesapeake Bay. By August 25, the troops put ashore at Elks Ferry, Maryland, and within two days Howe's advance corps was at the Head of Elk, only four days' march from Philadelphia.[59]

On learning of the landing of the British force in Maryland, General George Washington marched his tattered Continental Army from north of Philadelphia through the city, and encamped at Wilmington. On August 26, Washington and his aides Generals Nathaneal Greene and Marquis de Lafayette, rode forward to recon-

A Dazzling Enigma 303

noiter the territory between his troops and General Howe's. They rode to Iron Hill, only six miles from Howe's troops, but turned back in the middle of a wind and rain storm. Washington and his men found shelter in a "farmhouse at the foot of Chestnut Hill near the Welsh Tract Baptist Church in Pencader Hundred."[60]

It is a mistaken belief by some historians that Morgan Edwards was pastor of the Welsh Tract Baptist Church, as reported in the following quote from a historical paper.[61]

> The Rev. Morgan Edwards, pastor of the Welsh Tract Baptist Church during the Revolution, was a man of great distinction. He was the author of a history of the Baptists in Delaware, written about 1791. He is credited with the founding of Brown University at Providence, Rhode Island.
> Rev. Edwards is said to have been the only Baptist minister in America who was pro-British. His congregation, being pro-American, objected to his radical utterances, and refused to permit him to occupy the pulpit. Their opposition continued until he had admitted his error and reduced the admission to writing.

Two days after his reconnaissance, Washington moved an advance unit under General Greene's command up to the crossroads at Cooch's Bridge, near Iron Hill. It was the site Washington chose to fight his adversary, and it was located almost on top of the Welsh Tract Baptist Church. Washington, changed his plans and made a stand at Stanton further to the northeast. It was too late for Greene's troops under Brigadier General Maxwell to escape battle at Cooch's Bridge.

On the morning of September 3, the British under the command of Lord Cornwallis and General Knyphausen advanced with considerable force. Cornwallis's troops attacked Brigadier General Maxwell's men, who, retreat-

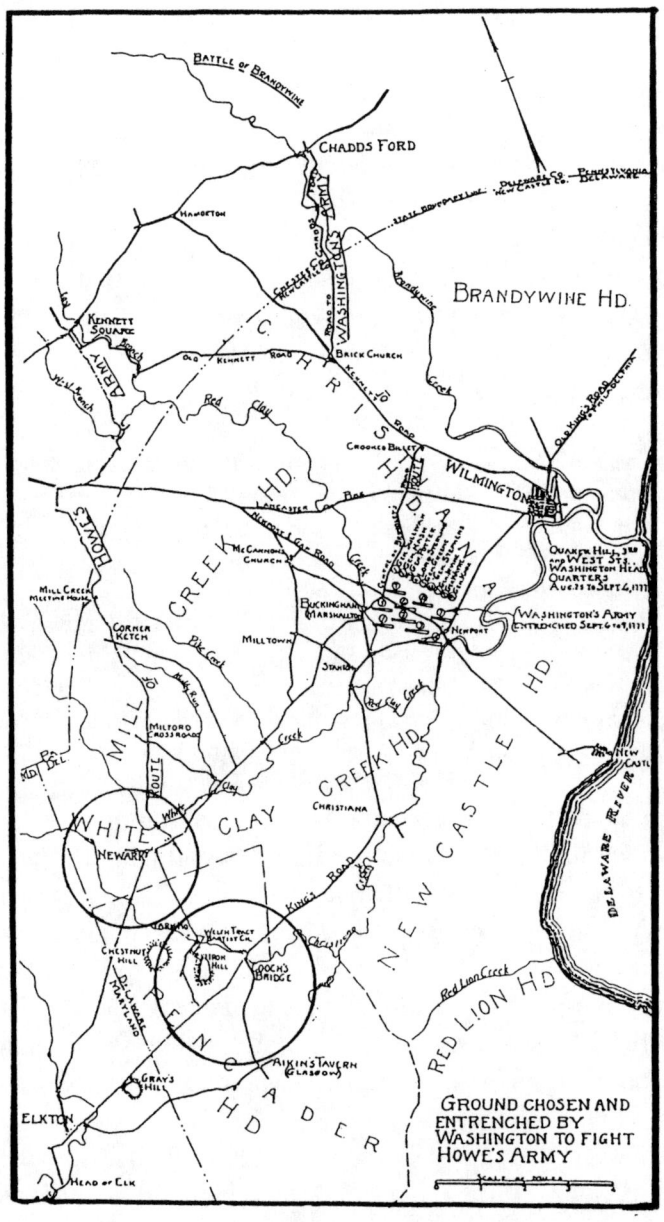

Map of the Battle of the Brandywine

ed after a short resistance over White Clay Creek with about forty casualties. The British losses were greater as Continental marksmen hidden behind the trees and rocks, fired with deadly accuracy into the advancing Redcoats.

The battle was little more than a skirmish, with the British advancing only about two miles, and then withdrawing to a line one mile back. It was the only battle fought in Delaware during the Revolution, but it was significant as it was the first time the stars and stripes, the new flag of America, was unfurled in battle.[62] At this point, Morgan Edwards' house was still standing.

The advance of the British toward Cooch's Bridge on that morning of September 3, involved only the right flank of the whole British army moving on Stanton. The left flank continued on its march toward Newark. On the morning of September 8, the Royal troops moved through the town, burning the houses of Patriots and Tories turned Patriots. Morgan Edwards's home was one of those set afire by the British.

In the preface to his history of the New Jersey Baptists, Edwards described something of his loss:[63]

> ...in the late war; the insufficiency of them which remain; and the burning (with his house) a volume which he had prepared for the press upwards of twenty years ago.

Welsh Baptist historian Joshua Thomas reported in his manuscript history of the Welsh Baptists that he had received a letter from Morgan Edwards in which he reported suffering much during the Revolution. He wrote that he had to flee for his life when the British burned his house.[64] From his home in Pencader, Edwards fled south to Middletown, Delaware, and eventually made his way back north to Philadelphia. Later he would resettle in

Delaware.⁶⁵

Though Howe would swing his left flank through Newark on his way to the Battle of the Brandywine, there was no way for the residents to get protection from Washington's forces. It cost Edwards as high a price to renounce his loyalty to the King as it would have to retain it.

But he was not the only Baptist minister in America to profess loyalty and recant. Isaac Backus reports on one "Brother Leach...Oct. 21 when I visited him he lamented his wanderings, and confessed that he had listened too much to Tory's in our public contests...." McLoughlin notes that Leach was one of the few Baptists in New England known to have Tory leanings.⁶⁶

Edwards himself reported another Baptist Tory in North Carolina by the name of William Cook "who established a church in Dutchman's Creek section of Davie Co. Accused as a Loyalist in 1772 he 'professed his sorrow' to the Rowan Committee of Safety."⁶⁷ Indeed, information exists which cites other Loyalist Baptist preachers.

In Summary

Morgan Edwards was loyal to the British Crown until his renunciation, but his Tory sentiments were practical, not political. His loyalty was more in principle than in action. It was Morgan Edwards's commitment to religious liberty which kept him in the Tory camp until 1775, and on occasion he fired a volley of biting satire and sarcasm against those who oppressed Baptists.

Edwards had difficulty accepting the loud calls for freedom by the Patriots of New England, Virginia, and North Carolina, who would in the same breath call for taxing Baptists to support Established churches.

Morgan Edwards had options other than humbly and

publicly retracting his loyalty. He could have gone to Canada, as did many Tories, or he could have returned to his homeland, as did many others. He made the retraction before his neighbors, kept his pledge, and in so doing may have demonstrated the greater courage.

A sermon he preached on Christmas Day in 1763, best expresses the convictions which undergirded his actions.[68]

> Nor is there any room for invidious comparison between establishment and dissenters in this land [Pennsylvania] as in our mother country, and in most of her colonies [New England or Virginia]___Every sect is here upon an equal footing. None can say "The temple of the Lord are we and ye are Samaritans"___ The law calls not your meeting-house by the approbrious [offensive] name of conventicle [meeting place of an illegal religious assembly]___Nor turns the charming word liberty into *toleration*___Nor obliges you to pay the tenth part of your substance to a minister you never go to hear___Nor forces you to subscribe, and take oaths or to pay fines or go to prison___So that your faith requires not the accession of heroism in this respect___You breathe free air___You do that which is right in your own sight; nor is there any as much as to make you ashamed, or to ask "What doest thou?"

Morgan Edwards never lost the trust of most of his fellow Baptist leaders, and his quick recovery to leadership after the Revolution, demonstrates their understanding of his loyalty to the Crown. It was not anti-independence, but proreligious liberty which motivated his Tory utterances. He believed religious liberty was better safeguarded under British law than under the political control of Patriot leaders who still believed in an Established church, and the taxing of non-conformists.

A perspective of Edwards' loyalty to the Crown which was closer in time and relationship may be a better gauge of the true character of Edwards' attitude toward America. It is contained in the sermon preached by William Rogers at Edwards's memorial service on February 22, 1795.[69]

> He also met with dishonour; but he complained not much of this, as it was occasioned by his strong attachment to the Royal Family of Great Britain, in the beginning of the American war, which fixed on him the name of Tory: this I should have omitted mentioning, had not the deceased precisely enjoined it upon me. For any person to have been so marked out in those days was enough to bring on political opposition and destruction of property; all of which took place with respect to Mr. Edwards, though he never thought of doing the least injury to the United States by abetting the cause of our enemies.

Morgan Edwards may have been conquered by the chain of events leading up to the American Revolution, but he was not subdued. The same can be said of another problem area in his life--the use of alcoholic beverages.

ENDNOTES

1. George Washington Paschal, "Introduction to Morgan Edwards' Materials on the North Carolina Baptists." North Carolina Historical Review, Raleigh, N.C.: Vol. III, 1930, 365
2. William Cathcart, *The Baptists and the American Revolution.* (Philadelphia: S.A. George & Co., 1876), 70,71.
3. North Callahan, *Royal Raiders.* (Indianapolis: Bobb-Merrill Co., 1963), 7.
4. Ibid., 36.
5. Ibid., 40.
6. Ibid., 41.
7. Wallace Browne, *The Good Americans.* (New York: William Morro and Co., Inc., 1969), 32.
8. Ibid., 33.
9. Ibid., 34.
10. Carl Van Doren, *Benjamin Franklin.* (New York: Penquin Books,

1938), 322.
11. Ibid., 327.
12. Ibid., 330.
13. Ibid., 418.
14. Ibid., 450.
15. Samuel Eliot Morison, *John Paul Jones.* (New York: Little Brown and Company, 1959), 32.
16. Charles Chauncey Langdon, *Everyday Things In American Life.* (New York: Charles Scribner, 1937), 194-195.
17. Ibid., 191.
18. E. James Ferguson, "Currency Finance - An Interpretation of Colonial Monetary Practices," *Essays In American Colonial History,* ed. Paul Goodman. (New York: Holt, Rinehart and Winston, 1967), 343.
19. Ibid., 353.
20. Morgan Edwards, *Materials Towards A History of the Baptists,* (Danielsville, GA.: Heritage Papers, 1984), Vol. 1, 47, App. II.
21. Ibid., 80,81.
22. Ibid., 122.
23. Ibid., 96.
24. From an anonymous article on Morgan Edwards written in 1874, and pasted inside the back cover of a copy of his *Materials Towards a History of the Baptists of Maryland.*
25. Edwards, Vol. 1, 106.
26. Robert G. Torbet, *A History of the Baptists.* 3rd ed. (Valley Forge: Judson Press, 1963), 242.
27. Ibid.
28. Edwards, Vol. 2, 101.
29. Paschal, 365.
30. Edwards, Vol. 2, 91.
31. Thomas R. McKibbens, Jr., and Kenneth L. Smith, *The Life and Works of Morgan Edwards.* (New York: Arno Press, 1980), 155.
32. Edwards, Vol. 2, 101.
33. Ibid.
34. Ibid., 91,92.
35. William G. McLoughlin, *New England Dissent, 1630-1833:The Baptists and the Separation of Church and State.* (Cambridge: Harvard University Press, 1971), 531-546.

36. _____, *The Diary of Isaac Backus*. 3 vols. (Providence: Brown University Press, 1968). 914,915.
37. Reuben A. Guild, *Early History of Brown University Including the Life, Times, and Correspondence of President Manning*. (Providence: Snow and Farnham, 1897), 15.
38. McLoughlin, 914,915.
39. Ibid.
40. Isaac Backus, MS Copy, A Journey To Philadelphia 1774. (John Hay Library, Brown University, Providence), n.p.
41. McLoughlin, *Diary*, 917
42. The author encountered some of the folklore surrounding Morgan Edwards' silence during an interview with Hywell Davies on May 11, 1991, in Cardiff, Wales. Dr. Davies, a Baptist historian, raised the question of whether Edwards might have been intimidated by Robert Strettle Jones who, with the Quakers, put the brakes on the entire Grievance Committee.
43. Backus, n.p.
44. Ibid.
45. W.B. Sprague, *Annals of the American Pulpit*. (New York: Robert Carter & Brothers, 1865), Vol. 6, 83.
46. Delaware State Archives, Dover, Delaware, Deed Z 603, Orphans Court 310.
47. Edwards, Vol. 2, 5.
48. The author has drawn this biographical sketch from the following sources: MS. Autobiography, Samuel Miles, Philadelphia: Historical Society of Pennsylvania, AM 1042. Ellis P. Oberholtzer, *Philadelphia, A History of the City and Its People*. (Philadelphia: S.J. Clarke Publishing Co., n.d.), I, 295. MS. Churchbook, First Baptist Church, Philadelphia, 15.
49. MS. Letter of Richard Webster to Horatio Gates Jones, July 20, 1853. American Baptist Historical Society, Rochester, N.Y.
50. Ibid.
51. J. Thomas Scharf, *The History of Delaware, 1609-1888*, (Philadelphia: L. J. Richards & Co., 1888), I, 224.
52. Ibid.
53. MS. Letter of Thomas Rodney to Dr. Evans, March 20, 1791. Historical Society of Delaware, Wilmington.
54. The orignals are housed in the Historical Society of Delaware at

Wilmington.
55. Webster.
56. Delaware State Archives, Dover, Delaware.
57. Harold Bell Hancock, *The Delaware Loyalists*. (Wilmington: Historical Society of Delaware, 1940), 1.
58. Ibid., 2,3.
59. John P. Nields, "Washington's Army In Delaware in the Summer of 1777." Address at Cooch's Bridge, New Castle County, Delaware, on September 9, 1927, incident to the Celebration of the 150th Anniversary of the Battle of the Brandywine, 2.
60. Ibid., 5.
61. Edward W. Cooch, *The Battle of Cooch's Bridge,* 1940. The author of this treatise wrote several historical papers related to the events surrounding this battle. This paper was presented to the Historical Society of Delaware by the author on November 30, 1942.
62. Nields, 8,9.
63. Edwards, Vol. 1, 77.
64. Joshua Thomas, MS., Materials For A History of the Baptist Churches in the Principality of Wales, 1630-1782." Bristol Baptist College, 278.
65. MS. Letter from Samuel Jones to James Manning, March 9, 1777, Jones Collection, A 26.
66. McLoughlin, *Diary.* II, 287.
67. Edwards, Vol. 2, 108.
68. MS. Sermon, "And Beside This," Philadelphia: December 25, 1763. Crozer Collection, 1738, Box 1, Vol. XI, No. 5.
69. John Rippon, ed., Baptist Annual Register, London: 1796, 309.

CHAPTER TWELVE

CONDUCT UNBECOMING A BAPTIST MINISTER

> "A letter...was read informing the church
> of Rev'd Morgan Edwards' immoral conduct,
> and disorderly walk."
> Philadelphia Churchbook, 1781

The Nature of the Charge

By mid-year 1781, the Philadelphia Baptist church was a divided congregation. It was split over the preaching of their pastor, Elhanan Winchester, because he advocated the unacceptable doctrine of universalism. The situation deteriorated to the point that a major block of members demanded his resignation.

Amid that crisis, the church received a letter from one of its former members who had moved to Delaware. His name was Andrew Edge and his letter brought serious charges of misconduct against a former pastor, the Reverend Morgan Edwards. An entry in the churchbook reports it.[1]

A letter from Andrew Edge with two certificates signed by

Saml. Woodbridge and Hugh Grafford was read informing the church of Revd. Morgan Edwards conduct, and disorderly walk___The church take Mr. Edwards conduct under consideration but declining any decisive measures in the business until our next meeting of business.

Edge had once been an active member of the Philadelphia church, and Samuel Woodbridge was still a member. It seems ironic that the letter was presented to the church almost ten years to the day after Edwards presented his letter of resignation as pastor of the church. The charges brought against him continued for three years before he was excommunicated. Four more years would elapse before he would be restored.

This unhappy episode in Edwards's life requires an examination of the use of alcohol in the Welsh culture and in eighteenth-century America, Edwards's excommunication and restoration, and his commitment of sobriety.

The Use of Alcohol in Welsh Society

Morgan Edwards was a Welshman, and both ancient and modern Welsh scholars concur on the Welsh love for intoxicating drink. Giraldus Cambrensi, a twelfth century Welsh scholar, said of his countrymen, "They are immoderate in their love of intoxicating drink, being parsimonious in bad times and extravagant in times of plenty."[2] Twentieth century historian Jan Morris pointed out that "the convivial side of the Welsh character has often been encouraged by a taste for strong drink," and "the ordinary people in many periods of their history to have been besotted by drink."[3] Knowing the acceptance of alcoholic beverages in Welsh culture may help us to comprehend the reason why drinking was part of Edwards's life.

During Edwards's early years, alcoholic beverages figured conspicuously in most public events and private occasions. These would include "fairs and markets, at christenings, weddings, funerals, wakes and revels."[4] The basic drink was beer and its use consumed one-seventh of the total national income.[5]

Because fairs and markets were exempt from the limited hours imposed on licensed pubs, huge quantities of beer would be consumed at these events. It was not unusual for most guests at christenings to end the day in a helpless stupor, and weddings frequently became opportunities for "drinking, wooing, dancing...fighting."[6]

Even funerals did not escape excessive drinking. The friends of the deceased sat a vigil the night before a funeral. Gathered around a long table, with the corpse underneath, they smoked and drank until dawn, then they adjourned to the local pub to continue the drinking until time for the funeral service.[7]

One contributing factor to this behavior was the ancient belief in the Tylwyth Teg. These were mythical little people of Welsh folklore, who were believed to have been the souls of the ancient Druids or Romans. For centuries the Welsh believed them to be very real and to be powerful, small, and invisible. They appeared on special occasions to indwell a person, usually when drunk, and to change that person's character into a complete opposite.[8]

By the eighteenth century the early Methodists railed against the Welsh as a "heedless, feckless people."[9] These revivalists saw the Welsh as unconcerned for their moral life and for their chances of eternal life.[10] But the old ways of "merrie Wales" persisted strongly until the latter part of the century, and the conduct of clergy in the Established church did not encourage it to be otherwise.

It was accepted that "many clergymen, for various reasons, were apt to sip."[11] Some did so to enter the more polite society of the squires and rid themselves of the stigma of poverty. In turn, numbers of these became intoxicated and fell into indiscreet behavior. Still other clergy drank because they were unable to live up to "increasingly high standards of personal morality and pastoral care demanded of them."[12]

The connections between drinking and religion in Welsh life were quite pervasive. For example, the tradition known as "Cwrw' Achos", or the "beer of the cause," consisted of giving the minister a beer or two before the worship service so the alcohol would release him from any inhibitions during his preaching.[13]

"Cwrw' Achos" occurred at Sunday festivals in church yards and included dancing, boisterous games, swearing, singing, and drinking. It was not uncommon for such revelries to degenerate into quarrels and brawls. Because such behavior was not conducive to quality worship, many simply adjourned from the churchyard to the local alehouse.

During the restoration of older church buildings in the nineteenth century many were found to have private staircases leading from the parish pub next door to the church. Niches were also discovered in which were hidden special ale given for the vicar's use.[14]

With the coming of the revivals in the first half of the eighteenth century, Anglican clergy began preaching in opposition to excessive drinking. Underlying their efforts was the desire to educate the people to resist drunkenness as a snare of the Devil. Drunkenness received less attention in the Dissenting churches because the standard of conduct was higher than in the Anglican congregations.[15]

For most people, alcoholic beverages were essentials in the diet because water frequently was unsafe. Tea and coffee were seen as drinks for gentle ladies. Moderate use of alcoholic beverages was accepted even in the most puritan settings, whereas drunkenness was condemned. There was a clear distinction between "drinking and being given to drink."[16]

Another factor in the Welsh drinking culture was the pub or tavern. The pubs were accepted social centers in the communities. Here the people could find good food, entertainment, light, heat, comfortable furniture, news, town gossip, and camaraderie. In fact, the board of the Particular Baptist Fund held their meetings in London taverns.

But Welsh culture was changing. An example of the changes taking place in the second half of the eighteenth century was the passing of the practice of "terming." Terming referred to a man who became so frustrated with the sheer drudgery of his life that he deserted his family for several days at a time, going from pub to pub, in a drunken stupor. When the frustration had worn off he returned to his home and work until the next "terming." By 1770 this practice had all but disappeared.[17]

Two elements of this drinking milieu may have impacted Morgan Edwards's drinking habits. First, his sermonic references to his preconversion lifestyle described it as very sinful and wild. It does not take too much stretching of the imagination to picture that young man in his mid-teens being a part of the Anglican churchyard revelries of the times. The bawdy songs, loud and profane shouting, and brawls could have been part of his life then. Second, there was a sense of despair for a way of life that had slipped away.[18] Life had become more somber and austere, and drinking seemed to revive "merrie Wales."

Morgan Edwards's life must have turned somber as well. The emotional upheaval attendant upon his retraction of loyalty to the Crown, the deaths of his second and third wives after brief marriages, the burning of his house and most of his possessions, and the disappearance of his son William in England may have brought on a sense of despair.

Edwards would not have used life's tragedies as excuses for intemperance. His Welsh upbringing, and the American drinking climate, plus his adversities, however, may have lowered the threshold of his resistance to over-indulgence.

Drinking In Eighteenth Century America

Alcohol permeated every level of society in eighteenth century America. It crossed all regional, sexual, racial, and social lines. Americans drank alone and together, at home and abroad, at work and at play, in fun and in earnest.

They drank from dawn to dusk and in between. Taverns were crowded at night with boisterous, fun-loving drinkers. The people drank before, during, and after their meals. Americans drank in their youth, and if they lived long enough, into their old age. Drinking was part of all formal events, from weddings to ministerial ordinations, as well as informal times, such as sitting quietly by the fireside in the evening.

No place was spared as Americans drank in sophisticated Andover and on the Illinois frontier. They drank in the crude lumbercamps and on satin settees, in log cabins and at fashionable hotels. The American greeting was,

"Come, Sir, take a dram first."[19]

In the ten years before the American Revolution, Americans were annually consuming an estimated 3.7 gallons of alcohol per capita.[20] By 1790 that rate reached nearly six gallons absolute alcohol per year, more than twice that of today. In the late eighteenth and early nineteenth century, the per capita rate of alcoholic consumption in America was higher than ever before or since.

White males were trained to drink as children, even as babies. Year-old children were given drinks and toddlers were coaxed to drink the sugary residue in their parents' glasses. The intention was to teach temperance, but the children developed their parents' intemperate patterns. Teen-aged boys viewed a visit to the pub as a sign of manhood. A not uncommon sight was that of twelve-and fourteen-year old boys in a tavern drinking before noon.[21]

Another distinction made about American drinking was the ability to tolerate large quantities of alcohol. A Scotsman by the name of Peter Neilson said of Americans at that time, that they were "in a certain degree *seasoned*, [italics supplied] and consequently it [was] by no means common to see an American *very* intoxicated."[22]

Americans were no different from their European counterparts in the belief that alcoholic beverages were nutritious and healthful. They were seen as supplements to diets and medications for the relief of life's tensions. Americans believed as well that the only evil in drinking was intoxication. Hence, their ability to consume such huge quantities before getting drunk was really a self-deception.

As in Wales, so in America, the tavern was a focal point in the community. Americans enjoyed themselves as they transacted business, debated current issues, and even settled cases "out of court" because so many attorneys, judges, defendants, and jurymen gathered there.[23]

In New England, taverns were often located next to meeting houses so parishioners could be warmed up before and after sitting in the unheated meeting houses. In fact, many of these taverns were owned by deacons and ministers.[24] Because the colonial elite controlled most of the pubs, they were able to control the drinking of the common people until the introduction of cheap New England rum after 1720.

Before 1720, Jamaican rum was too costly for the average person to drink frequently. Early in the eighteenth century, however, New England farmers began to manufacture a cheaper brand of rum, and by 1740 it had become the common drink. With the increase in the drinking of rum came a rising tide of drunkenness, violence, and crime.[25]

These social ills brought a loud reaction from prominent clergy. Whitefield spoke out publicly against the abuse of alcohol, but he followed many New England ministers who had voiced opposition decades before. Cotton Mather, for instance, feared the "flood of rum could Overwhelm a good Order among us."[26] By mid-eigtheenth century many better educated people were joining the chorus of voices raised against intoxication and its resultant disorders. In 1760, Ben Franklin called the pub "the Pest of Society."[27]

The direction in which America was moving in its drinking patterns by the 1780s made it clear that while the amount of drinking had not yet reached its peak, a temperance surge was discernable on the horizon. Neither Edwards nor other clergy who might overindulge would find the moral climate as tolerant as in decades past.

Indeed, Edwards's voice was heard among those who spoke out against Demon Rum. In 1772, he recorded the experience of one Baptist minister who fell victim to drink. The minister was James Stephens of the Ashley River church in South Carolina.[28]

> [James Stephens] Came to Ashley-river in the month of May, 1750, and on the 22nd of June following became pastor of the church; but by an unhappy fondness for liquor was obliged to quit both the church and the ministry in 1769. But has not a dumb spirit, a deaf spirit, an unclean spirit etc. been cast out? And who knows but Jamaica spirit will one day be exorcised out of this country where it makes such dreadful havock? The Indians themselves lament its being brought hither though they are excessively fond of it. Surely if any creature of God were not good, rum would be it.

In 1757, Isaac Backus reported the case of a New England Baptist pastor, Jedidiah Hide, "who fell last August into the sin of excessive drinking."[29] A church council called to hear the matter judged him with greater strictness because he was an Elder. He was forced to resign his pastorate. Backus reported a similar situation involving one Ebeneezer Snow who was censured for drinking to excess.[29]

Despite occasionally errant ministers and lay persons, Baptists did maintain a tolerant attitude towards alcohol. They even engaged in the rum traffic, as seen in a letter from George Gibbs of Newport, Rhode Island, to Baptist businessman Nicholas Brown in Providence:[30]

> I this Day received a line from Capt. Anthony at Philadelphia he Writes us that he Expects to be here by Next Sunday as Mr. J. Brown Talk of sending 20 casks of Rum I Request you will get them Ready if you Continue of the same mind as we are Deter-

mined The Sloop Shall Not Lay above five days for fear of the Loss of the Market which is Very good at Present in Newengland Rum 2/3 sd at Philadelphia.

The use of alcoholic beverages had been a normal part of Morgan Edwards's life from childhood. While he probably abused alcohol during his preconversion teen years, he managed to practice moderation after his conversion. He was like most Baptists of his day.

Historian William G. McLoughlin has summed up the climate among Baptists in the latter part of the eighteenth century.[31]

> While the Baptists, like the Puritans, had no objection to moderate drinking (of beer, cider, rum, wine or flip) drinking was always a censurable evil, since it deprived a man of his reason, making him subject to his sensual passions and an easy victim of Satan's wiles. With increased consumption of hard liquor from distilled corn, a more scientific attitude toward the dangers of alcoholism, and a greater emphasis upon the dignity and reason of man in a democratic and Christian society, the pietists of America began to conclude that to drink alcohol in any form was to defile "the temple of the soul." Eventually teetotalist prohibition replaced temperance and moderation as a criterion of Christian morality.

The Baptists in Philadelphia did not escape the growing opposition to excessive drinking in their city because the Quakers were among the first to condemn the use of distilled beverages.[32] Their numbers included the educated, reform minded, and merchants of the city, and by 1780 that opposition was widespread.

The Philadelphia Baptist Church, however, was slow to go on record in their opposition to strong drink. It was not until January 5, 1789, fifteen months after restoring

Edwards to full membership, that they endorsed an earlier action of the Philadelphia Baptist Association opposing distilled beverages.[33] The question then is, how did they handle Morgan Edwards's situation?

Excommunication and Restoration
Following the reading of Andrew Edge's letter on July 2, 1781, the church decided not to take any action until the August church meeting. The reason for postponing action was to hear Morgan Edwards's side of the story.

By the time the next meeting was held on August 6, the church had received a letter from Edwards through Thomas Shields. Edwards defended himself against the charges, but the church minutes do not contain his letter. They reported only that the whole matter was considered and a unanimous vote taken to write a letter of admonition to Edwards. Colonel Miles and Thomas Shields, a silversmith, were to write the letter, which suggests two things might have occurred.

Either Edwards's defense did not satisfy the people at the meeting, or he acknowledged there was some truth to the charges. Otherwise there would have been no need to send a letter of admonition. The latter seems more likely because Edwards later gave a detailed account of occasions when alcohol was used. Apparently the offenses were not serious enough to call for either suspension or excommunication, but only for an admonition.

Events continued to unfold at the September 4 meeting when Shields reported that Colonel Miles was "so ingaged in publick business that it was impossible for him to assist" in writing the letter. The call for Miles to help in writing the letter implies that the church wanted to involve someone who was close to Edwards. By that time

Miles had been returned to civilian life, having been a prisoner of war, and was busy providing war supplies to the Pennsylvania militia.

John McKim, the church clerk, was appointed to replace Miles as one of the letter writers. Shields and McKim were then requested to immediately dispatch the letter. In addition, they were requested to inform Andrew Edge of the latest action.

Two months later the situation worsened for Morgan Edwards. At the November 5 church meeting a paragraph from a second letter was read, further indicting him. It was read by a Mr. Watkins, who had received the letter some time before from Samuel Davis, another member of the church. The charges were specific enough to cause the church to take more firm action.

The clerk, Mr. McKim, was authorized to write a letter to Edwards requesting his appearance at the next church meeting on Monday, December 3 at 2:00 P.M. to answer the charges against him. McKim was also instructed to write to Edge and Davis to request their attendance as well. They were asked to repeat the charges in Edwards's presence and invited to bring others who could support their testimony. The letter to Edwards reveals the gravity with which the church was treating the matter.[34]

Philadelphia 6 Nov. 1781
Rev. Sir
    I am requested to inform you that in as much as severall charges have been lately brot before the church against you, it is the request of the church that you attend in person at our next meeting of business, which will be Monday the third of Dec. coming to answer to the said charges, some of which are___in attention to publick worship___joining yourself with drunkards___frequenting taverns___being often intoxicated with liquor___singing

imodest songs, and using abusive language. It may also be proper to inform you that the persons who have lodged the afforesaid complaints, are also requested to give their attendance at the same time by order of the church.
Respectfully I am Revd. Sir Your Obed. Servt. John McKim
To Revd Morgan Edwards
Near New Ark - Sent by Mr. Hughes the date above

It is possible the issue of Edwards's drinking may have brought a measure of relief and reconciliation in the church at that time. He had friends and detractors in both camps of the Winchester controversy, and the attention had shifted from Winchester to Edwards. The minutes do not indicate the number in attendance, but surely it was far more than usual.

The December 3 meeting began with the selection of a moderator, a Mr. Bowen, and then a second letter from Andrew Edge was read. This letter was written in November and restated the previous charges. None of those accusing Edwards of misconduct was present, but he was. He responded to each charge in the order it was made.

To the charge he had absented himself from worship, he said the whole congregation could attest otherwise. One has to assume he at least was present on communion Sundays, if not on others. Given the distance he had to travel and the Sundays he might be supplying a pulpit, he could not have been there every Sunday. He did acknowledge being absent when a Mr. Sutton was supplying the pulpit because Edwards had received word from Rev. Abel Davis that Sutton was jealous of him.

Edwards also responded to the charges of keeping company with drunkards, frequenting taverns, and being intoxicated. He stated that for the past two or three years he had not in any way been intoxicated except on one occasion. In that instance, he stated, a doctor had prescribed bark diluted with alcohol as a treatment. Later in his statement, he said he had used too much alcohol in the mixture.

Edwards also confessed that sometime before that incident he had been intoxicated, for which he was sorry and asked the forgiveness of the church. He emphatically denied keeping company with drunkards and that his companions were men of the highest reputation.

In answering the charge of singing bawdy songs, Edwards acknowledged singing a verse of a song, but nothing in it was of immodest character. As proof he referred the church to Mr. Shields to whom he had sent a copy of the lyrics.

The fifth charge was that he had used abusive language to excuse disorderly behavior. He acknowledged saying the Whig Battalion (Continental Army soldiers) ought to be hanged and that he said it when he was intoxicated with the mixture of bark and alcohol.

Morgan Edwards declared that the sixth charge against him was the most hurtful. The accusation was that "he makes his brags of being in holy orders and never called to acct."[35] His refutation of this charge sheds much light on Edwards' strong convictions about ordination and the preaching of the Gospel.

He said he had often remonstrated with tax collectors on the "iniquity of their ways" by taxing him (he was not then pastor of a church) and not their own ministers. The tax collectors declared he did not preach. His rejoinder was, that it was not preaching that made a man a minister in the eyes of the law, but being in holy orders, and he was in holy orders.

Edwards meant by this statement that the law of tax

exemption had to do with one's being ordained and not whether or not one was pastor of a church. Edwards asserted before the congregation that he never mentioned holy orders in an unbecoming manner, and only on occasions of the kind he described.

In the absence of any of Edwards's accusers, the church found itself in a quandary. It decided to drop the whole matter unless other evidence were brought forward.

Morgan Edwards's name does not reappear in the minutes until June 7, 1784, forty-two months later. It is listed with several others "who have long absented themselves from publick worship and other church duties."[36] A committee was appointed to wait upon these persons, including writing to those who no longer lived in Philadelphia.

Three months later at the September 6 meeting the committee reported they were having difficulty contacting the people assigned to them. By now, Thomas Ustick was pastor of the church, and life in the city and church had suffered much from the Revolutionary War. The church recognized the problem and assigned George Ingles to visit those who lived in the city and request their presence at the next church meeting.

The Philadelphia church was in a state of decline between 1775 and 1792. The Revolution and the Winchester affair had taken a heavy toll on its strength, and the membership declined from one-hundred-seventy-four to eighty-seven in this period. James Manning visited the church and described it as "in a broken state."[37] In a church book entry for November 6, 1779, "Joseph Watkins is desired to get the broken panes of the Baptist Church filled up with boards."[38] In this dire time, the church wanted to assess its strength.

Another effort was made on November 8, 1784, to ascertain the standing of the members who had moved away, including Morgan Edwards. It was decided on December 13, to write to each member and request that he or she write back within three months asking for letters of dismission to another church. It was further decided that failure to act within the specified time would constitute disorderly conduct, unless the person could justify not acting for sufficient reason. Edwards was among those listed to receive a copy of the minute.

On July 26, 1785, Edwards reacted with some ire to the copy of the minutes sent to him. His reaction is contained in a letter to his old friend Samuel Jones.[39]

> Sometime ago I received a minute of one of the meetings of business (addressed to me and five or six more) belonging to the baptist church in Philadelphia requiring complyance in six months on pain of excommunication___instead of complyance I wrote a remonstrance, and insisted on their giving it a place in their records___but whether they have done so or not___or whether I am excommunicated for non-compliance I know not___I therefore desire you to inform yourself of the premises, and conjure by our old friendship to give me a full account of the matter, for if my remonstrance is not upon record it will compel me to make it public and lasting some other way.

When Edwards wrote the above on July 26, he was not aware of what had already transpired. On May 9, 1785, the church had voted to "proceed against Morgan Edwards based on the minute of Dec. 13, 1784 and other information respecting his conduct."[40] It was a unanimous decision and the bill against him was readied for the next meeting.

The resolution of excommunication was passed on July 4, 1785, twenty-two days before Edwards's letter to Jones. It noted his service as pastor and stated that it was only their highest sense of Christian duty which compelled them to take the painful action of excommunication. It cited written and verbal accounts which charged Edwards with conduct unbecoming both a minister and a private Christian.

The resolution recognized Morgan's previous defense, and the church's decision not to act at that time. The indictment went on to imply he was still behaving in the same manner. In addition he had not responded to the letter from the December church meeting as to transferring his membership to a church closer to his home in Delaware. They assumed he had not acted because no other church would admit him, and no mention is made of his letter of remonstrance.

After quoting some related scripture verses, the resolution states, "That Morgan Edwards is now excluded from the communion of this church and cut off from a name and place in the house of God.[41] The action taken by the church was unanimous, and the resolution was to be read from the pulpit on July 24, 1785.

The process the church followed to excommunicate Morgan Edwards was of his design and is found in *The Customs of the Primitive Churches.*[42] The same must be said of the process by which he was eventually restored.[43]

On January 6, 1787 two and one-half years later in the middle of the winter, Morgan Edwards appeared before the church. He proposed "that 1st they should reverse the former judgement of the church relative to his exclusion and so admit him to a rehearing___ or 2nd as he now acknowledged his fault and had reformed, he wished to be restored and dismissed to another church."[44] The church did not act on either of his proposals. Of the first, they ruled that everything was done properly, and the decision could not be reversed. Of the second, they appointed a committee of the pastor, Thomas Ustick, former pastor William Rogers, and two laymen, Samuel Davis, Sr., and Joseph Watkins, to take two steps. First, check with the Welsh Tract church in Delaware to inquire concerning Edwards' reformation. Second, meet with him to determine what were the "signs accompanying of his repentance and reformation."

The church seemed to be taking Edwards's initiative seriously as two months later, on March 5 they authorized the pastor, Thomas Ustick, to meet at Chester, Pennsylvania, with John Boggs, pastor of the Welsh Tract Baptist Church. The purpose of the meeting was to determine when the Welsh Tract church was going to respond to their inquiries about Edwards's conduct. Ustick was also to write to Edwards, informing him of the church's intention to decide on his restoration at the next meeting if there were no further negative reports.

In a happy, chatty letter to Samuel Jones on February 28, 1787, we can discern Morgan's attitude during this period of inquiry. He said, "Tomorrow [March 1, 1787] will show how a certain Saint will fare in Welsh Tract___ What next?"[45] Apparently the "Saint" did not fare too well.

By the next meeting on April 2, they had apparently received unfavorable reports from John Boggs and/or the Welsh Tract church, so they delayed action on Edwards's restoration. It would be another nine months before the issue of Edwards's reinstatement be raised again.

On January 7, 1788, an unidentified person requested, on behalf of Morgan Edwards, that he be permitted to present evidence of his reformation at the next church meeting. It was clear, Edwards wanted to put this whole matter behind him. The Revolution was now history, the American states were in the process of forming a constitutional government, and the American people wanted to get on with their lives. The lingering remnants of that dark period needed to be settled, even in church matters.

Alas! Such was not the case for Morgan Edwards. He did appear at the next meeting on February 4, but the members present were not satisfied with the certificates verifying his reformation. This seems strange in view of the church's past history of restoring persons who, on verbal testimony, professed to have experienced a reformation from disorderly conduct. In his case, Edwards offered the written witness of others, and he was again refused restoration. More evidence was required and it would be another ten months before Morgan Edwards had another opportunity to seek reinstatement of his membership.

At the church meeting on October 6, 1788, it was evident that someone had been at work in Morgan Edwards's behalf. Samuel Miles brought before the church a request to restore Edwards to full membership. Edwards could not have had a more influential person speak for him than Miles, who was then mayor of Philadelphia. Only three months before he had marched through the city at the head of a parade marking the ratification of the Constitution of the United States of America.

After Miles presented Edwards's petition, "the question was put and carried in the affirmative."[46] Following the vote, Morgan came into the room and was received by those present. The quick dispatch of Edwards's restoration at this meeting suggests some comparisons with the other occasions on which it was attempted.

At the February meeting, Edwards appeared on his own

behalf and failed to win restoration. Samuel Miles appeared for him at the October meeting. Miles was Philadelphia's premier citizen and a long time prominent member of the church and a Revolutionary War hero. One concludes that Edwards and Miles settled on a strategy for the restoration and that Edwards had satisfied Miles that his sobriety and conduct were both as they should be.

Another comparison is the preparation made for the meeting. Miles evidently talked to a number of people in the church before the meeting to persuade them that Edwards' behavior had changed and that they should vote for restoration. The restoration vote went smoothly.

In retrospect, at the outset the church seemed to feel it had no other option but to excommunicate Edwards. It was a painful but necessary decision. By October 1788, however, it was clear the church was also ready to put the issue behind it.

It was on October 6, that Morgan Edwards reentered the mainstream of American Baptist church life. A few days later he attended the meetings of the Philadelphia Baptist Association, and for the first time in thirteen years, his name appeared in the minutes.

Morgan Edwards's Sobriety

Though Morgan Edwards was not restored to full membership until October of 1788, he had pledged himself to abstinence almost three years before. His commitment is contained in another letter to Samuel Jones on November 7, 1785.[47]

> You express sorrow at hearing Joe Watkins tell, *he saw a certain person far gone in liquor* --- I believe you -- I wish you had put down his words on the occasion -- Do that yet -- I am of opinion that an exhilerating glass is not a drunken glass -- what if it

freshens the cheeks, enlivens the eyes, gives a fillip to the spirits and tips the tongue with eloquence, and does not unfit a man for any business human or divine? is this drunkenness? -- and Big head saw no more let him call it what he will -- this I know by the quantity of liquor drank between Abel Davis and that same person which was only a nib of punch -- However you will hear no more such talk of your old friend from *all saints day* onward to the end of life -- I do not use lightness when I speak thus -- but tell you of a firm and abstinate resolution.

Morgan Edwards reported to Samuel Jones, that he had made a firm commitment as of October 31, 1785, to abstain from further drinking, even in moderation. The occasion referred to in the letter names one Abel Davis, a minister and member of the Welsh Tract church, as the one who shared a glass with him. Joseph Watkins was an active member of the Baptist church in Philadelphia and one of the first new deacons chosen shortly after Edwards arrived in Philadelphia. He was also a member of the committee authorized on January 8, 1787, to contact the Welsh Tract Baptist Church about the extent of Edwards's reformation. It was at this meeting that Edwards first appeared before the church seeking reinstatement.[48]

The incident was viewed differently by Watkins's and Edwards's people. Watkins must have seen Edwards in a tavern in company with Abel Davis and judged by their animated conversation that they were drunk. Edwards, on the other hand, saw the experience as two persons enjoying camaraderie over a glass of punch.

In colonial times, "communal gatherings such as weddings, house raisings or the ordination of a minister were occasions for the liberal provisions of cider, punch and rum."[49] While the punch was not just mixed fruit juices it was very much a watered-down drink. Edwards, as will be seen later, had a good sense of humor no doubt more freely expressed in the local tavern than in church meetings.

Edwards's feelings about the report were so strong that he emphatically said, "And Big head saw no more let him call it what he will." Morgan Edwards was never accused of dissembling in any matter. In fact, his forthright style frequently caused him problems. When he stated the drink consisted only of a "nib of punch," he spoke truthfully, even though Watkins perceived it otherwise.

What matters most in this statement is that Edwards came to the conclusion he could no longer drink, even moderately, and be restored in the church. So on October 31, 1785, he committed himself to total abstinence. It would be another three years before he was finally restored to full membership in the Baptist church of Philadelphia, on October 6, 1788. He had one more major hurdle to leap, however, and that was his involvement in the Winchester affair.

ENDNOTES

1. MS. Churchbook, First Baptist Church, Philadelphia, July 2, 1781, n.p.
2. Jan Morris, *The Matter of Wales*. (Oxford: Oxford University Press, 1964), 166.
3. Ibid., 193-194.
4. Geraint H. Jenkins, *Literature, Religion and Society In Wales, 1660-1730*. (Cardiff: University of Wales Press, 1978), 92.
5. Ibid.
6. Ibid.
7. Ibid.
8. Morris, 80.
9. Prys Morgan, *The Eighteenth Century Renaissance*. (Llandybie, Wales: Christopher Davis, 1981), 33.
10. Ibid.

11. Jenkins, 94.
12. Ibid.
13. Personal letter from the Reverend D. Hugh Matthews, dated September 4, 1992, in which he translates from a letter in Welsh from Professor Geraint H. Jenkins of the University of Wales.
14. Morgan, 37.
15. Jenkins, 29.
16. Ibid., 93.
17. Morgan, 35.
18. Ibid., 30.
19. W. J. Rorabaugh, *The Alcoholic Republic: An American Tradition.* (New York: Oxford University Press, 1972), 20,21.
20. Jack H. Mendelson, and Mancy K. Mello, *Alcohol, Use and Abuse in America.* (Boston: Little, Brown and Company, 1985), 13.
21. Ibid., 16.
22. Rorabaugh, ix, 11, 12, 14.
23. Ibid., 27.
24. Ibid., 28.
25. Ibid., 30.
26. Ibid., 31.
27. Ibid., 33.
28. Morgan Edwards, *Material Towards A History of the Baptists.* (Danielsville, GA.: Heritage Papers, 1984), II, 126.
29. William G. McLoughlin, *The Diary of Isaac Backus.* 3 vols. (Providence: Brown University Press, 1968), 466,467.
30. MS. Letter from George Gibbs to Nicholas Brown, May 18, 1770. (Providence: Brown Papers, John Carter Brown Library, Brown University), L 57 - 82 M.
31. McLoughlin, II, 1163.
32. Rorabaugh, 36.
33. Churchbook, January 5, 1789, n.p.
34. Ibid., November 5, 1781.
35. Ibid., December 3, 1781.
36. Ibid., June 7, 1784.
37. William D. Thompson, *Philadelphia's First Baptists.* (Philadelphia: First Baptist Church, 1989), 13.
38. Churchbook, November 6, 1779.
39. MS. Letter from Morgan Edwards to Samuel Jones, July 26,

1785.
40. Churchbook, May 9, 1785.
41. Ibid.. July 4, 1785.
42. Morgan Edwards, *The Customs of the Primitive Churches.* (No publisher nor place of publication are listed), 61, 62).
43. Ibid., 77, 78.
44. Churchbook, January 6, 1787.
45. MS Letter from Morgan Edwards to Samuel Jones, February 28, 1787.
46. Churchbook, October 6, 1788.
47. MS. Letter from Morgan Edwards to Samuel Jones, November 7, 1785. (Providence: Jones Collection, John Hay Library, Brown University) D 2470.
48. Churchbook, January 8, 1787.
49. Mendelson and Mello, 13.

CHAPTER THIRTEEN

THE WINCHESTER AFFAIR

> "Another difficulty for Edwards was his
> friendship with Elhanan Winchester."[1]
> William Henry Brackney, 1988

The Winchester affair was the forced termination in 1781 of the Reverend Elhanan Winchester as pastor of the Baptist church in Philadelphia. He was charged with preaching the doctrine of universalism. Universalism or universal restoration was heresy among Baptists, and a number of ministers, including Winchester, were charged with accepting and preaching the doctrine. "Among the others accused of this heresy was Morgan Edwards."[2]

What Was Eighteenth Century Universalism?
Universalism taught that all the wicked and unrepentant go to hell, and there suffer the penalty for the sins committed in this life. After a period of suffering, they will be redeemed from their torments and received into heaven.

Most eighteenth-century Baptists, however, adhered to the Philadelphia Confession of Faith, which quite clearly held an opposite view.[3]

> But the wicked who know not God, and obey not the Gospel of Jesus Christ, shall be cast into eternal torments, and punished with everlasting destruction, from the presence of the Lord, and from the glory of his power.

The Philadelphia Confession was adopted on September 25, 1742, and was taken seriously as an expression of the things which were surely believed among most of them. It was used to measure the orthodoxy of Winchester's preaching.

Who Was Elhanan Winchester?

Elhanan Winchester was one of thirteen children, mostly boys, born into a farm family that had moved from Chester, England, to Brookline, Massachusetts in 1750. He was born September 30, 1751, and had a conversion experience at nineteen. He was baptized at Canterbury, Connecticut.

Winchester did not learn to read until he was twelve years old, but he was gifted with an extraordinary memory, eloquence, and a charisma which drew great crowds to hear him. His early Christian experience and preaching were among the Particular Baptists, and his preaching kindled revivals in New England.

Winchester entered the ministry as a committed Calvinist and became pastor of his home church when only twenty years old. At that same age he married his first wife, who bore four children. Two children died at birth, and two died in infancy. His wife died with the birth of their fourth child.

In 1778, he left his home church and migrated to Welsh Neck on the Pee Dee River in South Carolina.

While there he came across a pamphlet on the final restoration of sinners though he rejected the pamphlet's message some of the ideas stayed with him. He began to move away from his Calvinistic roots to preach the general atonement of the General Baptists. As his preaching took on more of a "whosoever will may come" character, more and more people responded.

Meanwhile, he developed a strong compassion for the African slaves, and publicly acknowledged an abhorrence of slavery. As the slaves heard him preach, many converted, as did an increasing number of white people. In the summer of 1779 he baptized one-hundred-thirty-nine people, and his congregation grew to one thousand.

Winchester's Acceptance of Universalism
In 1779 Winchester lost his third wife, and he almost died of a fever. More and more, his mind was warming up to the restoration of all things. As he conversed with other ministers, he put forward his ideas and waited for their response. He found their answers too weak to change his growing acceptance of universalist teachings.

In September 1779, he left South Carolina to visit friends in New England. Along the way he preached in various churches to large crowds and had many conversions. Before he started his return journey to South Carolina, he had accepted the doctrine of the universal restoration. He began his return trip back to South Carolina in 1780.

One of his stops was Philadelphia, where he arrived on October 7, 1780. He planned to attend the annual meetings of the Philadelphia Association and visit the Baptist church. Since the church was without a pastor, he stayed to fill the pulpit. The response was so great that the congregation began holding services in St. Paul's Church, the largest in Philadelphia.

As might be expected, many in the congregation saw Winchester as their next pastor, but others wished to call Oliver Hart. Hart had been pastor of the Baptist church in Charleston, South Carolina, and had fled to New Jersey to escape British military authorities. His intense involvement in the independence movement made him a wanted man.

At a meeting of the Philadelphia congregation on October 19, 1780, it agreed to have Winchester preach at a Saturday service and Hart preach on Sunday. The congregation met on Monday to decide which one to call.[4] Winchester received a majority vote and accepted the call on October 23, 1780. This action was seen as "a most unfortunate decision."[5]

Within six months of accepting the call, Winchester was accused of preaching universalism. Ninety-seven persons signed a protest against him that had been drawn up on March 5, 1781. The Protesters asked him to desist from propagating universalist doctrine. Receiving no response, they locked the church against him and his followers. His supporters broke into the church and took possession of it. The Protesters later retook the church and managed to get legal protection to keep out the others.

In the meantime, the Protesters took their case to a council of neighboring Baptist ministers and each side presented its case. The council's opinion was that the doctrine of universal restoration was out of harmony with the Philadelphia Confession of Faith. It further ruled that the Protesters were the Baptist church and the others were not. They recommended that Winchester be dismissed.

After two more failed attempts to resolve the issues to the satisfaction of both sides, Winchester and his followers obtained the use of a hall at the University of Pennsylvania. Over one hundred people went with him and organized themselves as the Society of Universal Baptists.[6] Winchester resigned the pastorate of the Baptist church on October 27, 1781.

The Protesters took their own actions. They sent a circular letter to the churches in the Philadelphia Association outlining their five charges against Winchester. At the annual meeting of the association, official action was taken supporting the decision of the council of ministers and recommending that the church visit all who did not sign the protest. The purpose of the visits was to allow them an opportunity to sign the protest and present grounds for excommunication to those who failed to sign.

Eventually sixty refused to sign, and were excommunicated. Winchester's camp sued to regain possession of the meeting house, but the jury ruled in favor of the Protesters on July 9, 1784.[7]

Winchester began holding two preaching services at the university on Sunday afternoon and evening.[8] In December 1782, his audiences were described as "very thin assemblies," numbering between fifty and sixty hearers.[9] By September 1783, however, Thomas Ustick, Winchester's successor at the Baptist church, reported him as "flamingly zealous and great additions...are now making to his church."[10]

Winchester stayed at the university until 1787, when he went to London. By that time, he had married for a fifth time, and within a year he was preaching to large crowds. Abraham Booth, pastor of the Prescot Street Baptist Church in London, wrote James Manning that "loose professors begin to admire him."[11] Winchester's growing popularity in London gave rise to some anxiety because Booth asked Manning to tell him all he knew about his history and moral character.

Eighteen months later Booth wrote to Manning again and by now had formed an opinion of Winchester.[11]

> ...I have read some of his publications; my opinion, bear the marks of intoxication with the love of novelty, of ignorance, & of vanity. He appears in the pulpit...with all the pomp of a parish priest.

On May 1, 1794, Winchester disappeared, to escape from his wife who was physically abusing him. He soon reappeared on May 19, 1794, and left for America where he again preached to large crowds. His wife followed him in March 1795, and they were reconciled. He died on April 18, 1796, at the age of forty-six, and his movement died out following his death.

Winchester has been described as "colorful and controversial."[13] He certainly must have been attractive for he had been married five times by the age of thirty-two. James Manning was the only minister who seemed to adequately answer Winchester's questions about universalism, but Manning saw him as "an eccentric genius."[14]

Manning presented the most concise view of Winchester in a letter to John Rippon in London, August 3, 1784.[15]

> The apostasy of Mr. Winchester has been for a lamentation among us. Self-exaltation was the rock on which he split. Though he had from the first been remarkable for instability of character, he inflicted a grievous wound on the cause, especially in Philadelphia; but I think he is now at the end of his tether. His interest is declining, which will probably prove a deadly wound. I saw

him last May, and from his appearance think he has nearly run his race. His state of health will not admit of his preaching, and by a letter last week from Rev. Thomas Ustick, who now supplies the pulpit in Philadelphia, I learn that Winchester and his friends have lost their case in their suit for the meeting-house and the property of the church. It really appeared that God owned his labors in the revival in New England. Perhaps for attempting to take the glory to himself, he has laid him aside as an improper instrument for his work, who justly challenges the whole of it as his own. From common fame, and from what I myself saw, I really think this to be the case.

The perception Manning and others had of Winchester appears to agree with that of the Philadelphia church. It is contained in the circular letter from the church to the association churches.[16]

Popular applause, the idol which too many worship, was soon discovered to be an object zealously sought for, and courted by Mr. Winchester. To accomplish this, persons were every week *hastily* admitted to baptism, upon the slightest examination; though we really believe, that among the number are several sincere Christians, who, during the season of trial, have not been ashamed openly to discountenance *his errors.*

How Well Did the Church Handle the Crisis?

The Protesters, the name by which they called themselves, followed accepted Baptist polity in most of their actions. Despite the charges of intemperate behavior lodged against Morgan Edwards following the Winchester issue, they hewed to a straight Baptist line in both matters. Ironically, that was a tribute to Edwards who had trained the church leadership in Baptist polity.

When it became obvious that Winchester was proclaiming universalist doctrine, a church meeting was called. At the meeting Winchester's supporters defeated a vote to terminate him, twenty-four to thirty-five.[17] Nonetheless, the minority, calling themselves the Protesters, were the core leadership of the church and they elected a committee to meet with Winchester, present him with the protest, and call for his resignation. In their view, his preaching was not in accord with the Philadelphia Baptist Confession.[18]

The committee twice unsuccessfully attempted to see Winchester, even though an appointment was set for the second visit. They sent him a letter which was returned unopened. Out of frustration, the Protesters occupied the meeting house and locked out Winchester and his supporters. The majority broke into the meeting house and changed the locks.

The Protesters next turned to the leadership of Samuel Jones, pastor at the Pennepek church and moderator of the association. He advised them to meet with the Winchester supporters to explain the steps taken to rid the church of Winchester. Apparently the Protestors felt this would be a useless action, and so they asked five Baptist pastors to meet with them at Samuel Miles's home on April 2, 1781.

Out of that meeting came an agreement with the Winchester supporters for one of the ministers to debate the issue of universal restoration with him before the whole congregation. John Boggs of the Welsh Tract church was selected to speak for the Protesters, but he refused to debate, pleading insufficient knowledge of universalism.

Boggs, however, asked Winchester directly if he believed in the universal restoration. Winchester answered that he did. Boggs responded with an indictment of Winchester.[19]

> If you held these Sentiments and intended to propogate them when you came to this City, you are a *base Man* and a *Deceiver;* for you came here as a Baptist Minister, and if you came in with a Design to hold and propogate this Doctrine, you are an Imposter.

At that Winchester explained he was not confirmed in his universalism when he came to the church. He told of sharing his unsettled thoughts on the issue with two fellow Baptist pastors. They advised him not to preach it and he asked them to keep his confidence. It became public, knowledge, however, and Winchester was forced to make a more extended study of universal restoration. The result was full acceptance.

With that explanation, Boggs backed away from his judgment of Winchester and described him as "an honest Man and a *Christian.*" Such opinions held of Winchester were not uncommon.

Following that exchange, the Protesters suggested the formation of a joint committee to meet the next morning to work out their differences. The committee asked the five ministers to write an opinion to present to the congregation that evening. The ministers recommended the dismissal of Winchester because he had admitted to the heretical preaching of universalism. Furthermore, they stated, the Protesters were the true Baptist church of Philadelphia because they had followed the Philadelphia Confession of Faith.[20]

Two other attempts were made to reconcile the differences, one proposed by Samuel Miles and one by the Protesters. Both failed. On May 15, 1781, the Protesters broke into the meeting house and called on the magistrate and constables to protect against an attack on the building from the Winchester people.

The Protesters then set about getting a pulpit supply and informing the churches in the association of the events. In October the association voiced its support of the Protesters, and in December the church began to excommunicate those who still sided with Winchester. Like many other members, Morgan Edwards had signed the protest, but with a notation.

Morgan Edwards Labelled a Universalist

The protest which came out of the March 5, 1781, church meeting read as follows:

> Whereas the doctrine of the universal restoration of bad men and angels in the fullest extent has for a considerable time privately and of late more publicly been introduced among us, and is now openly avowed by some of the members, to the great disorder and confusion of the church, and wounding the hearts of many of the brethren contrary to our Confession of Faith___We whose naims [sic] are underwritten do in the sollam manner from Reall Conviction of Duty seriously protest against the same as a most dangerous heresy.

Before the protest was drawn up there had been considerable discussion over what action to take. The discussion indicated they could not take any action that night, and the hour grew late.

A motion was made to appoint a committee to "wait on Mr. Winchester and let him know that the church cannot admit of his preaching in their pulpit___on account of his holding the doctrine of universal salvation...."[21] The motion failed by a vote of twenty-four to thirty five. With that, the Protesters held an after-meeting, and selected a committee to call on Winchester for his resignation in spite of the vote.

Morgan Edwards was among those who signed the protest and he wrote as follows, "Morgan Edwards signs this protest against the doctrine of universal salvation under the character only of a doctrine that he does not believe."[22]

A commonly held notion is that Edwards made that notation because of his friendship with Winchester or because he was entertaining universalist thoughts himself. Neither of these suggestions were true.

Edwards may have known Winchester at the time of the protest, but not as a close friend. The date of the protest was March 5, 1781, but a letter from Edwards to Samuel Jones on February 28, 1787, makes it clear he did not have a closer relationship with him until 1786. The letter implies it might have been on the occasion of the annual meetings of the Philadelphia Association in the Fall of 1786.[23]

> I spent a good deal of time with Mr. Winchester___He is a man of more merit than I was aware of___He can read Greek and Hebrew and French rapidly___He is also expert in figures; & as you are a *figurative* man You may see a calculation of his in the Pennsylvania packet of Feb. 14th. which/ if his *datum* be just/ is certainly true___I do think he can preach night and day without study, and say things that will/ every now and then/ surprise & please.

Edwards wrote this letter six weeks after his appearance before the Philadelphia church in his first bid to restore his membership. It was also written in the same year in which Winchester sailed to England.

Edwards implies he was not well acquainted with Winchester prior to meeting with him in 1786. Given Edwards's directness, he probably sought the appointment in order to form his own opinion about him. Morgan Edwards always had an appreciation for those who had sharp minds and were diligent scholars. He often lauded a minister who used those qualities in effective preaching. The above quotation says nothing about Winchester's theology, but one must imagine they did discuss universalism. In any case, it was not friendship with Winchester which prompted Edwards's notation on the protest.

Neither did Edwards make the notation because he himself was entertaining universalist thoughts, as some have charged. In John Rippon's letter to James Manning on May 1, 1784, he asked Manning, "Is it true that Mr. Morgan Edwards, to whom I intend writing soon, has printed a book in vindication of him?"[24]

Manning responded on August 3 of that year.[25]

> Mr. Morgan Edwards has not printed in vindication of his [Winchester's] principles, but he read me a manuscript more than a year since on that subject, which he did not own, though charged then with being the author. He did not deny it; whereby he was entreated not to add the printing of this to the long list of imprudent things which had already so greatly grieved his friends and so injured his reputation. This plainness did not please him, but I thought the use of it was duty.

From Manning, then, one learn's that Edwards shared with him the Winchester manuscript more than a year before. What was in the manuscript is not known, but apparently it seemed to favor Winchester. Edwards neither acknowledged nor denied authorship, but word of its contents circulated. The gossip created some negative reaction against Edwards. One historian has speculated that it may have been a paper written by Winchester and published in London in 1788, under the title *The Univer-*

*sal Restoration: Exhibited in Four Dialogues Between a Minister and His Friend.*²⁶

It could be that Winchester's publication was his record of the 1786 meeting with Edwards. On the other hand, the title appears to convey four occasions when the subject was discussed, and Edwards gives no indication he met with Winchester more than once. There can be little doubt that Edwards would have reported it as four theological dialogues had it been so.

Another writer has suggested that Edwards made the notation to indicate he did not want Winchester ousted.²⁷ Given the emotional reaction to the doctrine of universalism at that time, it is easy to understand why some would paint Edwards with the universalist brush. Even William Rogers, his successor at the church and one of the four spokesmen for the Protesters, was accused at a church meeting in 1788 of being a universalist.²⁸

Rogers expressed his opinion of the labeling of Edwards as a universalist at Edwards's memorial service.²⁹

> *Evil reports* also fell to his share; but most of them were false reports, and therefore he gave credit as a species of persecution. And even the title of deceiver did not escape him. Often has he been told that he was an Arminian, though he professed to be a Calvinist; that he was a Universalist, & c. Yet he was **true** to his principles. These may be seen in our confession of faith, agreeing with that republished by the Baptist churches assembled at London, in the year 1689. He seldom meddled with the five polemical points; but when he did, he always avoided abusive language. The charge of Universalism brought against him was not altogether groundless; for though he was not a Universalist himself, he professed a great regard for many who were, and he would sometimes take their part against violent opposers, in order to inculcate moderation.

There was little patience for moderation in those days. Even John Leland, a loud Baptist voice in the cause of religious liberty in the eighteenth century, was accused of universalism. He was a Winchester convert in New England and traveled with him in 1783, two years after the Philadelphia church dismissed him. So Manning's advice to Edwards not to publish that paper on Winchester was good counsel. As it was, the "imprudent actions" Manning referred to were the glue which made the charge of universalism against Edwards stick whereas, it did not with Rogers and Leland.

For historical accuracy, Edwards said he did not believe in the doctrine of universal salvation. True, he was the only one of the ninety-two persons who signed the protest with a notation, but he was unequivocal in his denial of universalism.

Unfortunately, even today there is still the mistaken notion that Edwards "nearly joined the new denomination."[30] It has been suggested that his association with Winchester and the charges of intoxication led to his excommunication in 1785.[31] As shown, Edwards had little acquaintance with Winchester before 1786.

It is clear from Edwards's life and convictions why he made the notation. The lesson from his life relates to the pain and humiliation of his forced termination from the Baptist church in Cork, Ireland in 1759. His irenic nature would have led him to try to bring Winchester back into the fold rather than cut him off.

Secondly, Edwards believed all things should be done decently and in order. The majority upheld Winchester at the March 5 meeting, and the minority wanted Winchester to resign. Though some of his best friends were in the minority group, Edwards's would have taken the matter to the association sooner than did the Protestors.[32]

Edwards's notation indicates his conviction that it was too soon to call for Winchester's resignation. He wanted to take more time with Winchester and his supporters or call for help from the association. To take such a stand when his own membership was to be called into question took great courage and strong theological convictions.

The four dark shadows which crossed the pathway of his life--loyalty to the Crown, intoxication, excommunication and universalism--never subdued Morgan Edwards. He continued in the activities which occupied his life until his death.

ENDNOTES

1. William H. Brackney, *The Baptists*. (New York: Greenwood Press, 1988), 160.
2. Joseph R. Sweeny, "Elhanan Winchester and the Universal Baptists." (Unpublished PhD. Dissertation, University of Pennsylvania Library, Philadelphia, 1969), 103.
3. William L. Lumpkin, *Baptist Confessions of Faith*. (Philadelphia: The Judson Press, 1959), 295.
4. MS. Churchbook, First Baptist Church, Philadelphia, October 19, 1780.
5. William W. Keen, *The Bi-Centennial Celebration of the Founding of the First Baptist Church of the City of Philadelphia*. (Philadelphia: American Baptist Publication Society, 1899), 66.
6. Sweeny, 99.
7. Keen, 68.
8. MS. Letter, Thomas Ustick to Nicholas Brown, February 4, 1782. (Providence: Brown Papers, John Carter Brown Library, Brown University), L81-83M.
9. MS. Letter, Thomas Ustick to Isaac Backus, December 3, 1782. (Providence: Ustick Papers, John Hay Library, Brown University).
10. MS. Letter, Thomas Ustick to Isaac Backus, September 9, 1783. Ustick Papers, A 21316.
11. MS. Letter, Abraham Booth to James Manning, December 12,

1787. Manning Papers, A 728.
12. MS. Letter, Abraham Booth to James Manning, July 11, 1789. Manning Papers, A 730.
13. William D. Thompson, *Philadelphia's First Baptists*, (Philadelphia: First Baptist Church, 1989), 15.
14. Keen, 68.
16. MS. Letter, James Manning to John Rippon, August 3, 1784. (Providence: Manning Papers, John Hay Library, Brown University), A 792.
16. "An Address from the Baptist church in Philadelphia to their Sister Churches," 4.
17. Churchbook, March 5, 1781.
18. Ibid.
19. Sweeny, 93.
20. Churchbook, April 4, 1781.
21. Ibid., March 5, 1781.
22. Ibid.
23. MS. Letter, Morgan Edwards to Samuel Jones, February 28, 1787. (Providence: Jones Collection, John Hay Library, Brown University), D 2469.
24. MS. Letter, John Rippon to James Manning, May 1, 1784, (Providence: Manning Papers, John Hay Library, Brown University).
25. Manning Letter, August 3, 1784.
26. Thomas R. McKibbins and Kenneth L. Smith, *The Life and Works of Morgan Edwards*. (New York: Arno Press, 1980), 49.
27. Sweeny, 103.
28. Churchbook, Vol. 4, 29-30.
29. John Rippon, ed., *Baptist Annual Register*, (London: 1796), 310 (Memorial Sermon, William Rogers, February 22, 1795).
30. William G. McLoughlin, *New England Dissent, 1630-1833*. (Cambridge: Harvard University Press, 1971), II, 721.
31. Brackney, 160.
32. Morgan Edwards, *Materials Towards A History of the Baptists*. (Danielsville, GA.: Heritage Papers, 1984). I, 62.

CHAPTER FOURTEEN

A BAPTIST TO THE END

> "He died in 1795, having retained to the end
> the fullest confidence of his brethren."
> Alfred H. Newman, 1898

Life in Delaware

Morgan John Rhys was a Welsh Baptist preacher who came to America in 1794 and was something of a kindred spirit with Morgan Edwards. Rhys was born on a farm in Glamorgan, Wales, in 1760, when Edwards was serving at Rye, Sussex. After grammar school Rhys attended Bristol Academy and was ordained at Penygarn in 1787. At Bristol he was under the teaching of Hugh and Caleb Evans, who were an influence on his support for America and abhorrence of slavery.

More importantly Rhys was an ardent advocate for full religious liberty.[1] Indeed, his espousal of a form of government founded on the will of the people led popular preacher Christmas Evans to say a spirit of "rebellion was very strong in him."[2] Rhys lost all hope of seeing the political reforms he wanted and emigrated to America in 1794.

After arriving in America, he sought out the Welsh Tract Baptist Church in Delaware and found many Welsh people, including Morgan Edwards. In his diary he wrote of his meeting with Edwards, who was now in the last year of his life.[3]

> An old gentleman who resides here, and has travelled all over the Atlantic States has given me a particular account of their peregrinations from their first period of settlement to the present time.

If Morgan Edwards were that old gentleman, then he was still leading a very active life his last year.

Edwards's Life in Delaware

Morgan Edwards was seventy-two years old when he encountered Morgan John Rhys. He had moved to a farm he purchased in Pencader, Delaware, in 1772, after he married Elizabeth Singleton. While Edwards never served in another pastorate, he continued to preach in pastorless churches until the American Revolution began.

Following the war he began again to "read lectures on divinity" (i.e. to preach) in the Middle Atlantic and New England states, organize his many sermons, and continue work on his history of the Baptists.[4] His marriage to Elizabeth Singleton was short lived, and in 1774 he married the widow of Nathaniel Evans, a wealthy landholder. Edwards moved to the Evans home in Newark.[5]

A puzzling aspect of Edwards's life in Delaware is why he never served in another pastorate although asked to do so.[6] The explanation may be found in a 1792 postscript to his history of the Baptists of New Jersey.[7]

> There has started a question in divinity,...which has not been satisfactorily answered to this day, viz, "Whether a minister who

has fallen into a gross sin, should ever after reassume the ministry, let his repentance be ever so notorious."

"Yes (say some casuists): for (1) Peter sinned grossly; yet his master did not degrade him; but, after repentance, bid him go on to feed his sheep and lambs: besides (2) A gross sin is to a minister what the loss of virtue is to a woman; the scripture phrase for the one is, that the ravisher humbled her: and the remembrance of a gross sin will make and keep the minister humble whilst he lives."

The baptist association of 1790...are on the same side of the question; but a decision of a question in divinity by votes deserves no great attention, especially if most of the voters know nothing of the matter.

"But nay" (say others): [Edwards cited Old and New Testament examples as well as those from the early history of the church before continuing]. I have been personally acquainted with several of the same diversity of opinions. This diversity has induced some lapsed and restored clergymen to refuse the character of "ministers," and to assume only that of "lecturers in divinity," which requires neither holy orders nor a spotless character....

The weight of the evidence which Edwards marshalls tilts his position toward those who say "no." He seemed to be saying he should not be in the pastorate because of his conduct. He frequently used the term "lectures in divinity" when referring to his preaching opportunities during this period. As was shown earlier, Edwards still considered himself an ordained minister when a tax collector attempted to collect taxes from him to support the Established church.

We must also factor into this equation Edwards's ongoing spiritual struggle over sin in his life. He spoke of it in his preconversion and conversion experiences and revealed in his sermons that it was a continuing issue for him. One must conclude that Edwards did not assume another pastorate because he did not feel himself worthy of that office, or because he feared he might have moral relapses. He took very seriously the importance of a minister's living a morally upright life.

Though Edwards never assumed another pastorate, he did remain very active in the Philadelphia Baptist Association until the year of his death. With the exception of the Revolutionary War years through to the restoration of his membership in the Baptist church at Philadelphia, his name appears almost annually in the minutes of the association. He served as clerk, took pulpit supply assignments, served on committees, and participated in the deliberations. Finally, at the last meeting he attended in October 1794, he opened the sessions with prayer and presented the association with a bound copy of the minutes for the years 1707 to 1793.[8] Within three months he would be dead.

It must be noted that the pulpit supply work Edwards did began in 1772 and extended from Delaware to New England. His volunteering for such assignments argues well for his continuing commitment to the ministry despite his many personal problems. As he had in the south, however, he did in the other states. He used the horseback-riding preaching trips as opportunities to collect historical data on the Baptists and therein lies his greatest contribution to Baptist church life.

Edwards The Historian

In addition to the three-thousand miles Edwards travelled in the south he rode thirteen-hundred in New Jersey and hundreds more in New England. Edwards's method of research led him to visit the churches where he "examined their records, and the records of their townships; questioned ancient persons; and has taken every other step which promised him information and certainty in his undertaking."[9]

Edwards discovered a different attitude on the part of Baptists in 1792 toward writing their history than when he published the history of Pennsylvania Baptists in 1770. Because of opposition to that volume, he lost money on its printing, and a carton of one hundred copies was taken from him by the British.[10]

Edwards was a totally unselfish person, and he freely shared his notes with others. He sent the notes on the Baptists of New England to Isaac Backus for use in his history of New England Baptists.[11] There is good reason to believe that Edwards also shared his notes on the Southern colonies with Backus.[12] He indicated the material was loaned to Backus on October 12, 1773.[13]

There is some question of whether Backus returned the New England material. In a letter to Samuel Jones on June 11, 1784, Edwards said that the "materials towards the history of the baptists [sic]...northward of Pennsylvania are in Mr. Backus's hands."[14] Four years later Edwards sent Backus a direct request for the materials. He wrote, "Some years ago I sent you a manuscript..., a collection of some historical facts relative to the Baptists. If you have the book please to return it to me as soon as conveniency offers."[15] Backus never acknowledged Edwards's help. The only New England manuscript of Edwards's known to exist is the one on Rhode Island Baptists. Yet he gathered materials from as far north as New Hampshire.[16] In fact, by October 1773 he had visited churches from Nova Scotia to Georgia.[17]

In 1789, John Leland requested the use of Edwards's notes on the Southern Colonies, and these were sent to him.[18] They were evidently returned as Edwards later shared them with Richard Furman.[19] Edwards died before Furman returned the manuscripts and they remained with the Furman family. John Asplund also used his materials in compiling *The Universal Register of the Baptist Denomination in North America.*[20]

Edwards's histories included Particular, General, Separate, Keithian, Rogerene, Seventh-Day, and German Baptists. Each volume began with a brief introductory history of the province, followed by a short account of the earliest Baptist work, a history of each church, biographical sketches of the pastors, and statistical data. He positioned the churches by the direction and distance of their location from Philadelphia. Edwards kept notebooks for each province during his tours and then wrote out the histories when he returned home.

His intention was to publish a twelve-volume history of the Baptists, but was able to publish only two--Pennsylvania (1770) and New Jersey (1792). Volume III on Delaware was completed in manuscript form but not published by Edwards. Extracts of it were used by David Benedict in his 1813 history of the Baptists.[21] Benedict obtained Edwards's materials when he received Isaac Backus's historical papers following his death in 1806.[22] Edwards's Delaware manuscript was printed in a Pennsylvania historical journal in 1885.[23]

Edwards also completed Volume IV, *The History of the Baptists of Rhode Island*, but never published it. It was published in 1867, by the Rhode Island Historical Society.[24] The work done in preparing for that publication came under severe criticism by an eminent historian, Dr. Sidney S. Rider.[25]

The remaining extant historical materials of Morgan Edwards cover Maryland, Virginia, North Carolina,

South Carolina, and Georgia. In spite of all the materials he had collected and prepared, he believed the writing of a history of American Baptists was too great a task for any one person.[26]

> I could wish further that the history of the American baptists were made: a matter of general concern for the reasons I have published to the world: the longer it be delayed, the more difficult will be the task: I have publishd some materials towards such a history: and have collected many more: some of which I have sent to my brother Backus, the rest I will give to any that take upon him to accomplish the design.

Edwards's interest in historical research and writing is traced by one biographer to his time in Ireland.[27]

> He [Morgan Edwards] evinced a love for historical research long before he left for America, and some of his productions are said to have been published in Ireland.

A hint of Edwards' historical research in Wales is found in his correspondence with Samuel Jones.[28]

> Please to inform Mr. Thomas, ... that he may see in Mr. Backus's book an account of the first baptist ch[urc]h in Wales viz. at *Ilston* which transmigrated to America and settled with their minister (Mr. Miles) near *mount hope* in Rhodeisland government. I suppose he knows that the first in South wales [sic] was at *Llangwm* in monmouthshire [sic].

Edwards knew Joshua Thomas; Joshua's brother Timothy and Morgan Edwards were classmates at the Trosnant Academy.[29] Joshua Thomas and Morgan Edwards both had overlapping interests in Welsh Baptists. Thomas's interest in Welsh Baptists extended to those who had migrated to America and other places. Edwards's interest in American Baptists included those who had come to America from other places including Wales.[30] Both men were part of a new breed of Baptist historian, which began with Edwards himself.

With the publication of Morgan Edwards's first volume in 1770, a new type of Baptist history appeared on the scene, one which utilized the records of churches and associations in the process of doing critical research. Edwards may have been the first of the new historians, but he was not alone. Numbered with Edwards in America were Backus and Jones; in Great Britain were Joshua Thomas and Robert Robinson of Cambridge. They all viewed Baptist history in more universal terms than did Baptist historians before them, but it was Morgan Edwards' perspective on Baptist history and his method of research which ushered in the new era.

A twentieth-century Baptist writer may have best defined Morgan Edwards's place as a Baptist historian.[32]

> Edwards was far in advance of his time in his exact historical method. The history was left unfinished, but it remains a model for the writing historian and a mine of valuable information for the researcher.

There is another matter which must be touched on before discussing the death and burial of Morgan Edwards. It is the possibility that Edwards made a second trip to the British Isles in 1793. The evidence for such a trip is found in a letter from the British Baptist preacher, Robert Hall to Joseph Kinghorn.[33]

Robert Hall (1764-1831) served Baptist churches in Cambridge, Leicester, and Bristol. His great preaching drew overflowing crowds of people. He was a great protagonist for open communion, a hotly debated issue among Baptists in that day. His chief adversary in the debate was Joseph Kinghorn, pastor of the Baptist church in Norwich, England. Though on different sides of the issue, they were friends. In his letter Hall is quoted as follows:

> Dr. Edwards of Philadelphia has been here [London] a day or two; he is a very intelligent and agreeable man, spoke in the highest terms of the happiness of America and unless I am mistaken one principal end of his coming to England is to induce emigration.

One can only surmise the "Dr. Edwards" referred to in the letter was Morgan Edwards. He is not mentioned in the minutes of either the Baptist church at Philadelphia or the Philadelphia Baptist Association during this period. Both Hall and Edwards were graduates of Bristol Academy, were very well known preachers, and were known for occasional bluntness. Edwards also had a reputation as an intelligent conversationalist. Could he have gone to England for reasons of health?

In a postscript to his 1792 history of the New Jersey Baptists Edwards talked about his health.[34]

> The history of them [Baptists] in Delaware state is obtained already; and will be sent to the press as soon as a sufficient number of subscribers offer; the author cannot expect to see it printed, because of an asthma and atrophy, which may hurry him out of the world....

The reference to his asthma and atrophy indicates that his general health was declining. There is earlier evidence of this decline in a 1787 letter to Samuel Jones.[35]

> But what next? Thus---I arrived home safe the 61st day from

> the day I left it.---Billy Rogers accompanied me as far as the [Marcus] Hook out of yure [sic] kindness, saying, *that he could not bear to see an old man travailing alone*---He is very good---and so is his wife---My ankle is yet sore---and something more than old age ails the rest of me...I was so pleased with myself at Philadelphia, Pennepeck and the ridge that I meditate another visit if I live to see next fall.

The letter reports his return from the association meeting of 1787 and that he was then experiencing health problems. Edwards may have described his physical condition in worse terms than it was, but he was, nonetheless, not feeling in good health. It must be remembered that he had been consulting a physician as early as 1781 when he reported to the Baptist church in Philadelphia that he had mixed too much alcohol with the bark prescribed by his doctor.

So it is possible that Edwards's thought the ocean voyage and trip to his homeland might revive him. Hall's letter states that Edwards came to England "to induce emigration," so he now thought America was a good place to live and prosper. But there may also have been another reason for Morgan Edwards to go to England in 1793.

If Edwards's general health was beginning to wane and he had been living alone for some years, he may have decided to make an effort to find out what happened to his son Billy. As discussed in chapter six, his other son Joshua later went to England with the same purpose in mind. If that were part of Edwards's reason for the trip, then both Morgan and Joshua wanted closure and hoped to find some conclusive evidence of William's death. Hidden beneath the scholarly facade of Morgan Edwards was a father's warm heart.

If Morgan Edwards did travel to England in 1793, he

had returned in time to attend the meeting of the Philadelphia Baptist Association in October of 1794. He presented the leather-bound minutes he had prepared, received the appreciation of the assembled messengers, and returned to Delaware after the meeting. The state of his health at that time is unknown, nor is it known if he tarried to visit with friends or preached in churches.

The Death and Burial of Morgan Edwards

William Rogers described the death and burial of Morgan Edwards in a memorial sermon on February 22, 1795.[36]

> Our worthy Friend departed this life at Pencader, Newcastle county, Delaware State, on Wednesday the 28th of January last, in the 73d year of his age, and was buried, agreeable to his own desire, in the aisle of this meeting-house, with his first wife and their children.

With these words, William Rogers announced the date and place of Morgan Edwards's death, and the place of his interment during a memorial service in Edwards's honor on Sunday, February 22, 1795, at the Baptist meeting house in Philadelphia.

Edwards apparently died a quiet death, for Rogers went on to declare, "Our aged and respectable friend is gone the way of all the earth; but he lived to a good old age, and with the utmost composure closed his eyes on all the things of time."[38]

There are no known reports of Edwards suffering from a serious, life threatening malady. In a letter to Samuel Jones on July 26, 1785, he reported, "I suffer nothing but what is common to old age."[38] In 1787, he wrote to Jones, "Something more than old age ails the rest of me," but he never complained of any serious illness.

If there is a conclusion about the cause of Morgan Edwards's death, it would be that he died from a wornout body. Rogers said in his memorial sermon, "That the Baptist interest was ever uppermost with him, and that he laboured more to promote it than to promote his own."[39] In a modern understanding of that statement, Rogers was describing Edwards as a person who continued to expend himself for a cause, even when he should have stopped for his own good.

The classic illustration of Edwards expending himself physically and emotionally for Baptist interests is in his letter to James Manning from London on April 26, 1768.[40]

> I have been not only denyed by hundreds, but also abused on that score---My patience, my feet, and my assurance are much impaired---I took a cold in November, which stuck to me all winter, owing to my transpoosing---the streets in all weathers.

Edwards most critical point in gathering his materials on New Jersey Baptists came when he "was on foot, the ice making riding dangerous."[41] Welsh Baptist historian Joshua Thomas said of him, "He suffered much in the wars."[42] Since Edwards corresponded with Thomas, we must assume he provided more detail to him about his suffering than Thomas reveals to us. Suffice to say, then, that Morgan Edwards died a natural death, and was probably physically spent from his untiring efforts on behalf of Baptists.

While it was Edwards's request to be buried in the aisle of the meeting house,[43] he and his family were the only ones to be interred there.[44] The actual date of his interment is uncertain since it would have taken time to move his body from Delaware to Philadelphia and to open the grave under the church aisle.

In his memorial sermon on February 22, 1795, Rogers refered to Edwards's burial in the past tense so that occasion was not of the actual funeral, but a memorial service. There was, however, a second sermon at the service and it was delivered by Samuel Jones.[45]

Edwards could not have been buried in Philadelphia on the same day he died, so Jones's sermon was probably delivered on the same occasion as the Rogers eulogy, February 22, 1795. Both men were friends of Edwards, and he requested each to preach at his funeral from a different text.

Jones declared that his text had "been previously appointed by the Deceased."[46] It was Psalm 137:6, "If I prefer not Jerusalem above my chief joy." Jones' tribute to Edwards in the first paragraph of the sermon reveals clearly the perception he held of Morgan Edwards.

> I could not have fixed on any more pertinent words than those cited above, as they were so clearly exemplified in his Life that of Sentiment contained in them seemed to be a common center of all his Aims, wishes and Actions. If I prefer not Jerusalem above my chief joy. i.e. If I am not more anxious for the prosperity of Zion than for the accumulation of wealth; If I do not long for the conversion of sinners more than for worldly comfort; If I am not willing to sacrifice my ease and my reputation for the cause of God; In particular of the Baptist cause, the religion they profess and the truths they maintain be not dear to me than whatever this world can promise of this life enjoy, yea dearer than Life itself.

Jones later cited the ways in which Edwards exemplified the text in his commitment to the Baptist cause. First, he referred to Edwards' conversion from the Anglican faith to that of the Baptists. In Jones's mind one would not leave a church with "power, preferment, pomp, grandeur, and the powerful popular motive [of] numbers; being the religion of the state" for the "few, and those generally poor and despised, void of power and policy," except "to have power of truth on an enlightened and tender conscience".

Jones went on to call attention to Edwards's efforts to promote a "coalition of Baptists on the continent," and a "uniformity of discipline and practice among the churches." He further illustrated Edwards's commitment by focusing on his labors for Rhode Island College, "whereby with great address, and indefatigable pains, he layed the foundation for an endowment for that liberal and truly catholic institution." Jones also spoke of Edwards's "taking great pains to collect materials towards a history of the American Baptists."

Finally, Samuel Jones reported wherein Edwards's commitment "shined above all others was of the Ministry."

> On this he entered early in Life and this seemed to be his favourite Employ, wherein he laboured, and with no considerable success to magnify his office, being a workman that need not to be ashamed. If you consider how he gave in the the 19 year of his age, himself wholly to the ministry, and avoided entangling himself with the things of this life, how he was content with food and raiment, how he applyed himself to reading, study and meditation, how he endured hardness when his duty required it; and used meekness and passiveness in cases of provocations and ingratitude, rather than forebear his endeavour to save the abusive and them that were out of the way; how, as far as honesty and consistency allowed him, he made himself all things to all men, pleased all men in all things, and became the servant of all that he might save the more.

Morgan Edwards did not die in isolation and obscurity. One small paragraph in Jones's sermon indicates he had a large circle of friends.

> Yet who can refrain from shedding a generous tear on so affecting an occasion as this. Who among his intimate friends, to whom he was near and dear, of whom there are many now before me, and of whom I count it an honour to have been one?

The text Edwards requested William Rogers to preach was II Corinthians 6:8 which reads, "By honor and dishonour, by evil report and good report; as deceivers and yet deceived." Rogers began by setting a biblical and historical background for the text, and proceeded to his biographical sermon on Edwards. He stated that he wanted "to avoid what might appear like embellishment, and confine himself to a plain narrative of the facts."[47]

Rogers pointed to the two honorary degrees awarded Edwards by the College of Philadelphia and Rhode Island College. He also portrayed Edwards as a man who had been honored in both Europe and America.

Rogers pointed also to the dishonor accorded Edwards because of his loyalty to the British Crown. In fact, Rogers said he would not have mentioned the Tory episode except that Edwards insisted Rogers do so; that being called a Tory "in those days was enough to bring on political opposition and destruction of property; all of which took place with respect to Mr. Edwards."[48] He went on to say, however, that Edwards "complained not much on this," and that "he never harboured of doing the least injury to the United States by abetting the cause of the enemy."

In terms of "good reports" on Edwards, Rogers told of many letters Edwards brought with him when he came to

America which "reported handsome things of him," that letters sent to the home country did the same thing.

The "evil reports" Rogers spoke of were mostly false. Some people called Edwards a deceiver, especially referring to the charge of being a universalist. Rogers did not gloss over this incident, however, as he stated that while Edwards was not a universalist, his regard for some who were and defending them against harsh critics left him vulnerable to such a charge. True to his irenic nature, Edwards was characterized by Rogers as a Calvinist who "seldom meddled with the five polemical points [of Calvinism]; but when he did, he always avoided abusive language."[49]

Rogers then presented a lengthy sketch of Edwards's life, including a list of his publications and some of the practical principles he held concerning the pastoral ministry. There was one facet of Edwards's character which not only Rogers came to appreciate, but many others as well. It was the cosmopolitan nature of his personality.[50]

> There was nothing uncommon in Mr. Edwards's person; but he possessed an original genius. By his travels in England, Ireland, and America, commixing with all sorts of people, and by close application to reading, he had attained a remarkable ease of behaviour in company, and was furnished with something pleasant and informing to say on all occasions

Thomas and Ceasar Rodney, were leaders in the cause of independence in Delaware, and Thomas saw Edwards in a similar light.[51]

> The Reverend Mr. Edwards did me the honor of spending an Evening at my house on his way to the lower Baptist Churches. I felt myself highly pleased and Entertained by his company and conversation--He possesses a degree of pleasantry and humour

A Dazzling Enigma

Monument at the Grave of Morgan Edwards

which is so happily adapted to this age, that it enables him to Communicate the knowledge of years [of] study and experience in a most agreeable manner.

Rogers closed his eulogy by saying Edwards believed the Baptist cause "to be the interest of Christ above any in Christendom."[52] The Baptist meeting house was not the final resting place for either Edwards or his family.

By 1852 the First Baptist Church of Philadelphia had outgrown its building at Second and LaGrange streets. It purchased property at the intersection of Broad and Arch streets, and in 1856 moved into a new building.[53] While the move to a new building may have been an exciting experience, the disposition of the graves at the old location was marked by considerable controversy.

On July 11, 1859, the church purchased a large lot in the Mount Moriah Cemetery on the southwestern edge of Philadelphia. A year later the remains from the churchyard and from under the aisle of the church were moved to that location. The gravestones of the early pastors, including Morgan Edwards, were placed inside the new building in 1884. At the same time, a member of the church, Mrs. Ann D. Coffin, gave a generous gift for the erection of a granite monument. The names of all the pastors interred at that location are engraved on the monument. Morgan Edwards and his family were laid to rest in Mount Moriah Cemetery.

A final word must be said about Morgan Edwards's state of affairs at the time of his death. Samuel Jones described Edwards's circumstances at his death as "not worth a groat."[54] A groat was an old English silver coin worth about four pence, and as executor of Edwards's estate Jones knew he was worth more than four pence.[55] Edwards owned one piece of land in Delaware and he left

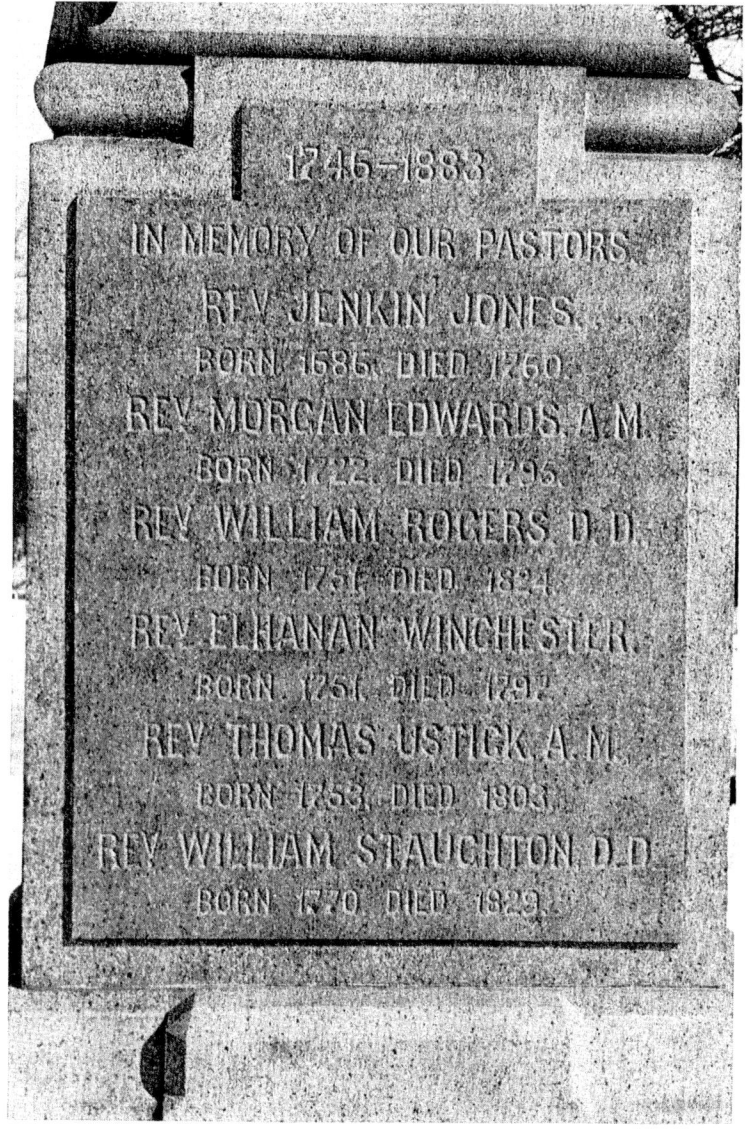

South Plate on Monument in Mount Moriah Cemetery

it and all of his personal effects to his youngest son Joshua.[56] Following the death of his father, Joshua went to Delaware and sold his father's land to a farmer named John Bayley on May 25, 1795, for the sum of two hundred and thirty pounds.[57]

Nineteenth century Baptist historian Albert H. Newman saw Morgan Edwards as retaining the full confidence of his fellow Baptists to the end.[58] If Edwards did enjoy such trust, it was in spite of being an enigma to his fellow Baptists, and to all Baptists since. The task remains then to close his story with a review of the perceptions people have had of him and to ascertain his place in American Baptist church life.

ENDNOTES

1. T.M. Bassett, *The Welsh Baptists*. (Swansea: Ilston House, 1977), 109.
2. Ibid., 110.
3. Hywell M. Davies, "Transatlantic Brethren: A Study of English, Welsh and American Baptists With Particular Reference to Morgan John Rhys (1760-1804) and His Friends," Unpublished PhD. Dissertation, (Aberystwyth: University of Wales, 1984), 40.
4. John Rippon, ed. *Baptist Annual Register,* London: 1796, 310, (Memorial Sermon, William Rogers, February 22, 1795).
5. Reuben A. Guild, *Early History of Brown University, Including the Life, Times and Correspondence of President Manning, 1756-1791* (Providence: Snow and Farnham, 1896), 16.
6. Rippon, 310.
7. Morgan Edwards, *Materials Towards A History of the Baptists* (Danielsville, GA:. Heritage Papers, 1984), I, 108-109.
8. The original leather bound volume is now housed in the American Baptist Historical Society at Rochester, N.Y. and was used by A.D. Gillette in his 1851 edition of the minutes.
9. Edwards, I, 77.
10. Ibid.
11. Ibid., 78.

12. Issac Backus, *A History of New England Baptists With Particular Reference to the Denomination of Christians Called Baptists, 1690-1784* (Providence: John Carter Company, 1784), II, 204.
13. MS. Sermon, *Lo, The People Shall Dwell Alone*, Philadelphia: October 12, 1773. Crozer Collection, 1738, XXXI, 1.
14. MS. Letter, Morgan Edwards to Samuel Jones, June 11, 1784.
15. MS. Letter, Morgan Edwards to Isaac Backus, August 18, 1788.
16. Edwards, I, 78.
17. Edwards, Sermon, October 12, 1773.
18. Ibid.
19. Letter from Alester G. Furman to Lorraine Whitehead, September 10, 1951, Baptist Collection (Furman University, Greenville, S.C.).
20. John Asplund, *The Universal Register of the Baptist Denomination in North America*, (Boston: John W. Folsom, 1794), 4.
21. David Benedict, *A General History of the Baptist Denomination in America* (Boston: Manning and Loring, 1813).
22. David Benedict, *Fifty Years Among Baptists*, (New York: Sheldon and Company, 1860), 90.
23. *The Pennsylvania Magazine of History and Biography*, Vol. IX. 1885, (Philadelphia: Publication Fund of the Historical Society of Pennsylvania, 1885).
24. Rhode Island Historical Collections, VI, 301-370.
25. Sidney S. Rider, "The Historical Society's Reprint of the Morgan Edwards Manuscript." *Book Notes*, Vol. III, No. 4, (June 6, 1885), 13,14.
26. Edwards, Sermon, October 12, 1773.
27. T.R. Roberts, *Eminent Welshmen: A Short Biographical Dictionary of Welshmen* (Cardiff: The Educational Publishing Company, Ltd., 1908), 80.
28. MS. Letter, June 11, 1784.
29. Ibid.
30. Davies, 39.
31. Ibid., 5,6.
32. John S. Moore, "Morgan Edwards: Baptist Statesman," *Baptist History and Heritage*, Vol. 6, No. 1, (January, 1971), 33.
33. MS. Letter, From Robert Hall to Joseph Kinghorn, November 26, 1793, (Rochester: American Baptist Historical Society).

34. Edwards, *Materials,* I, 145.
35. MS. Letter, From Morgan Edwards to Samuel Jones, February 28, 1787, (Providence: Jones Collection, John Hay Library, Brown University).
36. Rippon, 310.
37. Ibid., 314.
38. MS. Letter From Morgan Edwards to Samuel Jones, July 26, 1785, (Providence: Jones Collection, John Hay Library, Brown University).
39. Rippon, 314.
40. MS. Letter, From Morgan Edwards to James Manning, April 26, 1768, (Providence: Manning Papers, John Hay Library, Brown University).
41. Edwards, *Materials,* I, 148.
42. Joshua Thomas, MS. "Materials Towards A History of the Welsh Baptists' (Bristol: Bristol Baptist College), 278.
43. Rippon, 310.
44. William Williams Keen, *The Bi-Centennial Celebration of the First Baptist Church of the City of Philadelphia* (Philadelphia: American Baptist Publication Society, 1899), 171.
45. MS. Sermon, *If I Prefer Not Jerusalem,* (Providence: Henderson Collection, John Hay Library, Brown University).
46. Ibid.
47. Rippon, 308.
48. Ibid., 309.
49. Ibid.
50. Ibid., 313.
51. MS. Letter, From Thomas Rodney to a Dr. Evans, March 20, 1791 (Wilmington: Historical Society of Delaware).
52. Rippon, 314.
53. William D. Thompson, *Philadelphia's First Baptists* (Philadelphia: The First Baptist Church, 1989), 27.
54. Jones Sermon.
55. Edwards letter, July 26, 1785.
56. *Delaware Will Book, New Castle County,* (Dover: Delaware State Hall of Records), O-1, 57.
57. *Delaware Deed Book, New Castle County,* (Dover: Delaware State Hall of Records), P-2, 180-183.

EPILOGUE

AN ENIGMA STILL

> "For among all the Watchmen on Zion's walls,
> few in all respects were like him."
> Samuel Jones, 1795

Samuel Jones was right. There were few people like Morgan Edwards among eighteenth-century American Baptists.[1] He was a puzzle to his peers, and he has remained so to the present. The fact that Edwards was a multidimensional man is part of that puzzle. He was the "Renaissance man" of eighteenth-century American Baptists. He must be seen as a whole person. Jones attempted to do that in his funeral oration.[2]

> Was it my purpose to draw out his [Edwards'] character at full length, I might mention his natural endowments, and their happy improvement; I might mention his character as a divine, as a scholar, as a Christian, as a friend, as a husband, as a parent.

The epilogue seems to be the right place for one final, fleeting effort to see Morgan Edwards as a whole person. He may remain an enigma still, but perhaps less so.

Edwards as Seen by His Peers

Without his portrait it is hard to imagine Morgan Edwards's physical appearance. Samuel Jones describes him as of "comly form and manly deportment."[3] Thus, he was a handsome man who conducted himself in a strong, masculine manner.

Ezra Stiles described Edwards in his diary on September 18, 1769.[4]

> He is a solid, grave, learned Divine, tho'tful, penetrating, cool, judicious, without Enthusiasm. He is now in firm Health (except an incidental cold) robust & hearty; & at 48, as he tells me.

To Stiles, Edwards was a man who was firm and dependable in his views, solemn in manner, scholarly in his ministry, attentive to others, sharp in his thinking, controlled in his temperament, sensible in his judgments, and not given to emotional outbursts.

Another person who knew Edwards as a friend was William Rogers who succeeded him as pastor of the Baptist church in Philadelphia. Rogers's wife was the former Hannah Gardner, who had been reared as a devout Quaker, but in reading her Bible came to sense the importance of believer baptism. She began to attend the Baptist church when Morgan Edwards was pastor, and he baptized her. She and Rogers were married in June 1773, and she and Edwards remained close friends throughout the remainder of his life.[5]

Rogers spoke of Edwards as "my highly esteemed friend and Father,"[6] and he described him as "Very far from being a selfish person."[7] Rogers also saw Edwards as a unique person, for he said, "There was nothing uncommon in Mr. Edwards' person, but he possessed an original genius."[8] In its context this last statement could mean that Edwards was able to relate to persons from all walks of life.

> By his travels in England, Ireland, and America, commixing with all sorts of people, and by close application to reading, he had attained a remarkable ease of behaviour in company, and was furnished with something pleasant or informing to say on all occasions.

There were others who agreed with Rogers, such as Thomas Rodney, a leader in the independence movement in Delaware.[9]

More to the point, however, is that Edwards's peers perceived him as a good man, in spite of his faults. Oliver Hart described Edwards as "a great good man."[10] South Carolina Baptist minister Francis Pelot was even more effusive in his praise of Edwards:[11]

> We were favoured with the company of Rev. Morgan Edwards at my house for about a week in last Jany...also...at our Association. We all esteem him as a profitable good man. And he left us all full of love to him.

Finally, Edwards's contemporaries were very sensitive to his commitment to the cause of Christ by his participation in Baptist church life. On this score the same Francis Pelot had written earlier to Hezekiah Smith, and he described Edwards as "a talented man--a man who has served his Fellow[s] in a warm attachment to our Baptist interest."[12]

Oliver Hart, then also serving in South Carolina, said of Edwards, "He is...firmly attached to the Baptist interests; to promote which he cheerfully encounters all Difficulties."[13] In their funeral sermons, both Rogers and Jones gave strong witness to Edwards's total commitment to the Baptist church in his ministry for Christ. Rogers focused on a specific instance in the life of the Baptist church in Philadelphia.[14]

> The Baptist churches are much indebted to Mr. Edwards. They will long remember the time and talents he devoted to their best interests in Europe and America. Very far was he from being a selfish person; when the arrears of his salary, as pastor of this church, amounted to upwards of 372 pounds, and he was put in possession of a house by the church till the principal and interest be paid, he resigned the house, and relinquished a great part of the debt, *lest the church should be distressed*. [Italics mine].

Samuel Jones was less pointed but more graphic as he spoke of Edwards's legacy in ministry.[15]

> If leading a life of self-denial, and charity for the sake of Zion, and at last dying not worth a groat; If these be marks of a disinterested turn of mind and of warm and unabating Zeal in favour of Jerusalem, judge ye how far the spirit of the text was copied out in the life of him, whose too sudden, and as it were untimely death we mourn this day.

Edwards as Seen by Historians

When Morgan Edwards is discussed among Baptists today the conversations usually revolve around his eccentricities, while his positive contributions are bypassed. Actually, no other American Baptist leader has received so many accolades.

Samuel Jones, 1795: "For among all the watchmen on Zion's walls, few in all respects were like him."[16]

David Benedict, 1855: "...it is proper to say that for talents, industry and usefulness, he was preeminent in his day...emphatically, a pioneer in the history of the Baptists."[17]

William Cathcart, 1881: "In his day no Baptist minister equaled him, and none since has surpassed him."[18]

Thomas Armitage, 1887: "He was a noble, refined and scholarly servant of Christ as could be found in the colonies."[19]

Reuben Guild, 1897: "Mr. Edwards...is described by all the biographers as a man of wonderful magnetic influence, inspiring with enthusiasm all with whom he came in contact."[20]

William W. Keen, 1899: "...leaving a mark both in letters, education, executive ability and personal influence such as few have ever made."[21]

Henry C. Vedder, 1907: "His very faults had a leaning toward virtue's side, and in good works he was exceeded by none of his day, if indeed by any of any day."[22]

David Ashton, 1951: "The career of Morgan Edwards in review support the outstanding tributes paid to him by latter-day Baptist historians."[23]

Robert A. Baker, 1965: "These...activities show that Morgan Edwards was a busy man in his work, both pastoral and denominational, to say nothing of the demands of his family life."[24]

John S. Moore, 1971: "Edwards was far in advance of his time in his exact historical method."[25]

Thomas R. McKibbens and Kenneth L. Smith, 1980: "His sermons are examples of Baptist preaching at its best during the latter part of the eighteenth century."[26]

James A. Rogers, 1985: "Edwards was a statesman among Baptist leaders of the colonial period."[27]

H. Leon McBeth, 1988: "One of their [Welsh Baptists] greatest contributions was in the person of Morgan Edwards. He lent doctrinal and spiritual stability to

Baptists."²⁸

William D. Thompson, 1989: "Rev. Morgan Edwards was one of the most distinguished of all the church's pastors.²⁹

Norman H. Maring, 1990: "His gathering of the historical data was of great importance. For some...states we would know practically nothing if he had not furnished the information."³⁰

Hywell Davies, 1991: "Morgan Edwards was a man of strange ways, but also a man of refinement."³¹

What Was Morgan Edwards Really Like?

Available resources tell us of Morgan Edwards, a man who was a mixture of many ingredients; a man who experienced much personal tragedy in his life and may have internalized his emotional reactions to these events. If Edwards were an emotionally controlled person, that may explain the occasional caustic outbursts of his tongue and pen. It may also account for his brief bout with public drunkenness.

In contrast, he was a man who enjoyed all of life and was able to share much of it in camaraderie with others. This trait enabled him to befriend people of many different backgrounds.

Edwards was a man with an irenic spirit. He wanted to promote goodwill and understanding among people in general and Baptists in particular. Some have misunderstood this quality as theological compromise, but not so. Morgan Edwards was a convinced evangelical Calvinist.

Twentieth-century theologically liberal Baptists owned Morgan Edwards as a fellow traveller. However, a review of his sermons and writings would quickly demonstrate that he was theologically conservative to the core. Albeit, he did not use his theology as an instrument of divisiveness.

How Important Was Morgan Edwards?

Morgan Edwards's importance to Baptist church life in America was as an innovator and a motivator. He was a person who initiated action and inspired others to join in. Life for American Baptists was permanently changed because of Morgan Edwards's influence. There are at least nine areas in which he made a positive difference.

First, the area where he is perhaps most recognized is Baptist history. He introduced a new "historical method" and a new *raison d'etre* for Baptist history. His method was first-hand research in records and with persons. His aims were not apologetic but to tell the Baptist story and to promote Baptist unity. The history of early American Baptists cannot be written without using his materials.

Edwards's second place of importance is in higher education. Reuben Guild was correct in describing him as the "prime mover" behind the founding of Rhode Island College, which eventually became Brown University. He is not the only person who should receive credit for launching the school, but he did initiate the project and with immense effort and self-sacrifice, raised its first endowment funds in Europe.

His efforts represented the beginning of Baptist higher education in America. He received some severe criticism from those opposed to an educated ministry, but his persistence goaded American Baptists to see that Spirit-inspired preaching and an educated ministry are not antithetical.

The third area of Edwards's influence is in his plan for a national organization of Baptists. True, the seed of his plan lay on fallow ground for a long time, but he was the first to propose such a plan. There is no evidence that his plan in any way influenced the organization of the Triennial Convention in 1814, but the evidence does exist (see chapter nine) that his plan influenced the structure of the South Carolina Baptist Convention and the Southern Baptist Convention.

The fourth area of influence is in Baptist polity and practice. If polity is the principles and rules by which a group operates, Edwards' manual on the *Customs of the Primitive Churches* was the forerunner of many such publications to follow. It is difficult to assess how widely his manual was used, but a new day was ushered in for Baptists to do all "things decently and in order" when Edwards began using the principles in his book while pastor of the Philadelphia Baptist Church.

The fifth area of his influence is in connection with the Philadelphia church. Both in the church and in the Philadelphia Baptist Association, he brought order out of chaos to Baptist records. It was he who began the practice of including statistical data in church annual reports to the association.

The sixth area of Edwards's influence on Baptists is the printing of the minutes of the association meetings. Undoubtedly, this would have occurred eventually, but Edwards started it and at his own expense.

The seventh area is Edwards's prodding the Baptists to use the resources available to them. The recommendation he received from John Gill and the London board of the Particular Baptist Fund was known to all. It was an easy step, therefore, for him at his first association meeting in Philadelphia to urge the resumption of communication with the board after twenty-four years of silence.

An eighth area of influence is Edwards's idea to create an association fund to support a ministry to the churches. He was the first to use it several years later when he was appointed an associational evangelist. He thus became the precursor of all who served Baptist churches in the capacity of association or convention ministers or missionaries.

Finally, Morgan Edwards exerted his influenece for a better ministry among Baptists. This he did by leading the association to establish a library in Philadelphia for ministers and by holding high the torch for better preaching. As shown in chapters two and three, Edwards learned in his home and at Trosnant and Bristol academies the value of reading. It not only contributed to his preaching but enabled him to become a very cosmopolitan person. Morgan Edwards was one of the best Baptist preachers of his day, but he did not come by that reputation easily. He worked hard at producing and delivering outstanding sermons, and he was quick to express his convictions for the benefit of those who relied on histrionics alone.

In Summary

Morgan Edwards is seen as less of an enigma when viewed against the backdrop of his Welsh heritage and in the context of his times. His contributions gave much light to American Baptist church life because they are more in number than any other eighteenth-century Baptist leader. Isaac Backus and John Leland contributed more in the field of religious liberty; John Gano and Hezekiah Smith in the area of the military chaplaincy; James Manning to Baptist higher education; and what shall we say of Samuel Jones, William Rogers, Oliver Hart, and others?

Morgan Edwards was the outstanding American Baptist leader of the eighteenth century, simply because of being the primary contributor and motivator in more areas of Baptist church life than any other person. Therefore, let history judge him, not by focusing on his idiosyncrasies alone, but by focusing on him as a whole person. True, he was an enigma, but a dazzling one to be sure.

ENDNOTES

1. MS. Funeral Sermon, Samuel Jones, "If I Prefer Not Jerusalem Above My Chief Joy." (Providence: Henderson Collection, John Hay Library, Brown University, January 28, 1795)
2. Ibid.
3. Ibid.
4. F.B. Dexter, ed., *The Literary Diary of Exra Stiles*. (New York: n.p., 1901). 3 vols., I, 24.
5. William Rippon, *Baptist Annual Register*, (London: 1794- 1797), 58.
6. Ibid., 308
7. Ibid., 312.
8. Ibid., 313.
9. MS. Letter, Thomas Rodney to Dr. Evans, March 20, 1791.
10. MS. Letter, Oliver Hart to Hezekiah Smith, February 27, 1772.
11. MS. Letter, Francis Pelot to Hezekiah Smith, April 6, 1772.
12. MS. Letter, Francis Pelot to Hezekiah Smith, March 28, 1771.
13. MS. Letter, Oliver Hart to Hezikiah Smith, March 28, 1772.
14. Rippon, 312.
15. Jones Sermon.
16. Ibid.
17. David Benedict, *A General History of the Baptist Denomination in America and Other Parts of the World* (New York: Sheldon, Lamport & Blakeman, 1855), 602.
18. William Cathcart, ed. *The Baptist Encyclopedia*, (Philadelphia: Lewis H. Everts, 1881), 362.
19. Thomas Armitage, *A History of the Baptists*, (New York: Bryan Taylor & Co., 1887), 723.

20. Reuben A. Guild, *Early History of Brown University, Including the Life, Times, and Correspondence of President Manning, 1756-1791* (Providence: Snow and Farnham, 1897), 45
21. William W. Keen, *The Bi-Centennial celebration of the Founding of the First Baptist Church of the City of Philadelphia*, (Philadelphia: American Baptist Publication Society, 1899), 42.
22. Henry C. Vedder, *A Short History of the Baptists*, (Philadelphia: American Baptist Publication Society, 1907), 314.
23. David H. Ashton, "Morgan Edwards: First Historian of American Baptists," *The Chronicle*, (Philadelphia: The American Baptist Historical Society, April, 1951), XIV, No. 2, 79.
24. Robert A. Baker, "Profile of a Baptist Historian," *Baptist History and Heritage*, (Nashville: Historical Commission of the Southern Baptist Convention, August, 1965), I, No. 2, 6.
25. John S. Moore, "Morgan Edwards: Baptist Statesman," *Baptist History and Heritage*, (Nashville: Historical Commission of the Southern Baptist Convention, January, 1971), VI, No. 1, 33.
26. Thomas R. McKibbens, Jr. and Kenneth L. Smith, *The Life and Works of Morgan Edwards*, (New York: Arno Press, 1980), 210.
27. James A. Rogers, *Richard Furman, Life and Legacy*, (Macon: Mercer University Press, 1985), 170.
28. H. Leon McBeth, *The Baptist Heritage*, (Nashville: Broadman Press, 1988), 212.
29. William D. Thompson, *Philadelphia's First Baptists*, (Philadelphia: The First Baptist Church, 1989), 12.
30. Personal Interview, November 17, 1990, at Rock Hill, South Carolina.
31. Personal Interview, May 11, 1991 at Cardiff, Wales.

SOURCES CONSULTED

BOOKS

Armitage, Thomas. *A History of the Baptists*. New York: Bryan Taylor & Company, 1887.

Asplund, John. *The Universal Register of the Baptist Denomination in North America*. Boston: John W. Folsom, 1794.

Backus, Isaac. *A History of New England With Particular Reference to the Denomination of Christians Called Baptists*. 2 vols. Newton: n.p., 1871.

Ballard, G.J. *Connecting Links of About 200 Years History of the Sandhurst Baptists*. Rye: Adams & Son, n.d.

Barnes, William W. *The Southern Baptist Convention, 1845-1953*. Nashville: Broadman Press, 1954.

Bassett, T.M. *The Welsh Baptists*. Swansea: Ilston House, 1977

Belcher, Joseph. *George Whitefield: A Biography*. New York: American Tract Society, n.d.

Benedict, David. *General History of the Baptist Denomination In America and Other Parts of the World*. New York: Sheldon, Lamport and Blakeman, 1855.

_____. *Fifty Years Among Baptists*. New York: Sheldon and Company, 1860.

Brackney, William H. *Baptist life and Thought*. Valley Forge: Judson Press, 1983.

_____.*The Baptists*. Westport, Connecticutt: Greenwood Press, Inc., 1988.

Branberry, J.A. *A History of Monmouthshire, From the Coming of the Normans into Wales Down to the Present Time*. London:

Michael Hughes and Clark, 1907.
Bronson, Walter C. *The History of Brown University, 1764-1914.* Providence: Brown University Press, 1914.
Brown, A. Hedley. *The Rye Baptists 1750-1904.* Rye: Deacon's Printing and Publishing Works, 1904.
Brown, Wallace. *The Good Americans.* New York: William Morrow and Co., 1969.
Buffard, Frank. *Kent and Sussex Baptist Association.* Faversham, England: E. Vinson, n.d.
Callahan, North. *Royal Raiders.* Indianapolis: Bobbs-Merrill Co., Inc., 1963.
Cathcart, William. *The Baptists and the American Revolution.* Philadelphia: S.A. George & Co., 1876.
_____. *The Baptist Encyclopedia.* Philadelphia: Louis H. Everts, 1881.
Champion, L. G. *Farthing Rushlight, The Story of Andrew Gifford, 1700-1784.* London: Carey Kingsgate Press, 1961.
Christian, John T. *A History of the Baptists,* Nashville: The Sunday School Board, 1922.
Clark, Arthur. *The Story of Monmouthshire.* 2 vols. Llandybie, Wales: Christopher Davies, 1962.
Clark, J. H. *History of Monmouthshire.* Usk, Wales: County Observer, 1869.
Cook, Richard B. *The Story of the Baptists.* Baltimore: H. M. Wharton & Co., 1885.
Cramp, J. M. *Baptist History.* Philadelphia: American Baptist Publication Society, n.d.
Crane, Arthur, Bernard Derrick, and Edward Donovan. *Pontypool's Heritage in Pictures and Postcards.* Newport: Starling Press. 1990.
Davies, J. *History of the Welsh Baptists: From the Year Sixty-Three To The One Thousand Seven Hundred and Seventy.* Pittsburgh: D.M. Hogan, 1835.
Dexter, F.B., ed. *The Literary Diary of Ezra Stiles.* 3 vols. New York: n.p. 1901.
Douglas, Crerar, ed. *Autobiography of Augustus Hopkins Strong.* Valley Forge: Judson Press, 1981.

Edwards, Morgan. *Materials Toward A History of the Baptists. (1770-1792).* 2 vols. Danielsville Georgia: Heritage Papers, 1984.

_____. *Customs of the Primitive Churches.* n.p. 1774.

Edwards, Owen M. *Wales.* New York: G.P. Putnam's Sons, 1901.

Elmwood, Tonie Butler and J.W. Elmwood, Jr. *The Rebellious Welsh.* Los Angeles: The Ward Ritchie Press, 1951.

Evans, E. A. *A History of Wales, 1660-1815.* Cardiff: University of Wales, 1976.

Gano, Stephen, ed. *Biographical Memoirs of the Late Rev. John Gano.* New York: Southwick and Hardcastle, 1806.

Gardner, Robert G. *Baptists In Early America: A Statistical History, 1639-1790.* Atlanta: Georgia Baptist Historical Society, 1983.

Gill, John. *A Collection of Sermons and Tracts by the Late Reverend and Learned John Gill.* London: George Keith, 1773.

_____. *A Complete Body of Doctrinal and Practical Divinity: Or A System of Evagelical Truths.* 2 vols. Grand Rapids: Baker Book House, n.d.

Gillette, A. D., ed. *Minutes of the Philadelphia Baptist Association from A.D. 1707 to A.D. 1807.* Philadelphia: American Baptist Publication Society, 1851.

Goodman, Paul, ed. *Essays In American Colonial History.* New York: Holt, Rinehart and Winston, 1967.

Green, John R. *England.* New York: Peter Fanlon Collin, 1958

Greene, Samuel Arnold. *History of the State of Rhode Island.* New York: D. Appleton & Company, 1874.

Guild, Reuben A. *Chaplain Smith and the Baptists.* Philadelphia: American Baptist Publication Society, n.d.

_____. *Early History of Brown University, Including the Life, Times and Correspondence of President James Manning, 1756-1791.* Providence: Snow and Farnham, 1896.

Hancock, Harold Bell. *The Delaware Loyalists.* Wilmington: Historical Society of Delaware, 1940.

Harden, William. *History of Savannah and South Georgia.* Atlanta: Cherokee Publishing Company, 1981.

Harrison, Fred W. *It All Began Here: The Story of the East Midlands Baptist Association.* London: East Midlands Baptist Association, n.d.

Hoadley, Frank T. *By God's Own Hand: The Story of American Baptists in Pennsylvania and Delaware.* Valley Forge: ABCOPAD Press, 1986.

Hudson, Winthrop S. *Baptist Concepts of the Church.* Valley Forge: Judson Press, 1959

_____. *Baptists In Transition.* Valley Forge: Judson Press, 1979.

_____. *Religion In America.* New York: Charles Scribner's Sons, 1981.

Ivimey, Joseph. *A History of the English Baptists.* 2 vols. London: Isaac Taylor, 1830.

Jenkins, Geraint H. *Literature, Religion and Society In Wales, 1660-1730.* Cardiff: University of Wales Press, 1978.

Johnson, Katherine W. *Rhode Island Baptists.* Valley Forge: Judson Press, 11975.

Jones, Adolphe G. *Half-Hours in Monmouthshire.* Newport: J.E. Southall, 1906.

Jones, Brynmor P. *Sowing Beside Still Waters.* Cwbran, Wales: Gwent Baptist Association, 1985.

Jones, David. *Hanes y Bedyddwy-yn Nehenbarth Cymon.* Carmarthen, Wales: n.p., 1839.

Jones, E.K. *The Baptists of Wales and Ministerial Education.* Wrescham, Wales: Hughes and Sons, 1902.

Keen, William W. *The Bi-Centennial Celebration of the Founding of the First Baptist Church of the City of Philadelphia.* Philadelphia: American Baptists Publication Society, 1899.

Kelly, Joseph J., Jr. *Life and Times In Colonial Philadelphia.* Harrisburg: Stackpole Books, 1973.

Langdon, William Chauncey, *Everyday Things In American Life, 1607-1776.* New York: Charles Scribner, 1937.

Lemons, J. Stanley. *The First Baptist Church In America.* Providence: Charitable Baptist Society, 1988.

Lippincott, Horace M. *Early People, Its People, Life and Progress.* Philadelphia: J.B. Lippincott, 1917.

Lumpkin, William L. ed. *Baptist Confessions of Faith.* Valley Forge: Judson Press, 1959.

Maring, Norman H. *Baptists In New Jersey.* Valley Forge: Judson Press, 1964.

_____. and Winthrop Hudson. *Baptist Manual of Polity and Practice.* 2nd. ed. Valley Forge: Judson Press, 1991.

McBeth, H. Leon. *The Baptist Heritage. Nashville:* Broadman Press, 1987.

McKibbens, Thomas R., Jr. and Kenneth L. Smith. *The Life and Works of Morgan Edwards.* New York: Arno Press, 1980.

McLoughlin, William G. ed. *Isaac Backus on Church, State, and Calvinism: Pamphlets, 1754-1789.* Cambridge: Harvard University Press, 1968.

_____. *New England Dissent, 1630-1833.* Cambridge: Harvard University Press, 1971.

_____. ed. *The Diary of Isaac Backus.* Providence: Brown University Press, 1979.

_____. *Soul Liberty: The Baptist Struggles in New England 1630-1835.* Providence: Brown University Press, 1991.

Mendelson, Jack H. and Nancy K. Mello. *Alcohol Use and Abuse in America.* Boston: Little, Brown and Company, 1985.

Milford, Peter D., ed. *Manuscript Histories of Baptist Chapels.* Newport: Minister Cottage, Highmor Hill, Caldicot, 1978.

Moon, Norman S. *Education For Ministry - Bristol Baptist College.* Bristol: Bristol Baptist College, 1979.

Morgan, Prys. *The Eighteenth Century Renaissance.* Llandybie, Wales: Christopher Davis, 1981.

Morison, Samuel Eliot. *John Paul Jones.* New York: Little Brown and Company, 1959.

Morris, Jan. *The Matter of Wales.* Oxford: Oxford University Press, 1964.

Moss, Lemuel, ed. *The Baptists and The National Centenary.* Philadelphia: American Baptist Publication Society, 1976.

Muir, Richard. *The Lost Villages of Britain.* London: Michael Joseph, 1982.

Newman, A.H. *A History of the Baptist Churches In the United States.* Philadelphia: American Baptist Publication Society, 1898.

Oberholtzer, E.P. *Philadelphia: A History of the City and Its People.* Philadelphia: S.J. Clark Publishing Corporation, n.d.

Parker, Irene. *Dissenting Academies In England.* New York: Octogon Books, 1969.

Payne, Ernest A. *The Fellowship of Believers*. rev. ed. London: Carey Kingsgate Press, 1952.

Richards, William. *The Welsh Nonconformists Memorial*. Edited by John Evans. London: Sherwood, Neely and Jones, 1820.

Roberts, T.R. *Eminent Welshmen: A Short Biographical Dictionary of Welshmen*. Cardiff: The Educational Publishing Company, Ltd., 1908.

Rogers, James A. *Richard Furman, Life and Legacy*. Macon: Mercer University Press, 1985.

Rorabaugh, W.J. *The Alcoholic Republic: An American Tradition*. New York: Oxford University Press, 1979.

Rose, Ivan Murray. *The First Baptist Church: A Brief History and Interpretation*. Philadelphia: By the author, 1963.

Rothermund, D. *The Layman's Progress: Religion and Political Experience in the Middle Colonies, 1740-1770*. Philadelphia: n.p., 1961.

Scharf, J. Thomas. *The History of Delaware, 1609-1888*. Philadelphia: L.J. Richards & Co., 1888

Sears, Barna. *Celebration of the One Hundreth Anniversary of the Founding of Brown University*. Providence: Sidney S. Rider, 1865.

Shotwell, Malcolm G. *Renewing the Baptist Principle of Associations*. Ann Arbor: University Microfilm International, 1990.

Shurden, Walter B. *Associationalism Among Baptists In America*. New York: Arno Press, 1980.

Smith, Paul H. *Loyalists and Redcoats*. Chapel Hill: University of North Carolina Press, 1964.

Spencer, David. *The Early Baptists of Philadelphia*. Philadelphia: William Sychelmore, 1877.

Sprague, William B. *Annals of the American Pulpit*. New York: Robert Carter & Brothers, 1865.

Stanton, Frank M. *Anglo Saxon England*. Oxford: Oxford University Press, 1847.

Swaine, Stephen Albert. *Faithful Men or Memoirs of Bristol Baptist College and Some of Its Most Distinquished Alumni*. London: Alexander and Shepheard, 1884.

Taylor, Adam. *The History of the English General Baptists*. London: T. Boie, 1818.

Thomas, Joshua. *History of the Welsh Baptist Association.* London: n.p., 1795.
Thompson, Pishey. *Historical Antiquities of Boston.* London: Longman and Company, 1965.
Thompson, William D. *Philadelphia's First Baptists.* Philadelphia: First Baptist Church, 1989.
Torbet, Robert G. *A Social History of the Philadelphia Baptist Association.* Philadelphia: Westbrook Book Publishing, 1944.
_____. *History of the Baptists.* 3rd. ed. Valley Forge: Judson Press, 1963.
_____. and Samuel S. Hill, Jr. *Baptists - North and South.* Valley Forge: Judson Press, 1964.
Toulmin, Joshua. *An Historical View of the State of the Protestant Dissenters in England From the Revolution to the Accession of Queen Anne.* Bath: Richard Cuttrell, 1814.
Underwood, A.C. *A History of the English Baptists.* London: Carey Kingsgate Press, Ltd., 1947.
Valentine, Theodore F. *Concern For the Ministry, The Story of the Particular Baptist Fund.* Teddington: Particular Baptist Fund, 1967.
Van Doren, Carl. *Benjamin Franklin.* New York: Penquin Books, 1938.
Vedder, Henry C. *A Short History of the Baptists.* Philadelphia: The American Baptist Publication Society, 1907.
Vidler, William. *A Sketch of the Life of Elhanan Winchester.* London: T. Gillet, 1797.
Walker, David. *A New History of Wales: The Norman Conquerors.* Swansea: Christopher Davies, 1977.
Walker, Williston. *A History of the Christian Church.* 1st. ed. New York: Charles Scribner's Sons, 1939.
Whiteley. W.T. *A Baptist Bibliography.* London: Kingsgate Press, 1916.
_____. *The Baptists of London 1612-1928.* London: Kingsgate Press, 1932.
_____. *A History of the English Baptists.* 3rd. ed. London: Kingsgate Press, 1943.
Williams, Gwyn. *The Land Remembers: A View of Wales.* London: Faber and Faber, 1977.

Williams, Rufus. [Thomas Williams]. *The History of the Welsh Baptist Seminaries in Monmouthshire*. Aberdar, Wales: n.p., 1863.

Wood, J.H. *A Condensed History of the General Baptists of the New Connection*. London: Wood, Simkin, Marshall and Company, 1847.

Wood, James E. ed. *Baptists and the American Experience*. Valley Forge: Judson Press, 1976.

ARTICLES

Ashton, Dean H. "Morgan Edwards: First Historian of American Baptists." *The Chronicle*. XIV (1951): 70-79.

Baker, Robert A. "Profile of A Baptist Historian." *Baptist History and Heritage*. I (1965). 5-7, 26.

Brown, Raymond. "Baptist Preaching in Early 18th Century." *The Baptist Quarterly*. XXXI. (1984-1985): 4-22.

Byers, Catherine Fox. "More Than 150 Years Ago." *Focus*. III. (1983): 1-3.

Champion, L.G. "The Social Status of Some Eighteenth Century Baptist Ministers." *The Baptist Quarterly*. XXVIII. (1978-1979): 10-14.

Clipsham, E.F. "Andrew Fuller and Fullerism: A Study in Evangelical Calvinism." *The Baptist Quarterly*. XX. (1962-1963): 99-114.

Gummer, Selwyn. "Trosnant Academy." *The Baptist Quarterly*. IX (1938-1939): 417-423.

Jones, R. "Miles Harry." *Transactions of the Welsh Baptist Historical Society*. (1926).

Kirkby, Arthur. "Andrew Fuller - Evangelical Calvinist." *The Baptist Quarterly*. XV. (1953-1954): 195-202.

Langley, Arthur. "South Wales till 1753." *The Baptist Quarterly*. VI. (1918-1919): 163-182.

Laws, Gilbert. "Andrew Fuller, 1754-1815." *The Baptist Quarterly*. II. (1924-1925): 76-84.

Lovegrove, Deryck W. "Particular Baptist Itinerant Preachers During the Late 18th and Early 19th Centuries." *The Baptist Quarterly*. XXVIII (1978-1979): 127-144.

Manley, K.R. "John Rippon and English Historiography." *The Baptist Quarterly*. XXVIII. (1978-1979): 109-125.

Matthew, D. Hugh. "The Declaration of Llantrisan (1654): An Attempt to Impose Presbyterianism on Welsh Baptists?" *Aspects On The Growth of Puritanism In Wales in the 17th Century.* J. Gwynfor Jones, ed. (Edwin Mellen Press, 1992).

Moore, John S. "Morgan Edwards:Baptist Statesman." *Baptist History and Heritage.* VI. (1971): 24-33.

_____. "Writers of Early Viriginia Baptist History (1) Morgan Edwards." *The Virginia Baptist Register.* XI (1972): 519-526.

_____. "Morgan Edwards' 1772 Virginia Notebook." *The Virginia Baptist Register.* XVIII. (1979): 845-871.

Morgan, D. Densil. "Smoke, Fire and Light: Baptists and the Revitalization of Welsh Dissent." *The Baptist Quarterly.* XXXVII. (1987-1988): 224-232.

Nuttall, Geoffrey T. "The Letter - Book of John Davis (1731- 1795) of Waltham Abbey." *The Baptist Quarterly.* XXIV. (1971-1972): 49-64.

_____. "Welsh Students At Bristol Baptist College." *The Transactions of the Honorable Society of Cymmrodorian.*

Price, E.W. "Dr. Thomas Thomas of Pontypool." *The Baptist Quarterly.* III. (1926-1927): 132.

Price, Seymour J. "Dissenting Academies, 1620-1820." *The Baptist Quarterly.* VI. (1932-1933): 125-138.

Payne, Ernest A. "Caleb Evans, Founder of the Bristol Education Society." *The Baptist Quarterly.* XXIV. (1970-1971): 10-14.

Rider, Sidney. "The Historical Society's Reprint of the Morgan Edwards Manuscript." *Book Notes.* III. (1885): 13-14.

Rippon, John. ed. "Memorial Sermon." *Baptist Annual Register.* (1796): 308-314.

Roberts, H.P. "Nonconformists Academies in Wales." *The Transactions of the Honorable Society of Cymmrodorion.* London: By the Society, Session 1928-1929, 1930.

Robinson, Frank E. "Reviews: (A Baptist Bibliography)." *The Baptist Quarterly.* I. (1922-1923): 46.

Robison, Olin C. "The Legacy of John Gill." *The Baptist Quarterly.* XXIV. (1970-1971): 111-125.

Stevens, Walter. "Oxford's Attitude to Dissenters, 1646-1946." *The Baptist Quarterly.* XIII. (1949-1950): 4-17.

Thompson. Josiah. "A View of English Nonconformity in 1773." *Transactions of the Congregational Historical Society.* II. (1911-1912): 264.

White, Barrington R. "John Gill in London, 1719-1729: A Biograhical Fragment." *The Baptist Quarterly.* XXII. (1966-1967): 72-91.

Whiteley, W.T. "The Influence of Whitefield on Baptists." *The Baptist Quarterly.* V. (1930-1931): 30-36.

_____. "Baptists In The Weald of Kent for 290 Years, Sandhurst Bicentenary." *The Baptist Quarterly.* V. (1930-1931): 322-333.

In order to avoid excessive duplication in the documentation of original correspondence, documents, sermons and manuscripts the abbreviations used will be as follows:

NCRC   Ambrose Swasey Library, Colgate Rochester Divinity School, Rochester, New York.

NCRC-CC   Ambrose Swasey Library, Colgate Rochester Divinity School, Rochester, New York; Crozer Collection.

NRAB   American Baptist Historical Society, Rochester, New York.

RPJCB(B)   Brown Papers, The John Carter Brown Library, Brown University, Providence, Rhode Island.

RPB-JH   The John Hay Library, Brown University, Providence, Rhode Island.

RPB-JH(H)   Mary Henderson Collection, John Hay Library, Brown University, Providence, Rhode Island.

RPB-JH(J)   Samuel Jones Collection, John Hay Library, Brown University, Providence, Rhode Island.

RPB-JH(M)   James Manning Collection, John Hay Library, Brown University, Providence, Rhode Island.

WDHS   The Historical Society of Delaware, Wilmington, Delaware.

PPHS(MJ)   McKesson-Jones Collection, the Historical Society of Pennsylvania, Philadelphia, Pennsylvania.

LETTERS

Alison, Francis, Philadelphia to James Moody, Newry, Ireland, 9 February 1767. RPB-JH.

Booth, Abraham, London, to James Manning, Providence, 12 December 1787. RPB-JH(M). A 728.

_____. London, to James Manning, Providence, 11 July 1789. RPB-JH(M), A 730.

Brown, Nicholas, Providence, to Morgan Edwards, Newark, Delaware, 19 August 1775. RPB-JCB(B), OL74-77M

Crane, Arthur, Pontypool, Wales, to the author, Alhambra, California, 8 March 1993. Letter now in the possession of the author.

Edwards, Morgan, Philadelphia, to Gardner Thurston, Newport, Rhode Island, 9 November 1764. RPB-JH(M)

_____. Philadelphia, to Gardner Thurston, Newport, Rhode Island, 28 June 1765. RPB-JH(M).

_____. London, to James Manning, Providence, 26 April 1767. RPB-JH(M), I. 33.

_____. Philadelphia, to the Corporation, Rhode Island College, Providence, 8 September 1769. RPB-JH.

_____. Newark, Delaware, to Samuel Jones, Penepeck, Pennsylvania, 11 June 1784. RPB-JH(J).

_____. Newark, to Samuel Jones, Penepeck, 25 December 1784. PPHS(MJ).

_____. Newark, to Samuel Jones, Penepeck, 26 July 1785. RPB-JH(J).

_____. Newark to Samuel Jones, Penepeck, 7 November 1785. RPB-JH(J). D. 2470.

_____. Newark, to Samuel Jones, Penepeck, 28 February 1787. RPB-JH(J)>

_____. Newark, to Isaac Backus, Northhampton, Massachusetts, 18 August 1788. Andover Newton Theological School, Newton Centre, Massachusetts, Backus Collection.

Furman, Alester G., Greenville, South Carolina, to Lorraine Whitehead, Ann Arbor, Michigan, 10 September 1951. Furman University, Greenville, South Carolina, Baptist Collection.

Gibbs, George, Newport, Rhode Island, to Nicholas Brown, Providence, 18 May 1770. RPB-JCB(B), Brown Papers, L57 82M.

Hall, Robert, London, to Joseph Kinghorn, Norwich, 26 November 1793. NRAB.
Hart, Oliver, Charleston, South Carolina, to Samuel Jones, Penepeck, 1 December 1763. PPHS(M-J).
_____. Charleston, to Hezekiah Smith, Haverhill, Massachusetts, 27 February 1772. RPB-JH.
Jones, Samuel, Penepeck, to James Manning, Providence, 9 March 1777. PPHS(M-J)
Manning, James, Providence, to Samuel Stennett, London, 7 June 1770. RPB-JH(M), A 751.
_____. Newport, Rhode Island, to Hezekiah Smith, Haverhill, 1 May 1771. RPB-JH(M).
_____. Providence, to John Ryland, Northhampton, England, 1 June 1771. RPB-JH(M).
_____. Providence, to Thomas Llewellyn, London, 21, February 1772. RPB-JH(M), A 778.
_____. Providence, to Samuel Stennett, London, 3 November 1772. RPB-JH(M).
_____. Providence, to James Wallin, London, 10 May 1773. RPB-JH(M).
_____. Providence, to John Ryland, Northhampton, 10 May 1773. RPB-JH(M), A 986.
_____. Providence, to Samuel Jones, Penepeck, 31 May 1773. RPB-JH(M).
_____. Providence, to John Ryland, Northhampton, 25 November 1773. RPB-JH(M).
_____. Providence, to Samuel Jones, Penepeck, 26 June 1773. RPB-JH(M), A 20.
_____. Providence to Samuel Jones, Penepeck, 7 March 1774. RPB-JH(M), A 24.
_____. Providence, to Samuel Jones, Penepeck, 17 May 1774. RPB-JH(M), A 25.
_____. Providence, to Samuel Jones, Penepeck, 14 September 1775. RPB-JCB(B), L 74 76 M
_____. Providence, to John Rippon, London, 3 August 1784. RPB-JH(M), A 792.
Matthews, D. Hugh, Cardiff to the author, Alhambra, 4 September 1992. Now in the possession of the author.

————. Cardiff, to the author, Alhambra, 24 November 1992. Now in the possession of the author.

————. Cardiff, to the author, Alhambra, 13 July 1994. Now in the possession of the author.

Pelot, Francis, Euhaw, South Carolina, to Hezekiah Smith, Haverhill, 28 March 1771. RPB-JH(M).

————. Euhaw, to Hezekiah Smith, Haverhill, 27 October 1771. RPB-JH(M).

————. Euhaw, to Hezekiah Smith, Haverhill, 6 April 1772. RPB-JH(M).

Rhode Island College, Providence, to Moses Linds, Charleston, 1 January 1771. RPB-JH(M).

Rippon, John, London to James Manning, Providence, 1 May 1784. RPB-JH(M).

Rodney, Thomas, Polar Grove, Delaware, to Morgan Edwards, Newark, 5 March 1791. WDHS.

————. Poplar Grove, to Morgan Edwards, Newark, 10 March 1791. WDHS.

————. Poplar Grove, to Morgan Edwards, Newark, 11 March 1791. WDHS.

————. Poplar Grove, to Morgan Edwards, Newark, 20 March 1771. WDHS.

Stiles, Ezra, Newport, Rhode Island, to the College of Rhode Island, Warren, Rhode Island, 3 September 1766. RPB-JH(M), I 25.

————. Newport, to the College of Rhode Island, Providence, 1 June 1771. RPB-JH(M).

Thompson, Joshua, Belfast, Ireland, to the author, Alhambra, 12 June 1991. Now in the possession of the author.

Ustick, Thomas, Philadelphia, to Nicholas Brown, Providence, 4 February 1782. RPB-JCB(B), L 81 83 M.

————. Philadelphia, to Isaac Backus, Northhampton, 3 December 1782. RPB-JH, Ustick Papers.

————. Philadelphia, to Isaac Backus, Northhampton, 9 September 1783. RPB-JH, Ustick Papers.

Wallin, Benjamin, London, to James Manning, Providence, 20 March 1773. RPB-JH(M), 710

————. London, to James Manning, Providence, 17 August 1773. RPB-JH(M), 713.

Webster, Richard, Mauch Chunk, Pennsylvania, to Horatio Gates, Jr., 20 July 1853. NRAB, File 1.

DOCUMENTS

Delaware State Archives. (Dover: New Castle County Deed Book) V. 2, 180-183.

_____. (Dover: New Castle County Will Book) 0-1, 57.

Philadelphia Baptist Church. *Baptism Certificate*. (Rochester: American Baptist Historical Society Archives, 1762).

College of Philadelphia, *Minutes of the Board of Trustees*. 11 May 1762. University of Pennsylvania Archives, Philadelphia.

Rhode Island College. *Petition To Assembly*. August 1763. RPB-JH(M), I 1.

_____. *Charter*. Ausgust 1763. RPB-JH(M), I 3.

_____. *Charter*. August, 1763. RPB-JH(M), 1 5.

_____. *Petition To Assembly*. October 1763. RPB-JH(M) I 7.

_____. *List of Authorized Solicitors*. RPB-JH(M), I 11.

_____. *Rough Minutes, Corporation Meeting*. 6 September 1764. RPB-JH(M), I 15.

_____. *List of Trustees and Fellows*, 1764-1770. RPB-JH(M) I 105.

_____. *Authorization of Morgan Edwards to Solicit Funds in Europe*. 20 November 1766. RPB-JH(M), I 27.

_____. *Certification of Morgan Edwards to Receive Donations and List of Contributors*. RPB-JH(M), 1-D, Ed. 9.

_____. *Report on the College*. n.d. RPB-JH(M), I 177.

_____. *Minutes of the Corporation, 1767-1768*. RPB-JH(M), I 31.

_____. *Certification For Morgan Edwards to Solicit Funds Among General and Particular Baptists in England*. 25 May 1768 and 27 May 1768. RPB-JH(M), I 35.

_____. *Published List of Contributors*. 22 August 1768. RPB-JH(M), I 37.

_____. *Morgan Edwards' European Expense Account*. 6 September 1769. RPB-JH(M), I 45.

_____ *Certification that Money Raised In Europe Go Exclusively Toward the President's Salary*. 7 September 1769. RPB-JH(M), I 39.

_____. *Reasons for Relocating the College at Providence.* RPB-JH(M), I 61.
_____. *General Commission to Solicit Funds.* September 1770. RPB-JH(M), A 21416.
_____. *Minutes of the Corporation.* 4 September 1771. RPB-JH(M), I 119.
_____. *Morgan Edwards' American Expense Account and Record of Contributors.* RPB-JH(M), I 131.
_____. *List of Corporation Members, 1772.* RPB-JH(M) I 137.
_____. *Public Admonition of a Number of Students.* RPB-JH(M), I 191.
_____. *Disciplinary Report.* 1774. RPB-JH(M), A 191.
_____. *Laws of the College.* 1774. RPB-JH(M), I 191.

SERMON AND ADDRESSES

Sermons of Morgan Edwards. MSS. NCRC-CC
Sermon of Morgan Edwards, "A Farewell Discourse," 8 February 1761. Published in Dublin, Ireland, by S. Powell.
Sermon of Morgan Edwards, "I Magnify My Office," 2 January 1763. Published in Philadelphia by Andrew Stewart.
Sermon of Morgan Edwards, "A New Year's Gift," 1 January 1770. Published in New port, Rhode Island by Solomon Southwick.
Sermon of Oliver Hart, "A Gospel Church Portrayed and Her Orderly Service Pointed Out," 1791. Published in Trenton, New Jersey.
Sermon of Samuel Jones, "If I Prefer Not Jerusalem," 25 February 1795. RPB-JH(J).
Address of John P. Nields, "Washington's Army In Delaware in the Summer of 1777." 9 September 1827 at Cooch's bridge, New Castle County, Delaware.

MANUSCRIPTS

Llanwenarth Baptist Churchbook. National Library of Wales, Aberystwyth. Dep. 409, 410 B.
Thomas, Joshua. "Materials Toward A History of the Baptist Churches In The Principality of Wales, 1630-1782." Bristol Baptist College Library, Bristol, England.

Minutes of the Particular Baptist Fund, I. 4 April 1718 to 13 May 1718. Angus Library, Regents Park College, Oxford.
_____. II. 1740-1757. Angus Library, Regents Park College, Oxford.
Edwards, Morgan. "Academical Exercises, 1742-1743." RPB-JH(M-J) I-U, Ed. 97a.
Cork Baptist Churchbook, 1759. Cork Baptist Church, Cork, Ireland.
Thomas, Joshua. "History of Bristol Baptist College." Bristol Baptist College, Bristol, England.
Philadelphia Baptist Churchbook. American Baptist History Society Archives, Valley Forge, Pennsylvania.
Waterford Baptist Church Registry of Pastors, June 1805-December 1914. Irish Baptist Historical Society, Belfast, Ireland.
"History of the Llanwenarth Baptist Church" Gwent County Records Office, Cubran, Wales.
Backus, Isaac. "A Journey to Philadelphia 1774." RPB-JH.
Miles, Samuel. Autobiography. PPHS, AM 1042.
Edwards, Morgan. "Historical Sketch on the Founding of Rhode Island College. RPB-JH(M), I 183.
Jones, Horatio Gates, Jr. "Manuscript of Morgan Edwards Material Toward A History of the Baptists of Rhode Island." NCRC.
Birdsong, J.E. "Tour of Rev. Morgan Edwards of Pennsylvania To The American Baptists in North Carolina, 1772-1773." 24 June 1889. North Carolina State Library, Raliegh.

UNPUBLISHED DISSERTATIONS

Davies, Hywell M. "Transatlantic Brethren: A Study of English, Welsh and American Baptist With Particular Reference to Morgan John Rhys (1760-1804) and His Friends." D.Ph. Diss. University of Wales, Aberystwyth.
Manley, Keith. "John Rippon, 1751-1836, and the Particular Baptists." D.Ph. Diss. Regents Park College, Oxford.
Morgan, Dafyyd Densil James. "The Development of the Baptist Movement in Wales Between 1714 and 1815, With Particular Reference to the Evangelical Revival." D.Ph. Diss. Regents Park College, Oxford.
Sweeney, Joseph. "Elhanan Winchester and the Universal Baptists." Ph.D. Diss. University of Pennsylvania, Philadelphia.

Thompson, Joshua. "Baptists In Ireland, 1792-1922." D.Ph. Diss. Regents Park College, Oxford.

PERIODICALS
"Associational Minutes," *Southern Baptist and General Intelligencer,* 9 September 1836. Baptist Collection, Furman University, Greenville, South Carolina.

ANNUAL REPORTS
Iowa Baptist State Convention. *Annual Report.* Des Moines: Committee on Obituaries Report, 1893.

PUBLIC REPOSITORIES
Archives, International Geneological Society, London.
Archives, National Library of Wales, Aberystwyth.
Cork Archives Institute, Cork, Ireland.
County Recorder's Office, Cork, Ireland.
Gwent County Records Office, Cumbran, Wales.

PERSONAL INTERVIEWS
Brackney, William, Dean, Eastern Baptist Theological Seminary, Philadelphia, by the author, 4 December 1988.
McBeth, H. Leon. Professor of Christian History, Southwestern Baptist Theological Seminary, Fort Worth, by the author, 15 November 1990
Gardner, Robert, Professor Christianity, Shorter College, Rome, Georgia, by the author, 16 November 1990.
Maring, Norman H., Professor Emeritus of Christian History, Eastern Baptist Theological Seminary, Philadelphia, by the author, 17 November 1990.
Ohlman, Eric, Dean, Professor of Christian History, Eastern Baptist Theological Seminary, Philadelphia, by the author, 4 December 1990.
Torbet, Robert, Professor of Christian History, Retired, Central Baptist Theological Seminary, Kansas City, Kansas, at Lansdale, Pennsylvania, by the author, 5 December 1990.
Bradley, James, Professor of Christian History, Fuller Theological Seminary, Pasadena, California, by the author, 16 April 1991.

Gaustad, Edwin S., American Baptist Historian, by the author, Riverside, California, 22 April 1991.
Davies, Hywell, Welsh Baptist Historian, by the author, at Swansea, Wales, 11 May 1991.
Matthews, D. Hugh, Principal, South Wales Baptist College, Cardiff, Wales, by the author 13 May 1991.
McLoughlin, William G., Head of the Department of History, Brown University, Providence, by the author, 24 January 1992.

INDEX

Act of Supremacy, 16
Act of Union, 17
Acts of Conformity, 62-63
Adams, John, 278, 292-294, 301
Adams, Samuel, 293-294
Alison, Francis, 173, 263, 301
American Philosophical Society, 162
American Revolution, 142, 170, 248, 267, 286, 308, 319, 327, 331
Anabaptists, 50, 209, 288-289
Andover, Mass., 318
Andrews, Jedediah, 128
Anglicans, 16, 31, 33, 49-52, 62, 65, 68, 73, 95, 98, 225, 236, 238, 258, 286, 315-316
Angus Library, 107
Annals of the American Pulpit, 190
Anthony, Johannah, 168
Anthony, Stepehn, 122
Arminianism, 34, 41, 50-51, 77
Arminius, Jacobus, 34
Armitage, Thomas, 8, 332, 379
Ashfield, Mass., 120, 289, 291, 295
Asplund, John, 358
Babcock, R., 190
Backus, Isaac, 235, 237,241, 351-352, 291-294, 306, 357-358, 360, 383
Baker, Robert, 233, 379
Baptists: General, 34-35, 38-39, 77, 84-88, 208-209, 243, 258, 262, 338, 358; German, 358; Particular, 34-35, 37-38, 77-78, 92, 106, 119, 208-209, 262, 338, 358; Regular, 210, 235; Rogerene, 358; Seventh-Day, 358, Separate, 225, 235, Six-Principle, 86-87, 243
Barbadoes Trading Co., 127
Bassett, T.M., 29, 91
Battle of the Brandywine, 306
Battle of Cooches Bridge, 302-303, 305
Battle of Lexington, 280
Bayley, John, 372
Bedfordshire, 107
Benedick, David, 117-118, 190, 378
Bennet, Job, 244, 247
Bentley Affair, The, 94-96
Biddle, John, 165
Blackwood, Christopher, 105
Boggs, John, 330, 344-345
Boon, Benjamin, 265
Booth, Abraham, 341, 342
Boston, Lincolnshire, 77-78, 84-88, 90, 100; General Baptist Church, 87, 89; Particular

Baptist Church, 84-85, 87-92
Boston, Mass., 257
Boston Tea Party, 279
Brackney, William H., 337
Brine, John, 37
British Museum, 266-267
Bristol, Eng., 69, 73-74, 144, 171, 353, 360
Bristol Academy, 27, 36, 61, 64-65, 68, 71-78, 84-85
Broadmead Baptist Church, 72, 73-78, 171
Bucks County, Pa., 127
Bunyan, John, 72
Burkloe, Samuel, 154
Burlington, Iowa, 145, 147
Broadmead Trust, 72-73
Brookline, Mass., 338
Brown, A. Hedley, 103
Brown, Nicholas, 141-142, 321
Brown University, 59, 63, 137, 145, 227, 231-269, 381
Cadoc, Saint, 24, 33
Caffyn, Matthew, 86
Calvinism, 34-35, 38-39, 52, 84, 92, 210, 368
Calvin, John, 34-35, 39
Cambrensis, Giraldus, 18, 314
Cambridge University, 360
Canterbury, Conn., 338
Carter Lane Baptist Church, 189
Cathcart, William, 1, 190, 232, 277-278, 379
Celts: Brettonic, 12, Brythonic, 12, Decangli, 12, Dematae, 12, Franks, 13, Friesians, 13, Jutes, 13, Oridvices, 12, Saxons, 13, Silures, 12, Suevi, 13
Charles I, 17
Charles II, 62
Charleston Baptist Association, 209

Charleston Baptist Church, 225
Chauncey, Charles, 250, 254
Chesapeake Bay, 302
Chester, Pa., 330
Choules, J.D., 190
Christ Church, 125, 129, 162, 263
Church of England. *See* Anglicanism
Coffin, Ann D., 370
Cohansey, N.J., 209
Cold Springs, Pa., 127
College of New Jersey, 236, 241, 258
College of Philadelphia, 108, 125, 137, 162, 172-174, 263-264, 367
Columbia University, 236
Committees of Safety, 146, 280, 296-297
Condy, Jeremiah, 257-259, 268
Congaree River, S.C., 224
Congregationalists, 34, 47, 98, 234, 236, 238, 245-247, 249-252, 255, 290
Constitution, The U.S., 331
Continental Congresses, 279, 283, 291
Cook, William, 306
Cork Baptist Church, 83, 92-102, 121
Cork Presbyterian Church, 101
Cornwallis, Lord, 217, 303
Cornwell, Francis, 105
Crockerton, Eng., 89
Cromwell, Oliver, 61, 87, 92
Crozer Collection, 180
Cwrw Achos, 316
Dafoe, Daniel, 105
Dargan, Jeremiah, 225
Darby, Henry, 298
David, Saint, 8

Davies, Howell, 32
Davies, Hywell, 380
Davis, John, (America), 291
Davis, John, (England), 36, 119
Davis, Samuel, 167-169, 324, 330
Declaration of Independence, 30, 280, 282, 294
Delaware, 213, 215, 269, 297, 313, 329, 356: Newcastle County, 135, Newark, 148, 174, 295, 298, 301, 305-306, 354; Newark Academy, 301, Pencader, 26, 135, 203, 303, 305, 354; White Clay Creek, 298
Delaware River, Pa., 123, 261
de Lafayette, Marquis, 302
Devonshire Square Baptist Church, London, 121
Dissenters, 35, 37, 43, 47: Academies, 61-65; churches, 18, 31, 33, 47, 63-64, 91; Education, 62; Ministers, 60, Ordination, 98; Persecution of, 72
Druids, 315
Duc de Lauzon, 147
Duncan, Isaac, 260
Dungan, Thomas, 127
du Pont, Pierre de Nemours, 281
Dutch Reformed Church, 234
Dyke of Offa, 13
Eaton, Isaac, 237, 241
Ebenezer Chapel, 88, 89
Edge, Andrew, 313, 324
Edward I, 15
Edwards, Eleasor, 101
Edwards, James, 27
Edwards, James the Younger, 27
Edwards, Jonathan, 189
Edwards, Miles, 91
Edwards, Morgan: administrator, 166-172; associational clerk, 210-212; associational evangelist, 213-214; associational librarian, 214; associational moderator, 212; associational preacher 213; Baptist commitment, 138, 281-283; baptism, practice of, 156-159; birth, 23, brother James, 24-28, 33, 92, 94, 268; call to Philadelphia, 118-123; church discipline, 160-162; communion practice, 159; conversion, 33, 35, 39-53; crowded church, 159-160; *Customs of the Primitive Churches, The*, 155, 160, 208, 214-219; 329, 282; death, 144, 363-372; death sermon, 102, 138, 179, 180-181, 184, 195-204, 211; drinking, 144, 363-372; father Morgan, 28-29; forced termination, 99-103; fund-raising, 150, 179, 255-268; grandson Morgan, 145, 147; Historian, 26, 39, 50, 157, 219, 224, 295, 305, 356-363; income, 91; love of singing, 155; loyalty to the Crown, 218, 145-147, 219, 277-308; marriages, 96-97, 193; national body of Baptists, 219-226; ordination, 98; preaching, 99-101, 175-179; premonition, 2, 102, 192-195; primary education, 29-31; reading, 29, 33, 59-61; resignation from the Philadelphia church, 181-184; Rye, Eng., 84, 101, 103-105, 117, 172, 253; Rye Baptist Church, 103-109; secondary education, 59-78; son Joshua, 96-97, 135-137, 139, 143-151, 163, 184,

296, 362, 372; son William, 135-145, 163, 184, 362; vote for women, 167-169; wife Mary, 25, 84, 92, 96-97, 123, 125, 135-139, 143, 148, 171, 179-180, 191-195
Edwards, Ruth, 27
Edwards, Sarah, 27
Edwards, Thomas, 28, 91
Eliot, Andrew, 257
Elizabeth I, 17
Elks Ferry, Md., 302
Ellery, William, 254
Ellys, Sir Richard, 266
Elmwood, J. W., 8
Elmwood, L. B., 8
Euhaw, S.C., 204
Evans, Caleb, 41, 68-70, 222, 239, 353
Evans, Evan, 31
Evans, Hugh, 74-75, 353
Eyres, Thomas, 246
Farewell Street Baptist Church, Newport, R.I. 214
First Baptist Church, Boston, Mass., 56
First City Troop, 296
Fish, Joseph, 235, 237
Foskett, Bernard, 64, 74-75, 78, 266
Fowke, Joseph, 93
Fox, Joseph, 292
Francis, Benjamin, 72
Francis, Enoch, 32
Fuller, Andrew, 37, 45, 78
Furman, Richard, 224, 358
Furman, University, 224, 225
Furman, Wood, 224
Gano, Daniel, 139
Gano, John, 240, 300, 383
Gardner, Hannah, 376
Gardner, John, 244

Gates, Horatio, 149
George II, 266
George III, 120, 142, 279, 281, 290
George, David Lloyd, 3
Gibbons, Ebenezer, 28, 83, 92-103, 192, 194
Gibbs, George, 321
Gifford, Andrew, 51, 74, 266-267
Gill, John, 36-37, 45, 84, 109, 117-122, 131, 189, 264-266, 382
Gillette, A.D., 211
Goochland, Va., 9
Goode, John, 87
Grafford, Hugh, 314
Grantham, Thomas, 87
Great Awakening, The, 209, 216, 225, 234
Greene, Nathaneal, 302
Greene, Samuel Arnold, 231
Greenville, S.C., 224
Griffiths, John, 67-68, 70, 118, 121-122, 126, 131
Griffiths, Morgan, 32, 67
Gruffydd ap Llywe, 13-14
Guild, Reuben, 59, 96, 145-147, 232, 268, 379, 381
Gummer, Selwyn, 68, 91
Gwent, 23-24, 32
Halifax, Nova Scotia, 243-244
Hall, Christopher, 103, 107
Hall, Robert, 107, 360-361
Hanbury Family, 24
Handy, Robert, 217
Hardcastle, Thomas, 72
Harris, Caleb, 27
Harris, Howell, 32, 50-51
Harry, Miles, 42-45, 47, 51-52, 68, 70, 76, 119-120
Hart, John, 139

Hart, Olver, 175, 217-218, 224, 243, 258, 340, 377, 383
Harvard University, 236-237, 258
Haverhill, Mass., 175, 204
Hastings, 14
Haw River, N.C., 169
Hellings, Benjamin, 155
Helwys, Thomas, 34
Henry II, 7
Henry IV, 16
Henry VII, 16
Henry VIII, 16
Heslam, William, 88
Heslam's Alley, 88-89
Higham Ferrar, Eng., 36
High Hills, S.C., 225
Hobbs, Elizabeth, 285
Hollis, Thomas, 236
Hopewell Academy, 120, 212, 237-238, 241
Horsleydown, London, 37
How, Samuel, 73
Howe, Sir Richard, 302
Howe, Sir Willia, 302-303, 305
Howell, David, 251-252
Hutchison, John, 87
Huntstown, Ma., 289
Hyder Alley, 147
Hywell Dda, 13, 15
Iberian, Peninsula, 12
Ireland-Ballymony, 263, Belfast, 263, Cork, 25, 42, 83-84, 91-103, 144, 192, 262, 265, 350; Dublin, 84, 99, 144, 265; Waterford, 92-93, 265
Irish Baptist Association, 83
Iron Hill, Del., 303
Ivimey, Joseph, 103
James, Tomas, 167
Jenckes, Daniel, 242, 245-247, 250-251, 254-255

Jenkins, Geraint, 18, 25, 29, 61, 65
Jenkins, William, 24-25, 30
Johnson, Katherine, 233
Jones, Edmund, 47
Jones, E.K., 232
Jones, Griffith, 32, 50-51
Jones, Horatio Gates, 232
Jones, Isaac, 122, 175, 213
Jones, Jenkin, 118, 129, 130-131, 157, 167, 216
Jones, John Paul, 282
Jones, Samuel, 59, 141-142, 150, 162-163, 184, 213, 216, 240, 246-247, 260, 266, 328, 332, 347, 357, 360-361, 363-372, 375-376, 378, 383
Jones, Robert Strettle, 246-247, 292-293
Jones, Rufus, 69
Jope, Caleb, 74
Josephus, 60
Keach, Benjamin, 127
Keach, Elias, 127, 216
Keen, William, 128, 136, 145, 153, 166, 232, 379
Keithian Quakers, 128-129
Kenny, Robert, 233, 269
Kent-Sussex, Eng., 105
Ketockton Association, 222
Kettering, Eng., 36
Kinghorn, Joseph, 360-361
King's College, 236
Kinnersley, Ebenezer, 122, 137, 146, 162, 173, 175
Kittrell, Peter, 74
Knight, John, 101, 121
Langley, Arthur, 88
Laud, Archbishop William, 105
Lee, Bishop Rowland, 16
Leicester, Eng., 360
Leland, John, 350, 357, 383

Levering Septimus, 161
Lincolnshire, Eng., 78, 84, 87
Liquor Pond Street, 88
Little Wild Street Baptist Church, London, 74, 76, 78, 84, 119, 266,
Llewelyn, Thomas, 72, 84, 120, 265,
London, Eng., 74, 76, 78, 84, 101, 119, 127, 189, 209, 212, 259, 264, 281, 241, 348
Lower, Dublin, Pa., 126
Luton, 107
Lyndon, Josias, 244-245, 247-248
Lynn, Eng., 265
Manning, Grace, 241
Manning, James, Sr., 241
Manning, James, 136, 139-142, 184, 193-195, 232, 238, 240-246, 248-252, 254-256, 258-259, 264, 267, 269, 291, 327, 341-343, 348, 364, 383
Manning's Academy, 136-138, 149, 180, 184, 256
Manning, Margaret Stites, 242
Maring, Norman, 218, 380
Martin, John, 37
Mason, Martha, 161
Mather, Cotton, 320
Mawson, Bishop, 70-71
Maxwell, Brigadeer General, 303
McBeth, H Leon, 208, 226, 233, 379
McKibbens, Thomas, 191, 233, 287, 379
McKim, John, 324
McLoughlin, William, 306, 322
Mennonites, 34
Mercia, 13
Mermaid Street, 106
Merrill, Benjamin, 288

Methodists, 41, 51, 301, 315
Middletown, Del., 305
Middletown, Pa., 209
Miles, Samuel, 146, 170, 278, 296-297, 302, 323, 331-332
Monmouthshire, 23
Moody, James, 263
Moore, Hester, 161
Moore, John, 203, 379
Morgan, Abel, 240
Morison, Samuel Eliot, 282
Morris, Anthony, 128
Morris, Jan, 3, 8, 314
Moreton, Hampstead, Eng., 102
Moulder, Isaac, 203
Mount Moriah Cemetery, 370
Muhlenberg, Henry, 124, 160
Munster, Germany, 50, 288-289
Negus, Elizabeth, 36
Neilson, Peter, 319
New Amsterdam, 283
Newark Academy, 283
Newark, Del., 148, 174, 295, 298, 301, 305-306, 354
New London, Pa., 173-174
Newman, Alfred, 232, 353
Newport, R.I., 145, 166, 180, 214, 234, 238, 242-244, 246, 250
New Road Baptist Church, Oxford, Eng., 63
Newton, Isaac, 60
New York, 258
Noble, John, 119
Normans, The, 15-15
Northhampton, Eng., 251
North Haven, Conn., 248
Northern Liberties Association, 180
Norton, Mass., 237
Nova Scotia, 222, 357
Norwich, Eng., 361

Nun, James, 265
Nun Joseph, 265
Nun, Joshua, 96
Nun, Mary, *See* Edwards, Mary
Nun, Ruth, 76
Nun, Sarah, 96
Offa, 13
Olney, Thomas, 239
Orange County, N.C., 286
Orthodox Creed, An, 86
Owain, ap Glyndwr, 16
Oxford, Eng., 63, 107
Oxford University, 62
Paine, Robert Treat, 294
Parker, Irene, 61, 63
Particular Baptist Fund, 70, 73, 76, 88-90, 120-121, 131, 212, 259, 317, 382
Pascal, George W., 277, 287
Patriots, 277-308
Patterson, William, 298
Peart, Thomas, 129
Peck, J.M., 190
Peedee Baptist Church, 295
Peedee River, S.C., 338
Pelot, Francis, 204, 377
Pemberton, Israel, 292
Pemberton, James, 292
Penn, John, 175
Penn, Thomas, 260, 264
Penn, William, 117, 123, 130
Pennepek Baptist Church, 126-129, 209-210, 246
Pennsylvania, 283
Pennsylvania Hospital, 126
Penygarn Baptist Church, 42, 45-49, 52, 69-70, 76
Perkins, John, 165
Petit, Joseph, 93
Petter, Thomas, 106
Philadelphia, 108, 118, 120-126, 138, 142, 144, 146-147, 170, 177, 211, 258, 261, 269, 331
Philadelphia Baptist Association, 120, 128, 131, 157, 181, 203-204, 207-227, 238, 243, 246, 251, 287, 291, 323, 332, 339, 341, 347, 363, 382
Philadelphia Baptist Church, 36, 70, 96-97, 100-102, 109, 117, 121, 126-131, 135, 148, 150, 153-184, 233, 247, 322, 333-334, 339, 343, 345, 347, 356, 362, 370, 382
Philadelphia Baptist Confession, 155, 209-210, 212, 218, 337-338, 340, 344-345
Philadelphia Luthern Church, 212, 234
Philadelphia Presbyterian Church, 127, 173
Phillips, Thomas, 68
Pilgrims Progress, The, 72
Piscataway, N.J., 209, 244
Plymouth, Eng., 74, 143-144
Powell, Vavasor, 31
Power and Duty of an Association, The, 216
Presbyterians, 35, 234, 236, 238, 286, 301-302
Prescott Stree Baptist Church, 341
Price, Seymour, 61, 67
Princeton University, 236, 251
Protestant Reformation, 33, 50, 193
Providence Baptist Church, 243
Providence Gazette, The, 136, 138
Providence, R.I., 137, 234, 254-255
Purdy, Thomas, 107
Puritans, 17, 29-32; Commonwealth, 18, 30, 61, 65; Parli-

ament, 17, 29
Quakers, 292-293, 322
Guested, George, 106
Redman, John, 172
Red-Man of Paviland, 11
Reese, Joseph, 225
Regents, Park College, 107
Regulator Movement, The, 286-289
Restraining Act, The, 283
Rhode Island, 137, 142, 144, 184, 198, 242
Rhode Island College, 63, 73, 91-92, 136, 138-140, 161, 171, 181, 208, 212, 217, 220, 226, 231-269, 278, 301, 366
Rhodri Mawr, 13,
Rhys ap Gruffydd, 14
Rhys, Morgan John, 72, 353-354
Richard of Bosworth, 16
Richards, Benjamin, 72
Richards, Walter, 121
Richards, William, 265
Rider, Sidney, 358
Riggs, Ann, 93
Riggs, Edward, 93
Roberts, Elizabeth, 124
Roberts, John, 124
Robinson, Robert, 360
Rodgers, Charles, 103, 107
Rodney, Caesar, 368
Rodney, Thomas, 299, 368, 377
Roffey, Samuel, 264
Rogers, James, 207-208, 379
Rogers, John, 100
Rogers, Captain William, 246
Rogers, William, 135-136, 143, 148, 150, 231, 247, 308, 330, 349-350, 362-372, 376, 383
Romans, The, 12, 13, 315
Roman Catholic Church, The, 16, 17, 130

Rose, Lucy, 100
Rowland, Daniel, 32
Ryland, John, 251
Salem Chapel, 88-89
Sandhurst, Eng., 106
Sandy Creek Association, 286, 288
Saint Paul's Church, Philadelphia, 340
Santee River, S.C., 244
Savoy Declaration, The, 210
Scotch Plains Baptist Church, 241-243
Sears, Barnas, 137, 231, 236
Second Baptist Church, Boston, Mass., 257
Second Congregational Church, Newport, R.I., 248, 250
Second London Confession, 209
Severn, River, Eng., 72
Shields, Thomas, 323, 326
Sievers, E.R., 145
Simons, Menno, 50
Singleton, Elizabeth, 135, 148, 295, 301, 354
Singleton, John, 148, 295, 301
Smith, Ebenezer, 289
Smith, Hezekiah, 175, 204, 232, 241, 268-269, 291, 377, 383
Smith, Kenneth, 191, 233, 287
Snow, Ebenezer, 321
Snow, Joseph, 136
Society for Promoting Christian Knowledge, 30, 120
Socinius, Fausto, 35
Socinius, Lelio, 35
Socinianism, 35
South Carolina Baptist Convention, 226, 382
Southern Baptist Convention, 226, 382
South Marsh, 87

Southwark, 37
Spencer, David, 130, 153, 190, 207
Spitalfields, Eng., 34
Sprague, William, 190, 195
Spring Mills, 296
Stamp Act, The, 279, 281
Stanton, Del., 305
Stennett, Joseph, 84, 119, 218
Stennett, Joseph, Jr., 51, 76-77
Stennett, Samuel, 259, 291
Stevens, James, 321
Stiles, Ezra, 173, 193-195, 237, 242, 244-245, 247-252, 254-255, 376
Stillman, Samuel, 258
Stites, John, 242
Strong, Augustus Hopkins, 202
Stuart, Gilbert, 126
Sussex, Eng., 118
Sutton, David, 213
Sutton, Isaac, 240
Sutten, John, 243
Swaine, Stephen, 59
Swansea, Mass., 256
Swift's Alley Baptist Church, 94
Taunton, Eng., 265
Terming, 317
Terrill, Edward, 72-74
Tewksbury Academy, 74
Thomas, David, 213
Thomas, Joshua, 75, 91, 120, 359-360, 364
Thomas, Philip, 161
Thomas, Timothy, 359
Thompson, Josiah, 88
Thompson, William D., 380
Thurston, Gardner, 145, 166, 214, 258-260, 268
Tillinghast, Nicholas, 194
Torbet, Robert G., 220
Tories, The, 277-308

Treatise on Church Discipline, A, 217-218
Trevithin Parish, 24, 30, 33
Triennial Convention, 223, 226, 382
Trinity Church, 124
Trosnant Academy, 22, 42-43, 45, 53, 61, 65-71, 76, 87, 119, 121, 222, 239, 267, 359, 383
Tryon, Governor William, 286-287
Universalism, 35, 103, 337-351
University of Delaware, 174
University of Pennsylvania, 236, 341
Unitarianism, 77, 86
Ustick, Thomas, 327, 330, 341, 343
Vane, Henry, 87
VanHorn, Peter, 120, 210, 212
Vedder, Henry C., 154, 232, 379
Virginia, 283
Wales: Abercar, 70; Afon Llwyd, 45; Arbertillery, 32; Blaenau Gwent, 43; Blaenavon, 28; Breknock, 32; Cardiganshire, 32; Cilfowyr, 47; Culture, 18-19; Cymry, 13, Glamorgan, 253, Gwent, 23-24, 32, 51-52; Hengoed, 67; Ilston, 256; Llandysul, 77; Llanwenarth, 27, 38, 52; Pencader, Old Man of, 7-8; Pengarn, 43, 47, 353; Pontypool, 24, 29, 31, 47, 52, 67; Trosnant, 47, 51; Wealas, 13
Wallis, Benjamin, 77, 90
Watkins, Joseph, 327, 330, 333
Watts, John, 127
Watts, Stephen, 162, 164-166
Warren Baptist Assoication, 219,

232, 291
Warren, R.I., 254-256, 268, 290, 293
Washington, George, 302-303
Webster, Richard, 87, 143, 145-146, 149
Weed, George, 162-164
Welsh Baptist Association, 47, 52
Welsh List, The, 76, 119
Welsh Neck, S.C., 338
Welsh Tract, Del., 148, 209, 215, 217, 219, 295, 303, 330, 344
Welsh Trust, The, 30
Wesley, Charles, 94
Wesley, John, 50-51, 77, 95
Westminster Confession, The, 210
Wheaton, George, 237
Whig Battalion, 326

White Clay Creek, Del., 298
White Horse Lane, 88
Whitefield, George, 9, 51, 77, 124-131, 162, 172, 201-202, 234-235
Whole Duty of Man, The, 32
Wilcox, J.P. 148
William and Mary College, 236
Williamsburg, Va., 9
Williams, Gwynn, 15
Williams, Roger, 239
Williams, Rufus, 28-29
Williams, William, 32
William the Conqueror, 14
Winchester, Elhana, 179, 313, 325, 337-351
Woodbridge, Samuel, 314
Woodrow, H., 122
Yale University, 174, 236, 248

ABOUT THE AUTHOR

Howard R. Stewart is a native of Philadelphia where he attended public schools. After serving in the U.S. Navy during World War II, he received a BA degree from Eastern College, three theological degrees from the Eastern Baptist Theological Seminary and his doctorate from the Fuller Theological Seminary.

He is an ordained American Baptist minister, and has served pastorates in Pennsylvania, Delaware and California between 1948 and 1988, when he retired. During that same period he also served as an adjunct professor in New Testament at Wesley College in Dover, Delaware; in Baptist history at both the American Baptist Seminary of the West in Covina, California, and the Fuller Theological Seminary in Pasadena, California. He is the author of *Baptists and Local Autonomy*, publlished by Exposition Press in 1974.

Dr. Stewart married the former Evelyn New in 1944 and they have two married sons and seven grandchildren.